ESSAYS
ON
INDIAN ECONOMICS

A COLLECTION OF ESSAYS AND SPEECHES

ESSAYS ON INDIAN ECONOMICS

A COLLECTION OF ESSAYS AND SPEECHES

MAHADEV GOVIND RANADE

GYAN

Published by

Gyan Publishing House
5, Ansari Road
Daryaganj, New Delhi-110002
Phone: 011-47034999, 9811692060
E-mail: books@gyanbooks.com

Distribution Network
gyanbooks.com
India, USA, Canada, UK, Australia

ISBN: 978-93-6433-304-7 (HB)

First Published, 1906

2nd Impression 2024

Printed at: Gyan Press, Delhi.

ESSAYS ON INDIAN ECONOMICS:
A COLLECTION OF ESSAYS AND SPEECHES

Author: MAHADEV GOVIND RANADE

ESSAYS
ON
INDIAN ECONOMICS

A COLLECTION OF ESSAYS AND SPEECHES.

BY

MAHADEV GOVIND RANADE, C.I.E.

SECOND EDITION: Rs. TWO.

PUBLISHED BY

G. A. NATESAN & Co., MADRAS.

1906.

PUBLISHERS' PREFACE TO THE FIRST EDITION.

THE twelve Essays on Indian Economics included in this Volume, represent the first instalment of the writings and speeches of the Hon'ble Mr. Justice Ranade, which his numerous friends have long desired to see in a collected form. The keynote of these Essays is furnished in the first Chapter on "Indian Political Economy", and the subsequent Essays only develop the main thesis in their practical applications to the subjects of Credit Organizations, State Encouragement of Agriculture and Industry, Emigration, Local Self-Government, Emancipation and Relief of the Agricultural Classes, and the Alienation of Land in British India. It is well known that on many of these points, the views held by the representatives of Indian public opinion are not always in full accord with those which find favour with the most popular English sentiments on these subjects. This divergence of views makes it the more important that the presentment of Indian thought should be made by one who has studied both sides of the question with a conscientious desire to arrive at the truth. The Essays now published cannot fail to satisfy the reader that Mr. Justice Ranade has stated the case fairly without exaggeration. He has spared no pains to make himself acquainted with first-hand sources of information. After setting forth the results of the study of the original authorities, the modifications suggested by the circumstances of this Country in the received Maxims of English Political Economy are stated without reserve and with a full sense of responsibility in terms which, it is hoped, will carry conviction to many minds, which have not lost the power of assimilating new truths. There are clear indications already of a change of feeling in the highest quarters on many of these subjects. Under the influence of the Imperialist sentiment, the hold of the old orthodox idea of Political Economy is gradually loosening, and a higher conception of the functions of the State is being more and more practically realized than was the case thirty years ago, when the *laissez faire* Policy was predominant. The circum-

CONTENTS.

stances of India, just emerging from the depression caused by manifold calamities of Famine and pestilence, also require a specially sympathetic treatment. The time, therefore, seems opportune for presenting to the public the most matured thoughts of modern India on these large Economical Questions, which call for immediate solution.

The public appreciation of this first instalment will encourage the publishers to bring out three more volumes of Mr. Justice Ranade's writings: (II.) His Chapters in Maratha History; (III.) Essays and Speeches on Socio-Religious Questions to which he has devoted considerable attention; and (IV.) lastly, his Theistic, Literary Educational and Miscellaneous publications.

——:o:——

by poor Tenants. In England the Landlords as such pay no special Tax to the State, but here Land is taxed on the ground that there is an unearned increment based on the Theory of Economical Rent, and that this unearned increment belongs of special right to the State. While the Nationalization of land is but a Socialist dream in England and Europe, it is in full swing here, and furnishes a scientific justification for periodical Revisions and Enhancements. Status and privilege form still the very cornerstone of English Social arrangements, but here every member of Society is only a mobile atom, without any differences marking him off from others, so far as the State is concerned. The Middle Class is the backbone of English Supremacy, but here there is no room for a Middle Class between the State and the poor Tax-payers. This change of front is a curious study by itself. For my present purposes, it is not necessary to cite more instances. Of course, if Political Economy is a Science of general and absolute Truths, like Physics or Astronomy, the tendency noted above to push its principles to their logical conclusions in all times and places, even when English Statesmen halt midway in their practical application of these principles, is intelligible, and may be even wise. There can be no doubt that those who thus give effect to these principles honestly believe in the scientific and absolute character of these Economical conclusions. But it is certainly a fair subject for consideration whether this belief is well-founded. If in Politics and Social Science, time and place and circumstances, the endowments and aptitudes of men, their habits and customs, their Laws and Institutions, and their previous History, have to be taken into account, it must be strange, indeed, that in the economical aspect of our life, one set of general principles should hold good everywhere for all time and place, and for all stages of Civilization. This conflict was one of the reasons which induced me to take up this subject for consideration on the present occasion.

Another reason which also influenced me in the choice of this subject was the fact that, at this time, when an appeal is being made to the popular will in two great communities to declare itself, the questions at issue are more Economical than Political in their character. The dreams of Cobden and Bright, of Ricardo and Mill, that the civilized world would, in a few years, with one accord embrace their principles, have not been realized. In America the issues are solely economical. One party favours free trade, the other favours protection. One party favours Silver Legislation, the other denounces it. In England also, as you are aware, the present Prime Minister has declared himself in favour of what is called Fair Trade, which is a modification dictated by Political and Economical considerations of the extreme doctrine of Free Trade, with a view to restrict the freedom to those who reciprocate it, and the Liberals have denounced this lapse from orthodoxy as unpardonable heresy. Even in Ireland, the Political issue is really at its base an Economical Dispute, which centres round the question of the extent of the rights of Private Property and Free Contract as between the Landlords and the Tenants. Similarly, here in our own Country, the Currency Association is also running a tilt against Economical Theorists, and boldly denies the universality of the equation of Supply and Demand as the best and only regulator of the exchange values of the precious Metals. On the Continent of Europe, and in the English Colonies, the same protest is being practically urged against the extreme rigour of the current theories of orthodox Political Economy. The Americans dispute the rights of the Chinese to settle in their Country, the Australians fear the same scafe, and even in England, legislation was contemplated against the immigration of alien Jews, on the ground that they were likely to underbid the indigenous labourer. The Trades-Union and Strikes, and the Knights of Labour, of which we have heard so much recently, furnish another form of this same general protest. This conflict of practice with theory, not in one, but in all points, not in one place or country, but all over the world, which distinguishes Contemporary History, furnishes another reason which appeared to me to justify a reconsideration of the question on broader lines than those you will find enunciated in the ordinary Text books.

In justice to some of these Writers, it must be admitted that they have taken good care to prevent many of the misapprehensions which are popularly entertained about the absolute and general character of the Economical Doctrines taught by them. Mr. John Stuart Mill, for instance, states in his preface that "for practical purposes, Political Economy is inseparably intertwined with many other branches of Social Philosophy. Except in matters of mere detail, there are perhaps no practical questions, even among those which approach nearest to the character of purely Economical questions, which admit of being decided on Economical premises alone." You will also recollect that one characteristic feature of Mr. Mill's work is his frank recognition of an essential difference between the Laws relating to the Production of Wealth, which he deems to be Universal and not arbitrary, and those which regulate its Distribution. The Laws of Distribution, Mr. Mill admits, are partly of human institution. Mr. Mill, and Mr. Cairns more clearly even than Mr. Mill, affirmed the hypothetical character of the Science. Mr. Mill contented himself with suggesting the necessity of verification to establish the soundness of the hypothetical demonstration, but Mr. Cairns went further, and asserted that "Economical Laws are no assertions respecting the character or sequence of phenomena, and that they can neither be established or refuted by Statistical or Documentary Evidence." It is true this was not the position of the earlier Teachers, Adam Smith, Ricardo, Senior, James Mill, M'Culloch, and Malthus, who never doubted that in all their reasonings they were dealing with Human Beings as they actually exist. Adam Smith, for instance, believed that Nature had made provision for Social well-being by that principle of the Human Constitution which prompts every man to better his condition, and in aiming at individual good, every man is led by an invisible Hand to promote general good. Human Institutions only interfere with this tendency, and when all restraints are removed, the obvious and simple system of natural Liberty establishes itself. Ricardo and Malthus were, if possible, still more dogmatic and absolute in their assertion of these necessary tendencies, and made no allowances, or at the best gave scanty recognition to, the one-sided character of their premises. Mr. Senior seriously thought that the whole Science could, like Geometry, be reduced from four axiomatic propositions. It will be useful at this stage to note the general features of these assumptions of the earlier Economists, which they believed to be as necessarily and universally true as the First law of Mechanics, that bodies move in straight lines, or the First Law of Physics, that they attract each other directly according to their mass, and inversely according to the square of their distance. These assumptions may be thus briefly stated:—(1) that National Economy is essentially Individualistic and has no separate Collective aspect; (2) that the individual, or typical Economical man, has no desire but that of promoting his own Self-interest, or at least that this is his strongest motive power; (3) that this Self-interest is best promoted by the largest Production of Wealth, *i.e.*, articles with value in Exchange, at the least trouble; (4) that such Pursuit of Private gain by each individual promotes best the general good; (5) that the free and unlimited Competition of individuals in the race and struggle of life is the only safe and natural regulator; (6) that all customary and State Regulation is an encroachment on natural Liberty; (7) that every Individual knows best his Interest, and has the capacity and desire of acting according to this knowledge; (8) that there is perfect Freedom and Equality in the power of contract between individuals and individuals; (9) that Capital and Labour are always free and ready to move from one employment to another, where better remuneration is expected; (10) that there is a universal tendency of Profits and Wages to seek a common level; (11) that Population tends to outstrip the means of subsistence; (12) and that Demand and Supply always tend mutually to adjust each other.

These assumptions lie at the root of all dogmatical treatment of the subject. It need not be said that they are literally true of no existing Community. To the extent that they are approximately true of any state of Society, the assumptions furnish valid explanations of its Economical Statics. Even then they furnish no suggestion as to its dynamical progress or development. As these assumptions do not absolutely hold good of even the most advanced Societies, it is obvious that in Societies like ours, they are chiefly conspicuous by their absence. With us an average individual man is, to a large extent, the very antipodes of the economical man. The Family and the caste are more powerful than the Individual in determining his position in life. Self-interest in the shape of the desire of Wealth is not absent, but it is not the only nor principal motor. The Pursuit of Wealth is not the only ideal aimed at. There is neither the desire nor the aptitude for free and unlimited Competition except within certain predetermined grooves or groups. Custom and State Regulation are far more powerful than Competition, and Status more decisive in its influence than Contract. Neither Capital nor Labour is mobile, and enterprising and intelligent enough to shift from place to place. Wages and profit are fixed, and not elastic and responsive to change of circumstances. Population follows its own law, being cut down by disease and famine, while Production is almost stationary, the bumper harvest of one year being needed to provide against the uncertainties of alternate bad seasons. In a Society so constituted, the tendencies assumed as axiomatic, are not only inoperative, but are actually deflected from their proper direction. You might as well talk of the tendency of mountains to be washed away into the sea, or of the valleys to fill up, or of the Sun to get cold, as reasons for our practical conduct within a measurable distance of time.

This hypothetical character of the entire fabric of Doctrinal Economy has been more or less freely recognized, as stated above, by Mr. Mill, Mr. Cairns, and other Teachers of Political Economy; and in our own time, Mr. Bagehot has gone so far as to assert that the traditional system rested on assumptions which were not only not true generally, but were true only of England of the present day. He calls it the Science of Business done in large and trading Communities. It does not explain the Economic life of earlier times, or of our own times in other Nations. It is insular, and has not obtained general recognition, by reason of its being chiefly a convenient series of deductions from assumed axioms which are in many times and places not true, and are only true in England, where Capital and Labour can freely transport themselves from one employment to another. Mr. Sidgwick, another contemporary writer, has expressed the view that the abstract method is useful only for the statical study of Economy, and that its conclusions, even within this province, are only hypothetically valid. In the dynamical study of the Progress of Wealth, the value of the deductive method is almost nil. Mr. Cliff Leslie has expressed himself in stronger terms. The Economy of every Nation, according to this writer, is the result of a long growth in which there has been continuity and change, and the economic side of this change is only a particular aspect. The Laws of Social Progress in Wealth must be sought in the history of the general Social Evolution which is different in different countries. Professor Jevons was filled with such despair by the sterile character of the hypothetical system that he thought the only way to cure its defects was to fling away, once and for ever, preposterous assumptions of the Ricardian School. It will be thus seen that in the land of its birth and highest development, the claims of Political Economy, as ordinarily taught in the Text-books, have been seriously questioned, and its value as a guide to practical conduct greatly discounted.

You will naturally desire to know how this revulsion of thought has been brought about in the course of a hundred years. It becomes necessary in this connection to take a retrospective view of the progress of the Science in Western Europe during the past two or three hundred years. Such a retrospect will help us to judge for ourselves how far the development of the Scientific

Theory of Political Economy can be regarded as even now complete. The ancient conception of Political Economy had regard chiefly to laying down the practical rules of prudent conduct for each private individual who desired to be rich. The conception of it as a Principle of Social Polity was more or less ignored. The general feeling in those days was that manual labour was below the dignity of a Freeman. Such work was done by slaves, or, as we would in this country describe them, by the Lower Castes. A Freeman could only devote his attention to Agriculture. Commerce and Manufactures were later developments. This circumstance also explains the interdict on Usury which was a common feature of all Ancient Institutes, excepting those of our own Country, which in this respect were more advanced than the Greek, or Mahomedan, or Christian notions on the subject. Gradually slaves became Serfs, and then Freemen, who worked for wages. These Serfs, seeking refuge in ancient coast towns and Roman Colonies, developed them into the Free commercial cities of the Middle Ages about the times of the Crusades, and later on into great manufacturing centres. The discoveries of the 15th Century gave a stimulus to trade, and later on to Colonization. The large imports of Gold and Silver helped to encourage the greater circulation of Money. The gradual rise of European Monarchies, and the decay of the Church and the Nobility, removed the pressure of Feudal ideas, and raised the status of those who were engaged in Commerce. The Republics of Italy developed Banking and Credit. It was when the national activity of Europe took such a varied form, stimulating Agriculture, Commerce, Manufactures, Banking, Currency, Exchange, Co-operation, Taxation, Colonization, and Foreign Conquests, that the ground was prepared for a systematic study of the Theory of the Laws which regulated economical arrangements, and made nations prosperous and strong, or the reverse. And the first speculative explanation attempted is known in history as the Mercantile Theory. It is too much the practice of Text-writers to cry down this Theory as one which confounded Wealth with Money and Bullion, and made the possession of precious Metals the test of National prosperity. This is, however, an utterly unfair and one-sided view of the subject. The leading feature of the system was that it set a higher value on Commerce and Manufactures than on agriculture, and on Foreign over Home Trade. It encouraged Exports, but desired to check Imports with a view not to retain money so much as to develop Home Manufactures. Lastly, it prescribed the directive control of the State in the way of stimulating domestic Manufactures and encouraging Commerce. Each State competed with the rest in Foreign Markets, and sought to secure the most advantageous terms and it sought also to extend its Colonies and Dependencies with a view to increase the sphere of open Markets for its produce. It is enough to state that men like Colbert, and Oliver Cromwell, Raleigh and Childe, could not have encouraged a system which had not some solid justification in the then circumstances of Europe. Cromwell's Navigation Laws have admittedly been the foundation of England's naval supremacy, and Colbert made France in his day the most prosperous State on the Continent. He had a keen perception that State protection and control were but crutches to teach the Nation to walk, and that they should be thrown away when the necessary advance had been made. It was under the influence of the same ideas that the Great East India Companies of Holland, France, and England were formed, and received the support of their respective Governments. Charters and Monopolies, Bounties and Subsidies, were freely granted under the influence of the same ideas, and State help and regulation did their work remarkably well.

In the next Century the natural progress of events made Nations alive to the abuses of the old system, and men began to feel the necessity of freedom in the Economical as well as in the Political field. This work of destructive and negative criticism began in England with the teachings of Hobbes and Locke, but was more earnestly taken up in France previous to the Revolution. The enormous abuses of State control and direction, of monopolies and restrictions, led to a reaction in favour of a theory which was founded on the idea of Natural Liberty. In this negative Philosophy individual man was, moreover, conceived as being solely guided by Private Interest, which it was supposed he understood better for himself than others could do for him, and the removal of all restrictions and prohibitions became the watchword of this School. The previous preponderance of State support in favour of Commerce and Manufactures was condemned and a preference for Agriculture as the only true source of all Wealth was developed into a mania. In grasping the conception that money alone was not Wealth, and that all Wealth is created by human Labour applied to Natural Agents, people ran to the other extreme of classifying Commerce and Manufactures along with service and professions under the head of Unproductive Labour. In protesting against Protection and prohibition, the extreme view went so far as to hold that Government itself was only a necessary evil, and that the State had no concern with Industry, and must confine itself to its sole function of keeping the public Peace. This conception of the domain of Natural Liberty in Economics was but a part and parcel of the great movement of Freedom which culminated in the French Revolution. Quesnay, Guorney, and the great Statesman Turgot, were the advocates of this New School of Thought which is known as the School of the Physiocrats.

Next in order of time we have Adam Smith, who was the direct product of the French negative School of Quesnay, but he improved upon his model and exposed the weakness of that School in two important respects. He established the fact that Agriculture was not the only source of wealth, and that Manufactures and Commerce were equally efficient in this respect, and that Nature helped man equally in all the three departments. While accepting the *laissez faire* doctrine of Free Trade as a general principle, Mr. Smith was alive to the fact that restrictive Navigation Laws had helped greatly to ensure English Commercial Supremacy, and he justified these laws on the express ground that defence was of more importance than opulence, and he advocated what are known as Fair Trade views, *i.e.*, views which permit retaliation by way of Differential Duties against non-reciprocating Countries on condition that such retaliation produces its desired consequences. He also approved of temporary concessions by way of Monopolies to Chartered Companies in enterprizes which involved risk and expense. Adam Smith never separated Economical from Social considerations, and thus occupied a position of advantage, which his Successors gave up by their too absolute assertion of his doctrines. I have already spoken of the rigid character of the system of Ricardo, Malthus, Senior, James Mill, Torrens, McCulloch and others, and shown how this dogmatic feature provoked a reaction in England, at first faintly represented in the protests of John Stuart Mill and Mr. Cairns, but more decidedly formulated by Bagehot, Leslie and Jevons. This strong reaction of feeling among English writers was due to the influence of the great French and German Teachers. August Comte was the first who denied the name of Science to the doctrines taught by the Deductive School, and he elaborated his own system of the Historical Method of Research, and these hints were taken up by the German and English Thinkers of our day. Sismondi was the first economical writer who gave expression to the dissatisfaction felt in France at the conclusions of the English Economists. He charged the Individualistic School with tendencies by which the rich became richer, and the poor were made poorer. He protested against the abuses of the *laissez faire* Policy, and invoked Government intervention for protecting the masses against the classes, and the weaker races against the pressure of the stronger and more advanced Nations under the *régime* of competition. Sismondi declared that the State was not merely an agency for keeping peace, but that it was an organization for securing the progress of the people as widely as possible, and for extending the benefits of the Social Union to all. Another French writer, Dunoyer, defined Liberty not as a mere negation of restraint, but a positive effort to increase efficiency of Labour in all its grades.

Two American Thinkers, Hamilton and Carey, sounded the same note of difference in more distinct terms. Hamilton was one of the Fathers of the American Constitution, and he stated that the English doctrine of Absolute Freedom was practicable only if all Nations accepted Free Trade views simultaneously, and he suggested a scheme of Protective Duties which were later on adopted as the leading feature of American State Tariffs. The Haileybury Professor Jones had before Carey attacked the Ricardian Theory of Rent as being true only of Farmers' rents, and as wholly inapplicable to the Indian Ryots' rent or the Metayer or Cottier rents. Carey went further, and denied that there was any Economic Rent proper, and contended that Rent was only a remuneration, in the same way as profits, of past invested Capital or Labour. Carey justified Protection to domestic Agriculture on the ground that the waste products of land must return to the soil to restore its powers, and this restoration was not possible where Raw Products were exported to, and consumed by distant Countries. Like the French Sismondi, Carey regarded the State as a co-ordinating power in Society, which checked the tendency of individuals to seek immediate gain at the sacrifice of permanent National interests, and he asserted that Protection was justified as being the only means by which the obstacles, thrown in the way of younger and less advanced Communities by more advanced Nations, could be removed. The immediate loss to the Nation was like the sum spent on the Education of youth by individuals, which more than repays itself in the long run.

Like the French and American writers, the Italian Economists of the modern period, Gioga and Ludovico, also advocated State Regulation of Industry, and asserted the Doctrine of Relativity as being an essential factor of all true Economic Theory. The work of positive exposition was, however, most successfully taken up by the German professors. Muller first suggested that Adam Smith's system, as elaborated by his more dogmatic disciples, was essentially English and insular. It succeeded in England, because the national life of England was preserved intact by its favoured situation and past history and conservative instincts, while it was unsuitable to the Continental Countries, because, with them the preservation of the National existence was a subject of greater importance than mere individual prosperity. It was the writings of List, which gave the fullest expression to this rebellion against the orthodox creed. He urged that the permanent interests of Nations were not always in harmony with the present benefit of individuals. National well-being does not consist only in the creation of the highest quantity of wealth measured in exchange value, independently of all variety of quality in that wealth, but in the full and many-sided development of all productive powers. The Nation's Economic education is of far more importance than the present gain of its individual members , as represented by the quantity of wealth measured by its value in exchange. In a sound and normal condition, all the three departments of national activity must be fully developed. Commerce and Manufactures are, if possible, more vital in their bearing on the education of the intelligence and skill and enterprize of the Nation than Agriculture. In a purely Agricultural Country there is a tendency to stagnation and absence of enterprize and the retention of antiquated prejudices. The function of the State is to help those influences which tend to secure National Progress through the several stages of growth, and adopt Free Trade or Protection as circumstances may require. In this view Free Trade may be good for a Country like England, but not for America and Germany.

The subsequent German Teachers further elaborated this historical view, and under the stimulus of the success of the comparative method in Philology and Jurisprudence, proposed to reconstruct Economy by the help of the new method. Raw, Knieys, Roscher, Hildebrand, Wagner and others worked on these lines. Their influence made itself felt on English thought, and Leslie and Jevons were directly influenced by these teachings. They advocated that Economy was only one branch of Sociology, and like all Social

Sciences, it must be studied both in its statical and dynamical conditions, and that the basis of a hypothetical economic man, guided solely by one motive of Self-Interest, must be given up, and man as he is, both selfish and altruistic, possessing rights as well as being bound by duties, must be studied in History, both Ancient and Modern. In brief, this German School regards that Universalism and Perpetualism in Economic Doctrine are both unscientific and untrue.

This resume of the past and contemporary history of the growth of economic Sciences in England, France, Germany, Italy, and America will satisfy the student that modern European thought does not at all countenance the view of the English writers of the Ricardian School, that the Principles of the Science, as they have enunciated them in their Text Books, are universally and necessarily true for all times and places, and for all stages of Advancement. Modern Thought is veering to the conclusion that the Individual and his Interests are not the centre round which the Theory should revolve, that the true centre is the Body Politic of which that Individual is a Member, and that Collective Defence and Well-being, Social Education and Discipline, and the Duties, and not merely the Interests, of men, must be taken into account, if the Theory is not to be merely Utopian. The Method to be followed is not the Deductive but the Historical Method, which takes account of the past in its forecast of the future;

and Relativity, and not Absoluteness, characterizes the conclusions of Economical Science. There are those who seek to get over this difficulty by differentiating the Science from what they are disposed to call the Art of Economy. This divorce of Theory and Practice is, however, a mischievous error, which relegates the Science to the sterility of an ideal dream or a puzzle, and condemns the Art to the position of a rule of the thumb. Theory is only enlarged Practice, Practice is Theory studied in its relation to proximate Causes. The Practice is predetermined by the Theory which tests its truth, and adapts it to different conditions by reason of its grasp of the deep-seated, permanent, and varied basal truths. I hope thus to have shown that the nature of the subject itself as a branch of Social Science, which is best studied historically and not deductively, the actual Practice of the most Civilized Nations and the history of the growth of its Theory given above, alike establish the doctrine of relativity, and the predominant claim of Collective Welfare over Individual Interests, as the principal features in which the highest minds of the present day chiefly differ from the Economical Writers of the Old School, with their *a priori* conclusions based on individual self-interest and unrestricted competition.

We have next to consider the bearings of this enlarged view of the science in its Indian aspects. The characteristics of our Social Life are the prevalence of

Status over Contract, of Combination over Competition. Our habits of mind are conservative to a fault. The aptitudes of climate and soil facilitate the production of raw materials. Labour is cheap and plentiful, but unsteady, unthrifty, and unskilled. Capital is scarce, immobile, and unenterprising. Co-operation on a large scale of either Capital or Labour is unknown. Agriculture is the chief support of nearly the whole population, and this Agriculture is carried on under conditions of uncertain rainfall. Commerce and Manufactures on a large scale are but recent importations, and all industry is carried on, on the system of petty farming, retail dealing, and job working by poor people on borrowed capital. There is an almost complete absence of a landed gentry or wealthy middle class. The land is a monopoly of the State. The desire for accumulation is very weak, peace and security having been almost unknown over large areas for any length of time till within the last Century. Our Laws and Institutions favour a low standard of life, and encourage sub-division and not concentration of Wealth. The religious ideals of life condemn the ardent pursuit of wealth as a mistake to be avoided as far as possible. These are old legacies and inherited weaknesses. Stagnation and dependence, depression and poverty—these are written in broad characters on the face of the land and its people. To these must be added the economical drain of wealth and talents, which Foreign subjection has entailed on the country. As a compensation against all these depressing influences, we have to set off the advantage of a free contact with a race which has opened the Country to the Commerce of the world, and by its superior skill and resources has developed communications in a way previously unknown. If we wish to realize our situation fully, we may not overlook this factor, because, it represents the beam of light which alone illumines the prevailing darkness. It cannot well be a mere accident that the destinies of this Country have been entrusted to the guidance of a Nation whose characteristic strength is opposed to all our weaknesses, whose enterprize, chiefly in Commerce and Manufactures, knows no bounds, whose Capital overflows the world, among whom Contract has largely superseded Status, and Competition and Co-operation play a predominant part, whose view of life is full of hope, and whose powers of organization have never been surpassed.

The first point which illustrates the divergence between the orthodox English doctrine and the enlarged views I have attempted to set forth, as characterizing the more developed modern European thought on the subject, relates to the so-called system of the territorial Division of Labour by which the orthodox economists assign to the backward Torrid Zone Regions of Asia the duty of producing Raw Materials, and claim for the advanced European Temperate Zone Countries, the work of transport and manufactures, as a division of labour in production which is fraught with the highest advantage to all, and is almost a Providential dispensation, against which it would be foolish to rebel. Of course, as far as the natural advantages of climate and situation force our hands, economically backward races must submit to such an arrangement, but it is fairly open to question whether there is any such inevitable necessity which justifies a line of separation, which has a tendency to accentuate natural deficiencies, and make them a source of permanent weakness. (1) In the first place, the Torrid Zone people may fairly appeal to past history, when their skilled products found a ready market in temperate kingdoms, and excited such jealousy as to dictate prohibitive sumptuary laws both in ancient Rome and in modern England. (2) They may also urge that the natural fitness of things requires that the manufactures should spring up where the raw materials grow, and where, besides, there is demand for the manufactured produce, rather than that bulky goods should be transported many thousands of miles over land and sea, and re-consigned the same way back. (3) The differences in favour of temperate regions are all modern growths due to the employment of Steam Machinery, and the abundance of cheap Iron and Coal. This is a real advantage, and has to be faced, but if it can be faced, there is no natural incongruity in an arrangement by which Industry would return to its ancient home with a double saving in time and cost. (4) Neither Mr. Adam Smith, nor even Mr. John Stuart Mill, recommend absolute freedom in such matters. Adam Smith was a Fair Trader, and Mr. Mill distinctly recognizes an exception to the general rule of Free Trade, where time is required to see whether new industries are or are not adapted to the natural resources of new countries. The late controversy between Mr. Blaine and Mr. Gladstone chiefly turned upon this point. Mr. Blaine contending that, with a large Continental Country like America, with all shades of climate and soil and position, the conditions of the problem were different from those of an isolated small territory like England. The Australian Colonies also justify their departure from the orthodox policy on this same ground. India may fairly claim the benefit of the experience and practice of these self-governing communities, and demand breathing time. (5) It is further to be noted that such a division of Production, if permanently stereotyped, consigns Asia to an Industry which is under the bane of the Law of Diminishing Returns, while the west of Europe appropriates to itself those forms of Industry which are not subject to any such law. The orthodox view thus condemns the poor to grow still poorer, and helps the rich to become richer—'it giveth much to him that hath, and taketh away from him that hath not the little that he hath.' (6) Lastly, people forget that the Agricultural Industry in the Torrid Regions has to work under the disadvantage of an uncertain rainfall, and suffer from famine visitations, which, when they come. paralyze Production, and condemn millions to violent or slow death. A due co-ordination of the three-fold forms of industrial activity, even if it be not immediately most advantageous to individuals in any one period, is a permanent National Insurance against recurrent dangers, and as such is economically the most beneficial course in the interests of the Community.

(2) The point noticed above has reference chiefly to Foreign Trade. In domestic interchange also, the same law operates, and every Nation which desires economical advance has to take care that its urban population bear an increasing ratio to its rural masses with every advance it seeks to make. Mr. John Stuart Mill has expressly laid down that no Agriculture can be really productive which is divorced from a neighbouring non-agricultural market represented by Thriving Towns and Cities. Under Native Rulers there was a sort of rude adjustment made in this direction, when the Courts of the Petty Sovereigns afforded so many centres of urban activity in industries patronized by the Court and its dependents. Mr. Mill suggests that in the absence of such near markets, the next available substitute is a large export trade to Foreign Countries. This substitute cannot, however, be accepted as really answering the purpose in view. The progress of rura-

lization in modern India means its rustication, *i.e.*, a loss of power, and intelligence, and self-dependence, and is a distinctly retrograde move. The growth of the Seaports and of the few Military and Railway Stations is not enough to counterbalance the enormous loss that has been inflicted by this retrograde movement. Every class of artisans, the Spinners, Weavers and the Dyers, the Oilsmen, the Paper-makers, the Silk and Sugar and Metal workers, etc., who are unable to bear up against Western competition, resort to the land, leave the Towns and go into the Country, and are lost in the mass of helpless people who are unable to bear up against scarcity and famine.

(3) The highest statesmanship may well feel aghast at this rapid change, and I know, as a matter of fact, that this subject weighs heavily on the conscience of the British Administrators in India. They, however, feel powerless to act under the influence of the all-pervading doctrine that these matters lie outside the province of Government. A regular system of Immigration from thickly populated poor Agricultural tracts to sparsely peopled new and virgin districts is a desideratum. The halting efforts made in this direction produce no good, for the concessions are not liberal enough, and there is no prescience about it. The Ancient Rulers who settled waste districts, and founded towns with flourishing and extensive Industries, made no difficulty about granting the most liberal conces-

comes up to the total value of landed property. In one generation, property thus changes hands, and when new men come in as purchasers for value, they do not enjoy any unearned increment of the past, but have to pay full value for the differential advantages of superior productiveness and vicinity. In the same way the Ricardian Theory that Economic Rent does not enter as an element of price, admittedly does not apply when all occupied land has to pay Monopoly Rent to the State Landlord. There is no competition among Landlords in this country, for there is only one true Landlord, and the so-called Land Tax is not a tax on Rents proper, but frequently encroaches upon the Profits and Wages of the poor Peasant, who has to submit perforce to a loss of Status and accommodate himself to a lower standard of life as pressure increases.

Lastly, the Advanced Theory expounded by the Modern School fully justifies the attempts made by the Government here and in England to check the abuse of Competition among poor tenants by conferring Fixity of Tenure, by adjusting rents judicially for a term of years, and imposing limitations on its increase. In this matter the Tenants of Government claim the same consideration as those of private Zemindars. The justification for this active interference is as valid in regard to Agricultural Labourers and Tenants, as it is in the case of Factory Labourers and Miners in Europe. These people are unable to combine for self-protection, or at least their combination is not so effective as that of the employers of Labour, and when their efforts fail to obtain regular redress, disorder and misery result as consequences, and threaten public peace and general well-being. In the same spirit, the regulation of the Freedom of Contract in regard to the fixing of rates of interest in transactions between the poor disunited indebted classes and the money-lenders, and the protection of immoveable property from being sold away for improvident debts, not secured on the same, are all legitimate forms of protection of the weak against the strong, and do not affect the real freedom of Distribution. The Advanced Theory concedes freedom where the parties are equally matched in intelligence and resources; when this is not the case, all talk of equality and freedom adds insult to the injury. It is in this spirit that the Distribution of Produce among the needy many and the powerful few has to be arranged, *i.e.*, in a spirit of equity and fair-play, and the orthodox Views of Finality in such matters must be reconsidered in all the relations of life.

Lastly comes the great department of Governmental interference. The meddlesomeness of the mercantile system provoked a reaction against State Control and Guidance towards the end of the last century in favour of Natural Liberty. The Doctrines of this Negative School have now in their turn been abused by a too logical extension of its principles. There is a decided

3

reaction in Europe against the *laissez faire* system. Even in England, the recent Factory Legislation, the qualified recognition by law of Trades-Unionism, the poor law system, and the Irish Land Settlement, are all instances which indicate the same change of view. Speaking roughly, the province of State Interference and Control is practically being extended so as to restore the good points of the mercantile system without its absurdities. The State is now more and more recognized as the National Organ for taking care of National needs in all matters in which individual and co-operative efforts are not likely to be so effective and economic as National effort. This is the correct view to take of the true functions of a State. To relegate them to the simple duty of maintaining peace and order, is really to deprive the Community of many of the advantages of the Social Union. Education, both Liberal and Technical, Post and Telegraphs, Railway and Canal Communications, the pioneering of new enterprize, the insurance of risky undertakings,—all these functions are usefully discharged by the State. The question is one of time, fitness, and expediency, not one of liberty and rights. In our own Country the State has similarly enlarged its functions with advantage. The very fact that the Rulers belong to a race with superior advantages imposes this duty on them of attempting things which no Native Rulers, past or present, could as well achieve, or possibly even think of. This obligation is made more peremptory by the fact that the State claims to be the sole Landlord, and is certainly the largest Capitalist in the Country. While the State in India has done much in this way in the working of Iron and Coal fields, and in the experiments made about Cotton and Tobacco, and in Tea and Coffee and Cinchona Plantations, it must be admitted that, as compared with its resources and the needs of the Country, these attempts are as nothing by the side of what has been attempted with success in France, Germany and other countries, but which, unhappily, has not been attempted in this country. Even if political considerations forbid independent action in the matter of differential duties, the pioneering of new enterprize is a duty which the Government might more systematically undertake with advantage. In truth, there is no difference of principle between lending such support and guidance, by the free use of its Credit and superior Organisation, in pioneering Industrial Undertaking or subsidizings private Co-operative effort, and its guaranteeing minimum interest to Railway Companies. The building up of National, not merely State, Credit on broad foundations by helping people to acquire confidence in a free and largely Ramified Banking system, so advantageously worked in Europe under different forms, has also not been attempted here. There is, lastly, the duty cast on it of utilizing indigenous resources, and organizing them in a way to produce in India in State Factories all products of skill which the State Departments require in the way of Stores. These are only a few of the many directions in which, far more than Exchange and Frontier difficulties, the highest Statesmanship will have a field all its own for consideration and action. They will, no doubt, receive such consideration if only the minds of the Rulers were once thoroughly freed from the fear of offending the so-called maxims of rigid Economical Science. It is time that a new departure should take place in this connection, and it is with a view to drawing public attention to this necessity that I have ventured to place before you the results of modern economic Thought. In this, as in other matters, the conditions of Indian life are more faithfully reproduced in some of the Continental Countries and in America than in happy England, proud of its position, strong in its insularity, and the home of the richest and busiest Community in the modern industrial World. If the attempt I have made leads to a healthy and full discussion of the change of policy I advocate, I shall regard myself amply repaid for my trouble.

The following extracts will show that the views embodied in the foregoing paper are not confined to the Native Community only, but that Anglo-Indian Thinkers of note are also becoming every day more and more alive to the evils of the present *laissez faire* policy of the Government of India. The first extract is taken from "A Modern Zoroastrian," by S. Laing, some time Financial Minister to the Government of India. The second extract is taken from "A Study in Indian Administration," by Sir William Wilson Hunter, and it represents the views entertained by the late Sir Maxwell Melvill on Indian Political Economy.

Extract from Mr. Laing's "A Modern Zoroastrian."

"When Sir Robert Peel some forty years ago, announced his conversion by the unadorned eloquence of Richard Cobden, and Free Trade was inaugurated, with results which were attended with the most brilliant success, every one expected that the conversion of the rest of the Civilised World was only a question of time, and that a short time. Few would have been found bold enough to predict that, forty years later, England would stand almost alone in the world in adherence to Free Trade principles, and that the Protectionist heresy would not only be strengthened and confirmed among Continental Nations such as France and Germany, but actually adopted by large and increasing majorities in the United States, Canada, Australia, and other English-speaking Communities. Yet such is the actual fact at the present day. In spite of the Cobden Club and of arguments which to the average English mind appear irresistible, Free Trade has been steadily losing ground for the last twenty years, and Nation after Nation, Colony after Colony, sees its Protectionist majority increasing and its Free Trade minority dwindling.

"It is evident there must be some real cause for such a universal phenomenon. In Countries like France and Russia we may attribute it to Economical ignorance and the influence of cliques of manufacturers and selfish interests; but the people of Germany, and still more of the United States, Canada, and Australia, are as intelligent as ourselves, and quite as shrewd in seeing where their interests really lie. They are fettered by no traditional prejudices, and their Political instincts rather lie towards Freedom and against the creation of anything like an Aristocracy of wealthy Manufacturers. And yet, after years of free discussion, they have become more and more hardened in their Protectionist heresies.

"What does this prove? That there are two sides to the Shield, and not, as we fancied in our English insularity, only one.

"Free Trade is undoubtedly the best, or rather the only possible, policy for a Country like England, with thirty millions of inhabitants, producing food for less than half the number, and depending on Foreign Trade for the supplies necessary to keep the other half alive. It is the best policy also for a Country which, owing to its Mineral resources, its accessibility by sea to Markets, its accumulated Capital, and the inherited qualities, physical and moral, of its working population, has unrivalled advantages for cheap production. Nor can any dispassionate observer dispute that in England, which is such a Country, Free Trade has worked well. It has not worked miracles, it has not introduced an industrial Millennium, the poor are still with us, and it has not saved us from our share of commercial depressions. But, on the whole, National Wealth has greatly increased, and, what is more important, national well-being has increased with it, the mass of the population, and especially the Working Classes, get better wages, work shorter hours, and are better fed, better clothed, and better educated than they were forty years ago.

"This is one side of the Shield, and it is really a golden and not an illusory one. But look at the other side. Take the case of a Country where totally opposite conditions prevail: where there is no surplus population, unlimited land, limited capital, labour scarce and dear, and no possibility of competing in the foreign or even in the home Market with the manufactures which, with Free Trade, would be poured in by countries like England, in prior possession of all the elements of cheap Production. It is by no means so clear that Protection, to enable Native Industries to take root and grow, may not in such cases be the wisest policy."

"Take, as a simple illustration, the case of an Australian Colony, imposing an Import Duty on Foreign boots and shoes. There is no doubt that this is practically taxing the immense majority of Colonists who wear and do not make these articles. But, on the other hand, it makes the Colony a possible field for Emigration for all Shoe-makers of Europe, and shoe-making a trade to which any Australian with a large family can bring up one of his sons. Looking at it from the strict point of view of the most rigid Political Economist, the maximum Production of Wealth, which is the better policy? The production of Wealth, we must recollect, depends on Labour, and productive labour depends on the Labourer finding his tools—that is, employment at which he can work. A labourer who cannot find work at living wages is worse than a zero; he is a negative quantity as far as the accumulation of wealth is concerned. On the other hand, every workman who finds work, even if it may not be of the ideally best description, is a wealth-producing machine. What he spends on himself and his family gives employment to other workmen, and the work must be poor, indeed, if the produce of a year's labour is not more than the cost of a year's subsistence. The surplus adds to the National Capital and thus Capital and Population go on increasing in Geometrical Progression. The first problem, therefore, for a new or backward Country, is to find 'a fair day's wages for a fair day's work,' for as many hands as possible. The problem of making that employment the most productive possible is a secondary one, which will solve itself in each case rather by actual Practice than by abstract Theory.

"This much, however, is pretty clear, that in order to secure the maximum of employment, it must be varied. All are not fit for agricultural work, and, even if they were, if the conditions of soil and climate favour large Estates and Sheep or Cattle Runs rather than small Farms, a large amount of capital may provide work for only a small number of labourers. On social and moral grounds, also, apart from dry considerations of Political Economy, progress, intelligence, and a higher standard of life are more likely to be found with large Cities, Manufactures, and a variety of industrial Occupations than with a dead level of a few Millionaires and a few Shepherds, or of a few Landlords and a dense population of poor Peasants. If Protection is the price which must be paid to render such a larger life possible, it may be sound policy to pay it, and the result seems to show that neither it nor Free Trade is inconsistent with rapid progress, while, on the other hand, neither of them affords an absolute immunity from the evils that dog the footsteps of Progress, and from the periods of reaction and depression which accompany vicissitudes of Trade."

Extract from Sir W. W. Hunter's "Study in Indian Administration."

"But Sir Maxwell Melvill, or Max Melvill as he was affectionately called throughout his career, was an important personality and a living influence quite apart from his official work. In Economics he did not shrink from declaring himself a Protectionist of the American type, that is to say, an advocate for Protection not for a single isolated Country, but for a great Continent like America or India made up of a number of States, possessing within them the resources for almost every kind of Production, indeed, for almost every form of human Industry, and capable of a self-sufficing economic development. One of those who knew him best believes that it was this consciousness of holding views not in accordance with the prevailing doctrines of the Government of India, which influenced him in declining the seat in the Viceroy's Council."

II.

THE RE-ORGANISATION OF REAL CREDIT IN INDIA.*

NO fact in the economic condition of this Country arrests attention more forcibly than the contrast presented by the hoards of unused Capital, stored up in the vaults of the Presidency and other Exchange Banks, and the high Premium Government Securities command on one side, and, on the other, the utter paralysis of industry in rural India, due to the poverty of the resources of the Classes engaged in the production of Wealth. It would appear as if some impenetrable barrier intercepted the overflow of wealth, and barred the channels of communication between the reservoirs of Capital and the parched fields of Industry, dried up for want of the wealth-bearing and fertilizing moisture. This is not a fancy picture. It is a stern reality which has to be faced by all who feel an interest in the well-being and progress of the Country. The Presidency Bank of Bombay alone, has at this moment more than Fifty Millions of Rupees of Deposit Receipts, which it

* Read before the First Industrial Conference, at Poona, in 1891.

does not know how to use, and which drives it in despair to refuse Municipal and other Private Deposits except as Current Accounts which bear no interest. Nearly Twenty Millions of Rupees are locked up in the Post Office Savings Banks in this Presidency alone, and as many as Fifty Millions of Rupees are similarly locked up all over India which the Government cannot turn to account except by buying its own Paper, and maintaining from the interests proceeds its Paper Currency Department. Government 4 per cent. Paper sells for Rs. 107 or 108, and 5 per cent. Municipal Loans fetch Rs. 111-12 per nominal value of Rs. 100. The average for ten years of Gold imports has been Forty Millions of Rupees and of Silver Seventy Millions of Rupees, the latter chiefly coined into Rupees, the former chiefly absorbed in ornaments. Meanwhile, the Cultivating and Artisan Classes can get no loans, except at rates of interest ranging from 12 per cent. to 24 per cent. In the four Deccan Districts, Poona, Satara, Nagar, and Sholapur, with a population of three millions and-a-half, for which information is available, the amount of annual borrowings on the mortgage of land exceeds four millions, and of simple loans one million and six hundred thousand, the interest rate on mortgage Loans being generally 12 per cent. and on simple Bonds 24 per cent. The slightest irregularity or delay in the annual rainfall deprives the whole population of food, and, what is far worse, leaves them without work, and Government finds it necessary to strain all its resources to arrest not only the Food Famine, but the Work Famine as well. Less than 3 per cent. of the land in the Presidency proper, excluding Sind, is protected by Irrigation. This is the actual situation, and it is clear that it is alarming enough. If there were no Capital in the Country seeking investment, there would be reason for despair. But, as things stand, the situation is not hopeless. There is Capital ready to hand awaiting secure investment. There is the broad dreary expanse of Industry which is thirsting for Capital, and offering the most secure investment for its fruitful employment. What is wanting is the necessary skill and patience which will adjust the capacity of the one to the wants of the other, and make both work in a spirit of harmony and co-operation.

In this connection it is very unfortunate that the Economic Conditions of England are so widely divergent from those of India that the Rulers of the Country, brought up in the traditions of their Native Land, find themselves more or less unprepared to grapple with the difficulties created by this novel situation. With its land owned chiefly by a few landlords, and its Peasantry representing a very small proportion of the Wage-earning Classes, with its large accumulations of Capital, and the vast development of its Manufacturing and Commercial activities, Great Britain is most peculiarly circumstanced, and its Economic History furnishes no guide for dealing with the difficulties of the situation in India, where, except in a few Provinces, the State claims to be the sole landlord, and agricultural classes form 80 per cent. of the total population, and there is no accumulation of Capital; and Manufactures and Commerce are in their rudimentary stage, and in that stage also, chiefly monopolized by strangers. On the Continent of Europe, however, Indian Problems are fairly reproduced with Indian conditions of life and property, and the lessons to be derived from the study of Continental Economy have a more practical bearing than the maxims contained in the usual Text-books of English Political Economy. The task of Re-organizing Credit, both Real and Personal, on a sound and progressive basis has been undertaken by Continental Statesmen and Thinkers during the last fifty years, and they have succeeded in bridging the gulf which separates the saving few from the producing many in a way which commands attention. If this task were undertaken in the same spirit by those who feel its importance here in the promotion of National Well-being, and a *modus operandi* established by which people seeking secure investment can be brought face to face with those who need their help and are prepared to offer that security, the Nation would soon start upon a new race of life with its powers invigorated, and its energies awakened in a way no other single agency can accomplish. This Conference will not have met in vain, if it succeeds in drawing public attention to the subject as one of paramount importance, and if it attempts to suggest ways and means for practical adoption, based on principles which will, in course of time, find their further development in far-reaching beneficial consequences. With this view, it is proposed to give a brief history of the growth of the organisation of real credit in the countries of Hungary and Austria, France and Italy, Belgium and Switzerland, during the past fifty years.

To take up the history of the movement in Hungary, it is noticeable that two important developments in the condition of the Agricultural Classes forced this subject upon the attention of the ruling classes in Hungary. As these developments find their counterpart in India, they deserve special notice. In the first place, after the Revolution of 1848, the Hungarian Peasants found themselves in the possession of personal freedom, and of proprietary right which they had only imperfectly enjoyed before. They were Serfs before, and though partially emancipated under Maria Theresa, their complete emancipation took place after the Revolution of 1848. The old Serfs were made proprietors of the lands they held under their landlords, who were bought off to give their consent by suitable compensation. Compulsory labour was abolished; Rents, Taxes, and Tithes were consolidated together, and the nobles were taxed like any other Classes, and had to pay wages to their old Serfs when they employed them on their diminished Farms. Copy-hold and Serf-hold Property became Freehold. As many as five lakhs (Five Hundred thousands) of families were thus restored to freedom, and, on an average, their holdings were about fifteen acres each. This, it may be noted, fairly corresponds with the change which has been brought about over the greater part of India by the survey settlements, except that the State in India has stepped into the position of the private landlord, and claims to be owner of all cultivable and cultivated land. The next change which took place in Hungary was also reproduced in the history of our own country. Owing to increased facilities of communication, new Markets were opened, and the Export trade was developed to a large extent. Old methods of cultivation, which did well enough under old conditions, were felt to be inadequate, and it was found necessary to abandon the old system. Owing to the poverty of good waste land, the cultivation had to become intensive in place of the old system of extensive cultivation.

Under the double influence of these two causes, the problem of re-organizing real credit, *i.e.*, of securing loans on easy terms on the security of Real Property, first presented itself for practical solution, and Real Credit Institutions, worked on divergent principles, were started, either in the interest of the borrowers who clubbed their resources together, and founded such institutions as the Boden Credit Institute, or in the interest of the lenders who opened departments for real advances in the great National Banks, such as the Austro-Hungarian Bank or the Provincial Savings Banks. The first Boden Credit Institute was started in 1863 by two hundred and nine land-owners who subscribed among themselves a large amount of Capital, about fifteen millions of Rupees, of which one-tenth was paid up in cash, and the remaining nine-tenths was represented by Bonds passed by the Founders in Favour of the Bank, which were gradually withdrawn as the Reserve Fund increased. Every borrower had to become a Member, and guaranteed with others, who joined with him, the solvency of the concern to all who had dealings with the Bank as Bond-holders or Depositors. The ordinary rate of interest on mortgage loans was much higher, but the Institute made its advances at a fixed rate of interest,—six and a half per cent.—which was gradually reduced to four and a half per cent. The advances made were limited to half of the assessed value of the property mortgaged. No property was taken in mortgage which did not yield a fixed and certain income, and no loan was made except by way of a first and sole charge. The rates of interest stipulated included interest proper, and one per cent. for the sinking fund or for the amortization charge, and twenty-five to fifty per cent. for the expenses and

4

the Reserve Fund. The repayment of principal and interest was secured by spreading the payment over a period of thirty-four to forty-one years. The Bank issued its Bonds of one Hundred or one Thousand or ten Thousand Florins at 4·85 per cent., and these Bonds were made payable to bearer, and, being negotiable, freely changed hands, and a portion of them was withdrawn by lot as each debt was paid off in part. The Bank was required by law to keep its Bonds strictly within the amount of the value of the mortgaged property. Besides this guarantee, the creditors had a first charge on the ten per cent. paid-up Capital of the Founders, and on the Reserve Fund, and the Mutual Guarantee Fund, and the subsidy paid by Government to help the Reserve Fund. It is very important to note the concessions granted to this Bank by the Hungarian Government. The Government granted a subsidy to the Reserve Fund of five hundred thousands of Florins. It exempted the Bank's profits from the income-tax, and its operations from all stamp duties. It lent the help of its officers for assessing the value of the property mortgaged. It ordered inspection of accounts with a view to secure obedience to the rules, and, finally, it permitted the Bank to foreclose or sell the mortgaged and also unmortgaged property of its debtor on default being committed in payment without requiring it to go to law, and take its chance of justice, with all its delays and costs. The borrower was required to pay six-monthly interest in advance, and the bank also paid the Coupons on its Bonds to the holders thereof after every six months. In consequence of these exceptional privileges, few defaults were committed, and it has been estimated that out of some fourteen millions advanced by the Bank to eleven thousand borrowers, the Bank had to suffer loss to the extent of twenty-five thousand pounds sterling only. The borrowers are allowed freedom to pay off their debts in anticipation, and a considerable minority took advantage of this privilege. The Institute has thus fully realized the leading ideas of its promoters. It acts as intermediary between the borrower and the lender; while procuring for the borrower easier terms and teaching him self-reliance and freedom, it favours the lender by offering its own guarantee for the money he advances to the borrower through its agency. These facilities have greatly helped the prosperity of all Classes in the Country, and lowered the rate of interest all round.

The Boden Credit Institute also deals with Communes and Municipalities, and advances loans on special terms favourable to these Corporations and to the Bank. This Bank is the best type of institutions worked in the interests of the borrowers, as the founders are content with five per cent. interest on paid up capital, and its Directors receive no payments.

There are other Institutions worked on the same principles in the interest of the lenders, and in their case dividends are declared as in ordinary Banks, varying according to the conditions of each year's operations. The Principle of all these Banks which make advances on Real Property is 'to interpose the Bank between the borrower and the lender, to guarantee the lender against all risks, and thereby secure a reduction of the rate of interest so as to help the borrower with loans at a slightly enhanced rate of interest, and provide for a Reserve Fund, and for the expenses of management, and by spreading the payment over a long number of years, generally forty years, provide for a gradual but certain satisfaction of both principal and interest. The Austro-Hungarian Bank is the chief of these Banks, which carry on business in the interests of lenders. Besides doing the regular work of a National Bank, it has a Real Credit Branch managed by a separate Committee. In consideration of the special privilege of obtaining speedy execution of its claims, and exemptions from Stamp Duties conferred on it, the Government has a hand in the supervision of the management of this Branch. A Government Commissary is appointed to this duty. The Bank issues Bonds at four per cent. and charges four and a half to five and three-quarters per cent. according as the period of amortization is long or short.

There are other Banks such as the Hypotheken Bank or the Credit Foncier, the Commercial Bank of Buda-Pesth, and the Savings Banks, which do not enjoy any special privileges, but do a large amount of work.

A smaller Boden Credit Institute was founded in 1879 to help poor Landholders. The Government granted a subsidy of half a Million Florins to its Reserve Fund, and its other rules and privileges, and the powers of Government control are very much the same as those described above in regard to the bigger Institution. It has helped land-holders with loans amounting in all to ten Millions of Rupees, secured on a total value of twenty-five millions, and has, in course of time, reduced the rate of interest from seven and a half per cent. to four and a half per cent.

All these Banks in Austro-Hungary have lately been empowered to advance loans for improvement purposes, and such loans are advanced at four and three-quarters per cent. including the sinking fund, and the period for extinction of liability ranges from thirty to fifty years. These advances are exempted from Stamp Duties and other charges, and the technical execution of these improvement works, which involve expenditure over a certain amount, is entrusted to the State Engineers as a portion of their charge. Default or difficulty of collection rarely occurs as advances are by rule limited to half the value of the assets.

In Austria, the Provincial Boden Credit Anstallen receive subsidies from the Provincial Governments, and in return the Governments exercise control and supervision through their Commissaries.

To come next to the Countries of the Latin Union,—France, Italy and Belgium,—it is to be noted that the establishment of a Credit Foncier, or Mortgage Bank for lending money on the security of lands, forced itself upon the attention of the French people about the time of the Revolution of 1848. Inquiries made at the time elicited the fact that the usual rate of interest on mortgage loans was nine to ten per cent., and the idea of the promoters was to remove the difficulties in the way of finding capital on the Credit of land felt by the Peasant Proprietors created by the French Revolution.

In 1852, three great Institutions were founded in Paris and in two other places, but they were soon amalgamated into a Central Institution with its head-quarters at Paris, and with an exclusive right to operate throughout France. The object of such Institutions was laid down to be the advance of loans to small land-owners at moderate interest, and provide for the repayment of the principal and interest of the same in a long period of forty or fifty years. The capital of this Central Bank was raised to sixty millions of Francs, one-half of which was paid up. In consideration of the exclusive privileges conferred on the body as the sole National Bank for the mortgage of Real Property in France, Government has insisted upon retaining in its hands considerable powers of control and supervision. The Governor and two Sub-Governors are appointed by the President of the Republic out of the larger shareholders, and there is a Council of Shareholders. In 1860, the Credit Foncier was authorised to lend money to Communes and Departments, secured on Municipal and Local Funds. The Credit Foncier cannot issue its Bonds over and above the value of the mortgaged property, and it must keep a Reserve of twenty per cent. of the total of the sum advanced. The capital of the Credit Foncier has been gradually raised from sixty millions to one hundred and eighty millions.

The amount of its mortgage advances rose from eight hundred and fifty-two millions in 1852 to two thousand and four millions in 1888, and its loans to Communes rose similarly from four hundred and seventy-eight to nine hundred and fifty-three millions. The net profits realized were seven and one-third million Francs in 1878, and twenty-two and two-thirds million Francs in 1889. No loan is advanced unless the property mortgaged yields a certain and durable return. It is not advanced beyond one-half of the value of the property as assessed by the Bank's experts. The expenses of negotiating the loan and satisfying the Bank about the title-deeds come to about 3 per cent., and are borne by the borrower. The interest charged is 4·85 per cent., and the period fixed for repayment may be either a short or a long term. The debtor may pay off the loans in anticipation. In all, three thousand and four hundred millions of Francs have been advanced as loans since 1852, and default was committed only in respect of debts amounting to eighteen millions, in regard to which the Bank found it necessary to buy the property itself. As a consequence of this improved organisation of Credit, the rate of interest has fallen throughout France from nine or ten per cent. to five per cent. The Government guarantees the Credit Foncier against competition and lends it the assistance of its officers.

France is pre-eminently a Country of Peasant Proprietors with small Holdings like those of India, and its agricultural interest is of considerable importance. Of course, the French people are differentiated from our countrymen by their remarkable thrift, industry, and forethought, and their powers of organisation and mutual help. These habits are, however, essentially the creation of the change that took place in the early part of the Century, when the estates of the Nobles and the Bishops and Monasteries were escheated to the State and parcelled out among the Peasant Farmers.

The accounts of the French Peasantry as given in the narratives of Mr. Arthur Young in times which preceded this great change, do not show that there was then any such advantage enjoyed by them over our people. The French peasant is, besides, the proprietor of his Holdings, and has no Land-Tax to pay. Barring these differences of history and character, the conditions in France are like those of Western India. The French peasant is heavily in debt, more than half the land being mortgaged, but his debts sit lightly on him, because they represent improvements made in the land, which cannot be said with equal truth of the debts due by our peasants. The re-organized system of Land Credit which has worked these wonders in France, and Austria, and Hungary, may, therefore, be safely expected to achieve equal success in India.

In regard to Italy, these observations apply with still greater relevancy. In 1861 it was ascertained that the average rate of interest on mortgage loans was eight to ten per cent., and the amount of the debts charged on the land in Italy, excluding Venice and Rome, was two thousand six hundred and ninety millions, while the net income was four hundred millions, and the Government charge on the land was one hundred and fifteen millions. Deducting Government and other charges, one hundred and twenty millions, and the interest amount, one hundred and forty millions, the owners had only one hundred and forty millions of revenue at their disposal. With the increase in Government taxes and in the interest charges, the balance left in the hands of the Land-owners grew less each year, and this drew the attention of the Italian Statesmen to the necessity of taking early action on the lines followed with such brilliant success in France.

In 1862 it was accordingly proposed to start a Central Credit Foncier for the whole Kingdom with a Capital of four millions of Pounds Sterling, and invested with exclusive privileges, and helped by a Government subsidy of four hundred thousand Pounds Sterling. It was not found possible to float the scheme in its huge proportions. and in 1866 a compromise was adopted by which the Agency of seven existing Banks was utilized, and powers were conferred on them to operate exclusively within their defined Zones, and deal in mortgage business. The rules of business were the same as those of the kindred Institution in working order in France. Loans were to be advanced up to half of the value of the property mortgaged, and gradual liquidation of principal and interest was to be provided for. The interest rate was to be a uniform one,—five per cent., and the Banks were to issue Negotiable Bonds, and withdraw them gradually as instalments were paid or satisfied. Between 1866 and 1885, thirteen millions of pounds were lent to eight thousand three hundred and fifty-five borrowers. After 1885, the zone System was done away with, and any Bank or Association with a capital of four hundred thousand Pounds Sterling was permitted to transact mortgage business under the condition mentioned above. The rigidity of a uniform rate of interest was also done away with, and discretion was allowed to charge four, four-and-a-half and five per cent. interest according as the period was long or short; the rule of limiting advances to half the value was also relaxed and loans were permitted up to three-fifths of the value under this New Law, the National Bank of Italy and seven other Banks carry on mortgage dealings in addition to their other business at Naples, Rome, Sienna, Bologna, and some other Towns. The Municipal Authorities of Sienna were the first to work the celebrated Monte Pia System of loans on pledges nearly three hundred years ago. The Italian Law allows to these Banks great facilities for the speedy and cheap recovery of mortagage debts, and the Government does not, as in France, exercise any active control in the management of the Banks' affairs The Banks which issue these Bonds undertake to sell. them on commission; the Bonds are made payable to bearer, and the holder has no claim against any private mortgagor, but only against the Bank. All the eight Banks cash each other's Coupons.

In Belgium, the First Institution of the kind we are

now considering, called Le Caissa Hypothecain, was established in 1855 with a view to offer facilities to capitalists for investing their monies safely, and to borrowers for borrowing money at low rates, and enabling them to clear off the principal and interest amounts by instalments spread over a long period. The powers of the Bank were enlarged in 1886, and it has since taken the name of Credit Foncier de Belgique. There are other Institutions which do the same business. The Belgian Authorities had under contemplation the creation of a Central Institution which was to have power to advance money on Houses, Forests and Woods up to one-fourth their assessed value, and on lands up to a half. The borrowers were to pay five and a quarter per cent. interest, which rate was to include the Sinking Fund and expenses of management and registration, and the period fixed for repayment was to be forty-one years. The Bank was to issue four per cent. Bonds fully covered by the value of the property mortgaged, and the Belgian Government agreed to undertake the work of collecting the instalments due by the Bank's debtors through its Treasury Agents, and in case of arrears special facilities were to be allowed for realizing the monies due, the Bank's Debts being allowed a priority over all other debts, and the transactions of the Bank were to be exempt from all taxes and duties. The Bill was passed by the Lower House, but before it received the assent of the Senate, a Political crisis occurred, and no further action was taken in the matter. The concessions proposed and accepted by the House of Representatives deserve, however, to be specially borne in mind, as they indicate the extent of support which Continental Governments are prepared to give in the work of Re-organizing Credit.

The Federal States of Switzerland furnish equally interesting examples of this same liberal policy. In these States, Private Capitalists seldom lend money on their own account. The Mortgage and Savings Banks virtually monopolize the business. These Mortgage Banks are either purely State Institutions, or of a mixed character. The Mortgage Bank of the Canton of Berne is a State Institution, and is the most important Institution of its kind in Switzerland. These State Institutions are more successful than Private or mixed Banks. Of course, the State Banks do not satisfy all demands, and there is thus full scope for private enterprize. The State Institutions have this advantage over private Banks that, they do not screw up the rates of interest, while their ample means enable them virtually to regulate the rate of interest all over the Country. The Berne Bank has reduced its rate of interest within the past fifteen years from five to four per cent., and has thereby doubled and trebled the volume of its business. The deposits have increased from £1,119,629 to £3,032,389, and the Loans from £1,600,000 to £3,200,000. Most of the Swiss Cantons have each their separate Mortgage Bank, and though Savings Banks, which deal in Personal Credit, are generally private, yet in many parts of the country the Communes assist even these Banks by taking a certain number of shares. Swiss Mortgage Banks lend by way of first charges only, and compel borrowers to discharge all previous claims. The amortization arrangements enable the indebted Agriculturists to pay off their debts, and free their lands from incumbrances with certainty and ease. Under the direct system of lending, creditors exercise a moral tutelage or dominion over the debtors who sink in dignity. The relations between a private debtor and creditor have a tendency, in course of time, to develop mutual misunderstanding and bitterness. The Emancipation of the population from this source of moral degradation by interposition of the Banks has proved of the highest value as an agency for the Education of the people in the best virtues of Citizenship. The Bank's relations to its debtors are of the simplest character and involve no useless expense. The men who have money, and want to invest it safely, find that they have not to hunt after their debtors, inquire into their solvency, and go to law to test the result. The man who has saved money which he wants to lend goes to the Bank, pays down his money as a Depositor, or buys the Bonds of the Bank, and when the six-monthly instalment falls due, he signs the Coupon, and cashes it. An immense waste of power, time, and money is thus saved to him and to the debtor. The business becomes specialized, like any other business, all risks are avoided, and all the benefits of a secure investment and cheap loan are secured to the monied and needy classes. These Swiss Mortgage Banks furnish, perhaps, the best example of genuine co-operative effort that is seen in any part of the world. Farmers club together for the purchase, in a joint way, of Agricultural Cattle, of Seeds, of Manure, Pasture Lands, Cheese Dairies, or for draining Marsh Lands, and constructing Country Roads, and the Banks help them to do so on very easy terms.

This principle of Co-operation for common purpose was first worked out in Germany on lines formulated by Raiffeisen, but they have been developed most widely and beneficially in Switzerland. Each Member contributes a fixed sum per month or year, and the Association also receives Deposits. Out of the Collections and Deposits, Loans are made to those who need them for buying Cattle or Seeds or Manure. The Association has a charge on the Cattle, etc., so bought, and the Swiss Law provides that if any one of the Members breaks his engagement to the Association, and sells the Cattle, the act is not only a civil but a criminal offence, of which a Magistrate takes instant cognizance. The engagement has in this case to be executed before the Magistrate so as to avoid all future complications. These small Associations receive help from the State Governments, and in return their accounts are open to inspection by State Officials.

This completes the summary I proposed to give of the most recent history of the Re-organization of Credit in some of the principal Continental Countries of Europe. The present circumstances of this Country demand that the efforts made by the Statesmen of so many countries, and which have been attended with such success, should be carefully studied by us with a view to practical action. There can be little doubt that, if similar attempts had been made in England, the Rulers of India would not have failed to take upon their shoulders the work of Re-organizing Credit on these lines in India long ago. The circumstances of England are, however, peculiar. The vast mass of her population consists mostly of wage-earners, who possess neither lands nor houses nor appliances of their own. The rich Capitalists and Landlords own the lands, and houses, and machinery, and factories, and being intelligent and well organized, need no special help. It is these peculiar circumstances which have made it superfluous for the Statesmen of England to devote their attention to these matters. They are naturally disposed to take care of their wage-earning Classes, to feed, clothe, and house them properly, to provide for smaller hours of work, to arrange for the compulsory safeguarding of the comforts and conveniences of Factory Hands. These traditions impel them also to turn their philanthropic attention to Factory Legislation here, which, though reasonable in its way, affects but a drop in the ocean of Humanity in India. Our agricultural and artisan Population are not wage-earners. They own their lands and houses, and implements of trade, and their small shops, and factories, and their cattle and carts. They mostly work on their own account, and if they have no store or savings of their own, as they generally have not, they must borrow money, and repay it as they best can. The necessity of Re-organizing Credit transaction is thus not confined to Agriculturist Classes. It is a general necessity created in this Country by its circumstances and habits, and any measures which tend to rescue this business from its present chaos, and restore certainty and honesty in it, are sure to put new life and energy in the body politic. The question of Credit, as observed above, does not concern Agriculturists alone. It equally concerns Spinners and Weavers, Carpenters, Smiths, Dyers, Potters, Brass and Copper, Silk and Embroidery workers, Shopkeepers, Carriers, and all the Trades and Professions that are now practised in this Country. It will have been seen from the summary given above, that the Statesmen of Europe have realized their duties in this matter of affording facilities for the Re-organization of Real Credit, and given it practical effect in various ways, (1) either by

5

lending the help of its Officials for control or management or inspection work, or (2) by subsidies, or (3) by undertaking Collections, or (4) by giving a Monopoly of business, or (5) by facilitating the work of Recovery, or (6) by exempting their business from all Stamp Duties and Income-tax and other charges. The circumstances of India furnish strong grounds why the Government here should help this work of Re-organizing Credit in all these ways according as local difficulties or aptitudes may suggest or justify. An effort was made in this part of the Country to start an Agricultural Bank on the lines laid down above. The Scheme was well supported by the Local Government, and by the Government of India also, acting under the advices of Sir E. Baring, now Lord Cromer. It was, however, negatived by the India Office Authorities. No blame need be laid at the door of any body for this untoward result. The English Rulers in India are brought face to face with the specialities of Indian life, and realize their responsibilities. In England the Authorities have not the advantage of this touch with actual life, and their English traditions naturally predispose them to regard that the State, as such, has no functions or responsibilities in this connection. The promoters of the Agricultural Bank desired that Government should sanction the experiment in one *Taluka* by undertaking an inquiry into the previous debts of the Agriculturists, which, when ascertained, were to be paid off by the Government, the Bank undertaking to make good the sum so paid on conditions of its being allowed a first charge on the mortgaged Estates of the *Ryots* so benefited. The Bank undertook to charge very low rates of interest, and to recover them in instalments fixed with the approval of Government Officers. To prevent all disputes, it agreed to leave this work of Collection of instalments due, in the hands of the Village Authorities, who were to realize the instalments as they now realize the Assessment of Government or its *Tagāi* advances. Lastly, the Bank prayed that Assessment within the area so dealt with should not be raised, so as to disturb the arrangements they might enter into, and that their transactions should be exempted from all taxes and charges. In consideration of their undertaking to finance and work the concern, and charge low rates of interest, the Government was to help them to obtain speedy and cheap execution. It will be seen that none of the special privileges and concessions asked for were without their precedent in the Credit Fonciers and Land Mortgage Banks subsidized and helped and controlled by the European States. The Scheme, however, fell through then, for reasons which it is needless now to relate. The difficulties of Indian life are, however, too serious and peremptory to be satisfactorily disposed of in any other way, and the question is sure to force itself soon upon public attention. Already we hear that the

Madras Government has appointed a Special Officer to inquire into the subject, and the time, therefore, seems opportune to press the matter once more upon the attention of Government. State help is needed for the very cogent reason that State control and supervision are necessary to inspire confidence. No other organization in the Country has such a deversified, intelligent and widely diffused Agency at its disposal. The interests of the State also, are materially involved in the matter of the well-being of the most numerons and least helpful Classes of the taxpaying population.

The State need not expend its Funds. The Funds will be forthcoming to any amount if it only promises to organize the Agency, and set it at work. The Post Office and Savings Banks deposits are ready to hand. All that Government has to do is to organize District or City Committees of Indian Capitalists, to empower them to receive deposits at fixed rates and lend them at slightly higher rates to the borrowers on the security of lands, or houses, &c., the excess rate providing for a gradual amortization of the debt in a definite period, as also, Insurance charges and working expenses. The loans of these District Committees should be allowed priority over all other debts, and exempted from all duties, and certain and speedy execution should be permitted to them. The experience of the working of similar bodies in Europe, and it may be noted in Egypt also, justifies the hope that the losses will be very trifling, and the benefits incalculable. What holds true of Agriculture holds equally good in this country about every other Trade and Industry. The recuperative powers of Nature and Art are limited, and cannot stand the dead weight of prohibitive rates of interest, made necessary by disorganized Credit, and the uncertainties and delays and expenses of Civil Proceedings. Remove these difficulties and hindrances, and Credit will rise to its natural and healthy level. The glories of peace are far nobler than those of war. The whole Country is looking up with wistful eyes for a Statesman who will guide its destinies in this great struggle, and help it to win the race of life and revived health, and national well-being.

III.

NETHERLANDS INDIA AND THE CULTURE SYSTEM.*

THE Economic Problem which the Government of India has to grapple with in the immediate future of this Country is of a far more peremptory character than even the question of Frontier Defences against Foreign aggression, and it presents difficulties and uncertainties by the side of which the difficulties and uncertainties of the military situation are but child's play. The Problem of settling New Continents, and planting on virgin soil 'Greater Britains,' has been so satisfactorily solved by the patience and genius of the British race, that it might, at first sight, surprise the superficial observer that the comparatively easy task of reclaiming India from the ancient bondage of Feudalism and Status, and bringing it into line with modern civilization, with its freedom of Contracts and the increasing activity of Commerce and Manufactures, which supplement the ancient single resource of Agriculture in Western Europe should have baffled the best

* Read at the Industrial Conference, Poona, in 1890.

efforts of British Statesmanship. After a Century of rule, the situation is as blank and dreary as ever it was before, nay, in certain aspects, it has grown worse by reason of the impact of civilized Foreign Rule and unrestricted Exchange, and undreamed of facilities of communication. The co-ordination of Industries, which establishes a healthy proportion between the Rural and Urban Populations, had been displaced to a greater extent than ever it was before, and has increased the dependence of multitudes on the soil exhausted by over-cultivation. The growth of Population does not represent to the same extent growth in material comforts, and has led to the absorption of waste lands till, in some parts of the Country, the last margin has been reached, and millions die or starve when a single Monsoon fails. The increased Trade and Commerce of the Country represents a steadily diminishing proportion of Native enterprise and skill engaged in it, and the monopoly of Political power is made more invidious by the monopoly of commercial Wealth and manufacturing activity. The Bible-promise that '*To him that hath, much shall be given, and from him that hath not, the little that he hath shall be taken away*' sums up the situation.

The Administration cannot be charged with either neglect or indifference to these changes. It has been honestly trying to apply palliatives, it ensures peace, protects Property and Labour, and secures the administration of Justice to all. It encourages emigration to foreign parts, and immigration from densely peopled portions to sparsely inhabited tracts. It has endeavoured to develop new sources of Wealth by encouraging pioneering enterprise. Above all, it has tried to open up the Country and utilize its Water Supply in a way which commands admiration. Its powers of action are limited and controlled by higher Authorities, and it is not, therefore, free to adopt certain remedies which commend themselves to Self-governing Countries in Europe, America, and the British Colonies, to protect themselves against the effects of foreign Competition, but, with this exception, everything has been done that human prescience could suggest, as possible remedies. Finally, it is open to conviction, and even prepared to retrace its steps, if it were convinced beyond doubt of its mistake. This circumstance justifies hope, and encourages the efforts of those who think that, notwithstanding past failures, a way may be found out of the difficulty, which involves no serious departure from established maxims of Civilized Rule, and promises success at no distant date.

I propose in the sequel to give a brief sketch of a great Experiment worked out by a European Power to improve the Economic condition of its Asiatic Dependencies, under circumstances very similar to those which obtain in India. There, as here, a civilized European Power was entrusted with the rule of vast Territories inhabited by a comparatively barbarous people, and the experiment was undertaken and preserved in, not purely from philanthropic motives, which prove weak in the long run, but from motives of Self-Interest, and resulted in a success, by the side of which the comparative failure of the efforts of British Rulers presents a very suggestive contrast. After being worked for thirty years, the experiment has been abandoned, because the special purpose, which dictated its adoption, has been to a large extent accomplished. The parallel is not, of course, complete in all respects. The Country where the experiment was tried was a small one, as compared with the vast expanse of India. The people, among whom it was tried, were a more homogeneous race than those who inhabit this Great Continent. The previous historical traditions were also not the same. But after making all allowance for these differences, there remains a sufficient substratum of common conditions, which justifies the assurance that an experiment undertaken in the same spirit here, with the necessary adaptations to suit local conditions, has a reasonable chance of attaining at least qualified success, so as to justify the venture.

The Experiment, to which the foregoing remarks relate, was tried by the Netherlands Government in their possessions in the East Indian Archipelago, Java and the Islands surrounding it. Java, it may be noted, became a Dutch conquest in the best days of Dutch domination on the Seas. It was administered by the Dutch East India Company in its own interests. The Company had the exclusive right of the Trade with Java, and it monopolized the production of Spices, the most paying produce of the Island, by continuing the ancient system of Forced Labour and Forced Deliverances. The Dutch Company left the Native Chiefs to rule the people, and confined their direct administration to the European Settlers in the Ports on the coast. In the French Wars, the Islands were under British management from 1811 to 1816, in which latter year, they were restored back to the Dutch, on the conclusion of Peace. Sir Stamford Raffles was British Governor during those years. Under the administration of this British Governor, the Indian *Ryotwari* System of fixed cash rates on land was introduced, the Native Magistracy was displaced, and European Agency in the Administration of Civil and Criminal Justice was substituted, and he declared that land was freely saleable for debts and arrears of Revenue. He abolished Forced Labour, and Monopolies of export and production, and threw open the trade of the Islands to all the world. These lines of policy will be easily recognized to be the lines of policy which have been steadily followed in British India. When the Islands were restored back to the Dutch, they, however, preferred to reverse this policy. They declared the lands to be unsaleable for debts or arrears of Government

Revenue. They abolished the *Ryotwari* System of small Holdings at fixed cash rates, and reverted to the ancient Native method of Joint Village Responsibility. The task of direct Government by means of an European Agency was given up, and the authority of Native Chiefs, or Regents as they were called, was utilized for the government of the Native population. They abolished Free Trade, and substituted Differential Duties on imports from foreign parts. The Old System of levying the Land Tax in the shape of one-fifth of the produce and one-fifth of the labour of Agriculturists for State purposes, was restored, with the modification that the Labour share was reduced to one-seventh, or one day in the week. The tax both in produce and Labour in respect of Government Land was paid to the Native Chiefs in Territories governed by Treaty Chiefs and to the Dutch Government in Territories acquired by conquest. In respect of these Government Lands, the Peasants who cultivated them had only the usufructuary interest, and could not sell or alienate their right of user. In regard to private lands, the Peasants paid the rent, in kind and labour, to the private Owners who could not raise the rent as fixed by Law, and the private Owner paid to Government one-fifth of the net income or rent, or three-quarters of one per cent. on Value. The Private Lands were liable to sale, and could be freely mortgaged or alienated. They could not, however, be sold until moveables were exhausted, and even then, the Judge fixed the price, and the creditor had to take it at that price, if no bid was made, or the bids were lower. The Peasant had recognized status both in the advantages and burdens of the Joint Responsibility System of the Village. If he reclaimed new land, no tax was levied for the first five years. The Tax of one-fifth produce was settled with the Village Chief (corresponding to our Patel), and he distributed the burden. The Labour-share of the rent, one day's work out of a week, was utilized on the Public Roads and Canals, and other Public Works, and Private Landlords used it for the cultivation of their own lands. Each Householder was required to furnish one adult male for Forced Labour, whatever might be the number of members in the family. In course of time, it came to pass that the Villagers jointly employed a certain number of hired hands at their own expense on State Works, and discharged this burden of Forced Labour. To a large extent these principles still regulate the Administration of the Dutch East Indies.

For the Native Territories, Residents are appointed, who discharge Judicial, Administrative, and Financial duties. These duties, however, are light. The judicial work especially is lightened by investing Native Chiefs with large powers of conciliation and arbitration. The Resident sitting with two Native Members, decides criminal cases as Session Judge. In regard to Europeans, there are separate Courts of Justice presided over by Dutch lawyers. The Resident's salary is £1,250 a year, and he earns by commission a similar amount. Assistant Residents receive £500 per year. The Resident's Secretary is also a European Official. He has charge of Registration work, and is a Treasury Officer and Record Keeper. Besides the Residents and their Assistants and Secretaries, there are Controllers of two classes charged with the duty of watching the condition of the Peasants, and of promoting their welfare. The Comptroller exercises no Judicial Powers, but is expected to act as Arbitrator or Conciliator. He has charge of Government Stores and is paid a salary which rises from £225 to £375 a year. The Residents with the Assistants and the Comptrollers of the several Provinces are under the authority of the Governor-General in Council. The work of actual government is, however, carried on by Native Chiefs. European Officers make suggestions or inspection Reports, but have no power to issue orders or enforce execution. Under the Resident there is a Native Regent for the Province, and there are District and Village Chiefs under the Regent. If a difference of opinion occurs between the Residents and the Regents, reference is made to the Central Authority. The Regent's salary ranges from £800 to £1,500 a year, and he also obtains a Percentage or Commission. He holds a sort of a Court, and is not only the Civil Ruler, but also the High Priest for his Province. The Regent exercises both Civil and Criminal powers except as regards Europeans, and the Residents are, at least in theory, deputed by Government to the Court of the Native Regent. The Regents are assisted by a Council of Vazirs, and have their own Secretaries and Clerks. The Regents preside over the Police Force, and have in their hands the appointment and control of the subordinate Native, District and Village Officials and Chiefs. These subordinate officials are called Mantries in Villages, and Vedanas in Districts, and receive salaries and commissions. They exercise Revenue and Police functions, and act as Conciliators, and no suit is entertained till conciliation fails. The Governor-General has a Council of four, and there is a High Court of Judicature with jurisdiction over Europeans and Natives of rank in the Coast Towns.

It was necessary to give these details of land management and Government in Java for a correct understanding of the experiment of the Culture System about to be described. It will be seen from them that the Dutch Government have steadily adhered to the Native model of Government, and limited the foreign Agency to the work of inspection and report, except in regard to the Dutch or other foreign Settlements in the Coast Towns. The difference between the British Indian System and the Netherland's method of Rule is radical, the latter being Conservative and Protective, while the former is based on modern ideas of equality and is worked out by a much larger foreign Agency, than is found necessary in the Dutch Indies. The one system is, therefore, necessarily costly, and requires checks upon checks, and a hierarchy of officials. Notwithstanding its costliness due to the larger employment of Europeans, there can be no doubt that in its educating influence the British Indian System compares favourably with the Dutch method of Rule. That method, however, has its own advantages. It does not dismember Native Society to the same extent, as is found to be the case in India.

To proceed with the narrative, the Netherlands Possessions in the the East Indies cover an area of 30,000 square miles. The population in 1885 was estimated to be about thirty millions. The Revenues in 1826 were eighteen million Florins, or one and a quarter Crores of Rupees, and they rose to thirty millions, or two Crores of Rupees, in 1833. In the years which preceded the introduction of the Culture System, the expenditure exceeded the revenue by three million Florins annually, for many years. This involved state of the finances first suggested to General Von de Bosch, Governor of the Netherlands East Indies, the necessity of taking urgent measures for developing the resources of the Island, and the plan followed by him is known as the Culture System. It was first introduced about the year 1831-33, and continued in operation for more than thirty years. The Theory of the System was that all Government Lands not required for Rice cultivation, which afforded subsistence to the cultivators, were to be planted with crops for which there was a demand in Europe, by means of advances to be made by the State to private Contractors, who undertook to plant the particular crops, and sell the produce to Government and fixed rates, and liquidate the advance made to them by instalments in a fixed number of years. These advances were of several kinds. The first in order, was the advance for initial expenditure necessary to start the concern. It might be a Planting concern or a Manufacturing concern. The Contractor received this advance under due regulations. In the first place, the advance to any particular Contractor was not to exceed two hundred thousands of Florins, or about £14,000. Though no interest was charged on this advance, it was repayable in twelve years by instalments of one-tenth from the third year. Care was taken to see that the Contractor was not a mere speculator, and the money was advanced to him under Official superintendence, which helped him to a choice of the site, as also in selecting and buying the machinery, and fitting up the mill, or making the water power available. In regard to the labour required for managing the concern, Government at first transferred to the Contractor the gratuitous or Forced Labour due to it from the peasants. The machinery was allowed to be imported duty free, and timber and other materials from Government Forests were supplied without charge. The Official experts assisted him with their advice. The Superintending Officer's certificate was necessary to satisfy Government that the money was spent for the purposes for which it was borrowed. Next to this initial advance, a yearly advance for the production or manufacture of crops was made on condition of being repaid out of the produce raised, at prices which were fixed in a way to leave a margin of profit, both to Government and to the Contractor. The Farms seldom exceeded four hundred acres. At first the whole of the produce was made over to Government at one-third above the cost price. This plan was found not to work well, and later on, the Government agreed to buy the produce at contract rates, which were fixed, so as to repay the yearly advance, and one-tenth of the initial or the building advance. Generally, the rates were so fixed that the delivery of two-thirds of the manufactured produce repaid the yearly advance, and left one-third as profit out of which the initial advance was repaid. The areas adapted for particular crops were chosen by Government Officers, who left in each Village sufficient land for Rice cultivation for the peasants, and required the villagers to plant one-fifth of their lands with the Contractor's crops. When one-fifth

6

area was thus set apart for the Contractor's crops, no Land-Tax was levied from that village. If, after paying the yearly advance and one-tenth of the building advance, any surplus was left, the Contractor had to share it with the villagers. In course of time, experience showed that the practice of remitting the Land-Tax worked unjustly, and it was accordingly given up, and in its place another plan was adopted by which the full rent was collected from the Village, and the labourers were paid individually in cash for the work done. Under this new arrangement, out of the cash payments made for wages, the villagers were enabled to pay the Government demand without the necessity of borrowing. In short, the Java Culture System may be described as a system of encouraging the planting of remunerative crops, and manufacturing them for the European market, by private agency and at private risk, with Government advances, and under Government supervision, and with the Government as the sole customer. All the three parties who worked the System, the Government, the Contractor, and Peasants, benefited by it. The Government borrowed money, as it alone could borrow, on Public Credit, and bought the produce so raised by Contractors to whom the money was advanced at low rates of interest, and it repaid itself, both principal and interest, by buying at rates which left a large margin of profit on sale in Europe. The Contractor, after he paid off the advances made to him, became the owner of a large and flourishing Concern, while the Villagers or Peasant labourers received much higher wages than they ever could obtain before, or shared in surplus profits. The Culture System was worked to best advantage in respect of First Class crops, such as Sugarcane, Indigo, Tea, Tobacco, and Cochineal, which required high planting, and skill in manufacture. There were, however, certain kinds of produce such as Coffee, Cinnamon, and Pepper, of the Second Class, which did not require planting or manufacturing skill. The intervention of Contractors was, therefore, dispensed with in their case, and advances were made to the Cultivators direct, and as with our own Opium Cultivation in Behar, prices were fixed beforehand through the Official Agency in such a way as to leave a margin of profit to the Cultivators as also to the Government, which had a right to buy the entire crop at fixed rates. The Sugarcane crop was the most remunerative, and next to it was Tobacco cultivation. The vigilance of the Official Agency was secured by a percentage as commission paid to them on the quantity of produce raised. The self-interest of the villagers was sharpened by a rule, which directed that if the crops failed, they should get nothing. In 1854, while two and a half millions of acres were under Rice cultivation, one hundred thousand acres were planted under the Culture System. The Land Rent paid to Government on these one hundred thousand acres was assessed at the Rice rates. The Government looked to the profits realized by it, on sale of the crops in Holland, as their only return.

The first Contracts were made for twenty years, and at the end of that period were renewed for another term. About thirty to forty Crores of Rupees were in all advanced under this System, and when the first advances were repaid, they were reinvested on similar terms. During the last twenty years, there have been no renewals. At present Independent Planters are encouraged to settle on Government lands, out of which large plots of uncultivated lands, measuring three hundred to four hundred acres, are leased for twenty years. No rent is charged for the first few years, and afterwards rent of Rupees two to three is charged as cultivation extends. The Reports of Local Authorities show that, notwithstanding the experience obtained under the Culture System, and the obligation on Government to buy produce at fixed rates, the Independent System of planting does not prove as profitable as the old system of protected and subsidized Planting and Manufacture. The two main defects of the most recent arrangements are: Firstly, the high rate of interest which the Planters and Manufacturers have to pay; and secondly, the absence of Official guidance which was secured under the old System. A Sugarcane Plantation, which cost two hundered thousand of Florins under the old System, was worth nearly three times as much at the end of the period, after the loans advanced had been paid off. The Independent System works well enough in regard to crops which do not require high skill and care. But, in the case of Sugar and Tobacco, the results are decidedly in favour of the Culture System.

This brief description of the Culture System will suffice to convey a general idea of the way in which General Von de Bosch succeeded in developing the resources of the Island. The experiment was undertaken merely for Revenue purposes, but indirectly it helped the Netherlands East Indies to attain a high degree of material prosperity. The deficits, which had, previously to 1831, been almost continuous for many years, were changed into surpluses of many millions of Florins. The Land Revenue, which was eighteen million Florins in 1817, and thirty millions, or two Crores of Rupees, in 1833, rose to one hundred and thirty-six million Florins in 1860, that is, nearly nine and a half Crores of Rupees. The advances required for the Culture System were made out of sums borrowed by the State, and this National Debt was repaid with interest in forty years out of the large profits which the State made by the sale of produce in Holland, so that in 1871 the Government of the Netherlands India had no National Debt. The surpluses of Revenue between 1831 and 1871 amounted to the large figure of seven hundred and twenty-five million

Florins, or fifty-two Crores of Rupees. An official report submitted to Lord Dufferin by Von Den Berg, the Governor of Java in 1885, admits that the Culture System greatly contributed to the development of Java in growing Tropical produce. In 1871 there were ninety-seven Mill-owners with whom Government had contracted for the production of Sugar. These ninety-seven Contractors planted seventy thousand acres with Sugarcane, and employed two hundred and twenty-five thousands of labourers. The Exports and Imports in 1860 were nine million pounds Sterling worth of Exports and five million pounds Imports. Since 1871, as observed above, the Java Government have discontinued the Culture System of encouraging production, and as a result of this change of arrangement, the prosperity of the Island has been almost at a standstill, and during the last eight years, from 1876 to 1884, there have been deficits of nearly seventy-five million Florins, which have had to be met out of the surpluses of one hundred million Florins of the first five years—1871 to 1876. The profits made by the sale of Government produce in Holland, which under the Culture System ranged from fifty to seventy million Florins, and were nearly equal to the Revenue raised in the Island by taxation, declined from sixty million Florins in 1871, to forty millions in 1884, and thirty millions in 1885. In consequence of this reduction, new Taxes had to be imposed, with the result that the Revenue raised by taxation, which was seventy million Florins in 1871, was one hundred and one millions in 1884, and one hundred and four millions in 1885. This increase of taxation has not, however, enabled the Government to avoid deficits. Financially speaking, therefore, neither the Dutch Government nor the people in Java, have benefited much by the change of System. There have been certain special circumstances which have contributed to produce this effect, notably the war with the Achines, and the efforts made by the Holland Government to shift a portion of her own burden of Debt to the Dependencies. The planting and manufacturing Industry encouraged under the Culture System has also suffered a collapse, and is not now as prosperous as it once used to be. The change of System was ostensibly introduced in the interest of the Native population, but the results do not show that the subjects of the Netherlands Government, both European and Native, have benefited much by the change, wages have gone down in most parts of the Island, while prices, both wholesale and retail, have not been kept up.

We have thus attempted to furnish in outline the leading Economic features of the condition of the Netherlands East Indies during the past sixty years, and contrasted, as far as published Records permit, the prosperity of the first forty years, when the Culture System was in force, with the comparative decline during the last twenty years when the Independent System has been more or less adopted in these Islands. This contrast is suggestive in itself, but it becomes more suggestive still when we compare Netherlands India with British India, and measure their relative progress under Foreign Rule. The Netherlands India is, as stated above, about thirty thousand square miles in area. The area of British India is thirty times more, being nearly nine hundred thousand square miles. The population of Netherlands India, however, is two and three-quarter Crores, or one-eighth of the population of British India. In other words, the Netherlands India is four times more populous than British India. The Exports and Imports of British India in 1885-86 were sixty-seven and eighty-five Crores of Rupees, respectively. The Exports and Imports of Netherlands India were in 1885 and 1886, one hundred and sixty and one hundred and ninety million Florins, or nearly twelve and fourteen Crores of Rupees, respectively. Seeing that British India has a population eight times that of Netherlands India, and an area thirty times as large, the Imports and Exports together of British India ought to be at least twelve times as large as those of Netherlands India. But the actual figures show that our Exports and Imports were only six times as large as those of Netherlands India. Netherlands East Indies had no National Debt in 1871. In 1876 the Dutch Government transferred a portion of its Home Debt, about thirty Crores, to the Dependencies, and it was the only debt charged on Netherlands East Indies in 1884. The British Indian Debt represents a charge which exceeds two hundred Crores of Rupees. The Dutch Government derived a Revenue of nearly forty million Florins, or of three Crores of Rupees in 1884 from Sales of Produce, which did not represent taxation proper. The Indian Government has no such resource except the Opium Revenue, and Railways, which, however, being constructed out of borrowed capital, do not, yet, pay their expenses and the full interest charged on the Loans. The Opium Revenue in British India, after deducting charges, represents a profit of six Crores of Rupees only. The Dutch Government, on the other hand, realises on sale of Government produce, Coffee, Sugar, Cinchona, Spices, etc., forty million Florins by an expenditure of twenty-five millions, and as regards Opium, that Government has a monopoly which yields twenty-one million Florins, or nearly one and a half Crore of Rupees. Opium and Government Produce thus yield three Crores of Rupees out of a total Revenue of ten Crores. Like the British Government, the Dutch Netherlands Government have a Monopoly of Salt, but the Revenue realised is only half a Crore against eight Crores realised in British India. In this respect the Dutch Government does not tax Salt, a necessary of life, to the same extent as the British Government. The Land Revenue, including Land Rent, yields to the Netherlands Government twenty-two and a half million Florins, or one Crore and sixty Lakhs of Rupees. The Land Revenue in British India is nearly twenty-two Crores. In other words, while the population of British India is eight times as large as that of Netherlands India, the Land Revenue is thirteen times that of the Netherlands India. The Forced Services, which have now been for the most part commuted into a Poll-Tax, yield about twenty-five Lakhs of Rupees to the Dutch Government. Even if this source of Revenue were included in the Land-Tax and Land Rent, the land Revenue in British India still shows a higher percentage, being nearly one Rupee per head, while in Netherlands India it is about three-fourths of a Rupee per head. The Salt-Tax is in British India six Annas per head, while in Netherlands India it is three Annas per head. Our Customs Revenue, having been needlessly sacrificed to Lancashire interests, scarcely yields one and a half Crores of Rupees. In the Netherlands India, the Customs Revenue exceeds seventy Lakhs. The taxes on Trades and Professions yielded in British India a Crore and a half of Rupees and in the Netherlands India the yield was thirty Lakhs of Rupees. Our Stamps Revenue yielded more than four Crores of Rupees or three Annas per head of the population. In the

Dutch East Indies, the Stamps Revenue was only eight Lakhs, and even adding Legacy and Transfer Duty, the Stamp Revenue was thirteen Lakhs, or less than one Anna per head. The Forest Revenue represents a charge of one Anna per head in British India, while it was less than half an Anna in the Dutch East Indies. It will be seen from this that the pressure of the Land-Tax, Salt, Stamps, and Forests, is much heavier in British India than in the Netherlands India, whilst the Customs, Duties, and the Trade or Income-Tax were much higher in Dutch East Indies than in British India. The net Interest charge in British India ranges from four to five Crores of Rupees or three to four Annas per head. In the Netherlands India this charge is almost nominal. In the Dutch East Indies, one-third of expenditure is met without taxation. In British India one-tenth of the expenditure is so provided for. Out of a total Export of one hundred and fifty-four million Florins, the Netherlands India exported to the extent of one hundred and twenty-five million Florins' worth of manufactured produce. The chief articles exported were Sugar worth seventy-two million Florins, Tobacco sixteen and a quarter millions, Tin four millions, Tea two millions, Oils three and a quarter millions, Indigo four millions and Coffee twenty millions. In British India, out of a total Export of ninety-nine Crores, manufactured Agricultural Produce was valued at about twenty Crores of

Rupees. The chief articles exported were Cotton manufacture worth six and one-third Crores, Tea five and a quarter Crores, Indigo four, Jute three and a half, and Coffee two Crores. We exported little or no Sugar or Oils. In other words, while the proportion of Raw to Manufactured Produce exported from British India was four to one, the proportion in Netherlands India was one to four.

These contrasts between the Economic condition of the two Countries will be sufficient to convey a general idea of the way in which the development of the resources of the two Countries has been carried out under the influence of two different Systems. We have developed only the faculty to produce Raw goods to send them to be manufactured in other Countries, and to bring them back again for our use. In Netherlands India efforts have been made not only to grow more raw produce of a high order, but to manufacture it, and this result is due to the working of the Culture System already described. All this change has been wrought without charge to Government, and to the evident benefit of the people at an expenditure which, at the highest, did not exceed thirty to forty Crores of Rupees. The British Government in India has spent in Railways and Canals four to five times as much, but so far from helping the Country to be more self-dependent in regard to its Manufactures and Commerce, it has only tended to increase our dependence on the single resource of Agriculture to a much larger extent than before. Excluding Canals, the Railway Expenditure of nearly two hundred Crores has only made competition with Europe more hopeless over larger areas, and facilitated the conveyance of Foreign Goods, to an extent not otherwise possible. The Government of India, when it adopted the Policy of constructing Productive Works out of Borrowed Capital, did in fact affirm the principle that, in the peculiarly backward condition of the Country, the development of its resources could not be left to independent private enterprise, and that as representing the general public, it was bound to utilise Public resources of Credit and its superior intelligence and organization, for the advantage of its Subjects by undertaking to be the great Railway and Canal Constructors in the Country. The principle of the Culture System was thus, tacitly affirmed more than twenty years ago. The difference lay only in the objects for which this State Credit was used and pledged. The success of Railway Policy, thus undertaken twenty years ago in Lord Mayo's time, has been questioned in some quarters. For our own part we are prepared to admit that this success, though not commensurate with the expectations formed at first, has been considerable, and taken along with the Political and Military advantages of Railway Construction, there can be no doubt that the borrowed money has been well laid out. The Policy which requires the State to be its own Railway Constructor, though formally acted upon twenty years ago, was really first initiated when Lord Dalhousie's Government sanctioned the System of Guaranteed Railways. The State Credit was pledged under that plan as effectively as under the arrangements adopted in 1870. In regard to Canals the same observation holds good. If the State assumes to itself the functions of Landlord and Sovereign, its duties naturally assume a wider scope, and no defence is, therefore, necessary for the position thus taken up. The State, as representing the Public, has a right, and is under corresponding obligation, to undertake all functions which it can best perform to public advantage. The principle underlying the Railway Policy of British India and the Culture System introduced in Netherlands India by Von de Bosch is thus one and identical. The difference lies only in the choice made of the objects of that Policy. The comparative figures given above show clearly that in the interests of the Dependencies, the objects kept in view by General Von de Bosch were of more paramount interest than those followed by the British Government in India. Facilities of communication are certainly desirable advantages, but more desirable still is the capacity to grow higher kinds of produce, and develop manufacturing and industrial activities. The sole dependence on Agriculture has been the weak point of all Asiatic Civilization. Contact with superior races ought certainly to remedy this helplessness, and not to aggravate it, as has been to a large extent the case in this Country. As the result of the two Systems at work in the two Countries, our proportion of Raw Produce to Manufactured Produce exported is four to one, while it is one to four with our Neighbours. The construction of Railways can never be compared, in their educating influence, to the setting up of Mills or Steam or Water Power Machinery for the production of Manufactured Produce in all parts of the Country. A Railway runs from one end of the Country to the other, and leaves no permanent impression upon the face of the Country, at least none so durable and penetrating as that which surrounds a great Manufactory. Now that the work of intercommunication has been well nigh completed, it seems to us that the time has come when Government should turn a new leaf, and venture upon a departure from its present received policy, on the model of the Culture System with suitable adaptations to Indian wants.

It cannot well be said that the policy thus recommended is entirely foreign to the genius of British Rule in India. In regard to Cinchona, Tea, and Coffee, the Government of India at great expense, pioneered the way for the introduction of these foreign products among the agricultural resources of the Country. These pioneering efforts were made entirely at State expense. What is now suggested is that similar efforts in other directions than Agricultural Development should be made, not at State expense departmentally, but on the plan followed in the case of Railways by Guaranteeing or subsidising private efforts, till private enterprise could support itself, or better still, by the plan followed in Netherlands India by advancing loans to private Capitalists at low interest, and helping them in the choice of places and the selection of the form of investment. The British Government in India recognizes the principle of making advances for improvements to agriculturists, known as *Tagai* advances, but this power is so niggardly exercised that it may virtually be said to have been ignored in practice.

Those who counsel non-interference in such matters on the authority of writers of Political Economy forget that Political Economy, as a hypothetical *a priori* Science, is one thing, while Practical Political Economy as applied to the particular conditions of backward Countries is a different thing altogether. American, Australian, and Continental Political Economy, as applied in practice, permits many departures from the *a priori* positions of the abstract Science. If authority were wanted for this assertion, we could refer to Mill's Political Economy. The quotation is peculiarly appropriate as it lays down the duties of Government in Countries circumstanced like India.

" A good Government will give all its aid in such a shape as to encourage and nurture any rudiments, it may find, of a spirit of individual exertion. It will be assiduous in removing obstacles and discouragements to voluntary enterprise, and in giving whatever facilities and whatever direction and guidance may be necessary. Its pecuniary means will be applied when practicable in aid of private efforts rather than in supersession of them, and it will call into play its machinery of rewards and honours to elicit such efforts."

"Government aid, when given merely in default of private enterpise, should be so given as to be, as far as possible, a course of education to people." Government must undertake to do "the things, which are made incumbent upon it by the helplessness of the public, in such a manner as shall tend not to increase and perpetuate, but correct this helplessness."

These principles justify a departure in the directions suggested above. The Railway Policy pursued by Government has, as a matter of fact, except in a few Presidency Towns, killed out Local indigenous Industries, and made people more helpless than before, by increasing their dependence and pressure on Agriculture as their only resource. The Policy adopted by the Dutch Government sixty years ago, has produced the opposite effects, and made Java export four times less Raw Produce and four times more of Manufactured Produce, than has been the case in British

7

India. Mr. Mill recommends pecuniary assistance in aid of private enterprise, and the Government recognizes this duty in its *Tagai* advances. So far, therefore, as authority is concerned, there is no heresy in the recommendation of a departure of Policy in the direction suggested by the experience of Java. We are aware that objection will be taken to the proposals made above on the ground that, finding Capital for Industries and Manufactures is a function which does not belong to Government. This is no doubt theoretically true, but at the same time, it does not lie in the mouths of those who advocate a vigorous Railway Policy to urge this objection, for, if the principle be accepted, it follows that Government has no business to find Capital for Railways or Canals, or for Pioneering Tea or Coffee Enterprises. Those who urge this objection forget that the great want of India is Cheap Capital ready for investment in large Enterprises. The Savings of the Indian population are but scanty. A large proportion of these Savings is taken up by Taxation, a still larger proportion is hoarded or buried under one form or another, and there is but a fraction less than four or five Crores of Rupees, all over the Country, left for industrial investment on a large scale. A large portion of these five Crores is in the hands of men in Presidency Towns, who have little relations with the Country at large. The habit of farming Joint-Stock Organizations is not developed, and the savings are invested in Government Stock or in Post Office Banks and bear no productive efficacy. Just as the Land in India thirsts for water, so the Industry of the Country is parched up for want of Capital. The evil is not of to-day, but is an old inheritance. Capital desirous of investment and content with low interest is a National want, and this want cannot be adequately supplied by any partial or local private efforts. These last are good as far as they go, but after all they are a drop in the ocean. The want being National, the Nation has a right to expect their Rulers to supply the want, more especially as these Rulers are not Afghans or Turks, but men belonging to a race the most gifted and the best endowed with material possessions, and lending their surplus Wealth to all the countries of the world, and capable of applying that Wealth in the most productive channels. In the case of Java, the Contractors to whom Government advanced loans were all Dutch Adventurers, but when these settlers went and settled in Foreign Lands, and invested their money and talent in local industries, the evils of Foreign Absenteeism were not felt to be so great as in the case of the Railway investments. In borrowing a lesson from the Dutch Method of conducting these operations, the British Government here need not confine their loans to British Capitalists only. Native enterprise, where the security was satisfactory, might well be allowed to hare in the new undertakings. This would remove one of the admitted evils of the Dutch plan of action. The loans need not be advanced free of interest, as was the case in Java. The British Nation will not tolerate any action on the part of the Government here, to have a Monopoly of sale of certain products. The East India Company had such privileges, but they proved a source of discontent, and the Monopolies had to be abolished in favour of Free Trade. These portions of the Dutch arrangement will, therefore, have to be dropped, but they do not form essential parts of the Scheme. The System of Forced Labour was, even in Java, given up, and in its place cash payments were substituted. The wages of labour in India are so low that there is no advantage in, or occasion for, this assistance of forced labour. These accidents of the Culture System thus eliminated, what remains for Government to do is to encourage Native and European enterprise in starting New Industries by advances, limited, as in Java, to maximum amounts, and made repayable at low interest in a certain number of years. The disbursement of these advances in the most profitable way should be subjected to the superintendence of Official Experts, who should help and guide private efforts, and watch the interests of Government by preventing abuse.

In the choice of Industries, Government may well prefer those in the prosperity of which it has a large
, and in respect of which India possesses special

advantages. As instances, the Iron and Coal Industries may be safely taken up for first trial. In regard to the Iron Industry, Mr. O'Connor observes in his last report that 'No practical development of the Iron Industry has as yet been made in India. The Barakpore works, where an industry of the first magnitude might be created by the expenditure of Capital and skill, are still limited to the production of Cast Iron in trifling quantities, although the State and Public require an import close on a quarter of a million of tons of Iron and Steel yearly, without including quantities imported as Machinery, Mill work, and Railway Material.' In regard to Coal, Government has for a long time worked the Warora Mines on its own account. In place of this costly departmental work, it may be suggested that private enterprise duly subsidised, or guaranteed, or helped with loans, should be substituted. Similarly, in regard to agricultural produce, Sugar is one of the Industries which needs help. Private efforts to establish Refineries fail, on account of the difficulties placed by the Abkari Department, in utilising the refuse or non-saccharine matter, for purposes of Rum or Liquor. Our competition in this article is not with England, but with China, Mauritius, and the Straits Settlements. With the Government assistance in money, and freedom from Abkari difficulties, India would produce its own Sugar. Similarly, in Oils, our competition chiefly is with

Ceylon, Mauritius, and the Straits Settlements. We export Seeds of all sorts to the extent of eight Crores, and import Cocoanut Oil from the Mauritius and from Ceylon, Ground Nut Oil from Java, and Linseed Oil from England. In the case of Beer, there has been a considerable development of Indian Breweries, but the importations are still many times the quantities produced in India. Woollen manufacturing, Industries and the Tanning of Hides and Skins and the Manufacture of Paper and Glass also afford large scope for the springing up of new enterprise.

We might multiply the list, if it were necessary to go into details, but it is unnecessary to do so, for the struggle, at present, is to secure the recognition of the principle advocated. All that I contend for is that on the principle followed by Government of borrowing two to three Crores each year for so-called productive Railways, it should borrow or divert this amount for the encouragement of New Industries in the Country by means of advances, or subsidies, or guarantees according as circumstances require.

Even if the Government be not prepared to take this risk on its own shoulders from fear of English criticism and jealousy, a way might be found, giving effect to arrangements proposed on a small scale by empowering the existing Local or Municipal Boards, or creating Special Corporate Boards of Trade and Commerce, to borrow from the Government at low interest the moneys required, and advance them as loans for the improvement of Rural and Urban Industries. The Savings deposited with Government, are at present wholly unproductive. The Depositors are paid $3\frac{3}{4}$* per cent. by investing their moneys in Government Stock at 4 * per cent. This benefits nobody. If instead of the present arrangement, the District and the City Deposits were lent by Government to Municipal and Local Boards or District Corporate Banks, and these Bodies, empowered to make advances, say at five or six per cent. to private persons with skill and energy to turn them to account, an annually increasing Fund of four to five Crores will be at the disposal of the Government, for purposes more calculated to benefit everybody than the present plans. Each District might thus have a Fund to develop its resources in its own way, and several Districts might combine together to support a strong undertaking for common advantage. If the powers of these Boards were thus enlarged, there would be no risk of loss to Government, and the Boards might make considerable profit by the use of the money, and thus relieve the burden of Local Taxation. Of course, the Government through its Officers would have a potent voice in the proper disbursement of these borrowed moneys, and with judicious supervision the whole face of the Country might be changed in the course of a few years. The

* Since reduced to $3\frac{1}{4}$ per cent. and $3\frac{1}{2}$ per cent.

Government might also help these efforts by giving its own custom to these manufacturing concerns in respect of the articles required for its Stores. When the Country was thus enabled to obtain a new start, and Factories and Mills on a small or large scale were set up all over the land, the present paralysis would give way to a play of energies which would far more effectively than Schools and Colleges give a new birth to the activities of the Nation. This then is our plan. The alternative suggested above may do as an experiment, but it would be far better if the Government recognized this function of developing New Industries in the Country, to be as legitimate a part of its duty as it now regards Railway Construction to be. The principle underlying both functions is the same. The one has been tried and has attained its success, but has not cured the particular weakness which has crippled the growth of the Nation. The experimental trial of the other principle in a Neighbouring Country has to all appearances supplied this defect, and this experience warrants a similar trial in this Country.

IV.

PRESENT STATE OF INDIAN MANUFACTURES & OUTLOOK OF THE SAME.*

DR. WATTS, Reporter on Economic Products to the Government of India, has, in his recently published Memorandum on the Resources of British India, devoted an entire chapter to the consideration of the "Present State of Indian Manufactures and Outlook of the Same" for the future which is eminently suggestive, and deserves most careful consideration by the Members of an Association, such as that under whose auspices we meet here to-day. The political domination of one Country by another attracts far more attention than the more formidable, though unfelt domination which the Capital, Enterprise, and Skill of one Country exercise over the Trade and Manufactures of another. This latter domination has an insidious influence which paralyzes the springs of all the varied activities which together make up the life of a Nation and this influence was so paramount at one time in British India, that there were grave reasons to fear the worst consequences of this inevitable

* Read at the Industrial Conference, Poona, in 1893.

change. In the Eighteenth Century, England, like the other Countries of Europe, desired to have Colonies of its own race in all parts of the World, chiefly for the command of the markets, thus opened up to the Home Manufacturers and Traders. The Colonies were looked upon as, and in fact were actually called. Plantations, where raw produce was grown to be sent to the Mother Country, to be manufactured and exported again back to the Colonies and to the rest of the World. This Policy suggested restrictive measures of action intended to foster domestic Trade and Arts at the sacrifice of the best interests of the Colonies. The American War of Independence put an end to this scheme of Economic Government, and since then, though the sphere of English colonization has been multiplied during this Century beyond all previous record, yet these new Colonies have from the first been allowed to work out their own destinies, free from the leading strings of domestic control. The great Indian Dependency of England has, during this Century, come to supply the place of the Old Colonies. This Dependency has come to be regarded as a Plantation, growing raw produce to be shipped by British Agents in British Ships, to be worked into Fabrics by British skill and capital, and to be re-exported to the Dependency by British merchants to their corresponding British Firms in India and elsewhere. The development of steam power and mechanical skill, joined with increased facilities of communication, have lent strength to this tendency of the times, and, as one result of the change, the gradual ruralization of this great Dependency, and the rapid decadence of Native Manufacture and Trade, became distinctly marked. Even now the danger is not over. It is, however, a most fortunate circumstance that, during the last twenty years, there has been a clearly distinguishable departure from the till then unimpeded process of ruralizing a vast Continent long known for its great resources and aptitudes. The rationale of the existence and working of such a body as the Industrial Association of Western India is that it seeks to encourage this tendency, and check rustication. It is no doubt, a struggle of a very unequal character, a struggle between a Giant and a Dwarf, and yet the struggle has to be maintained against great odds; and those who are engaged in the struggle cannot do better than note from time to time, whether the direction of the movement is correct, and its velocity satisfactory. I propose in this paper to bring together certain facts, chiefly based on Official Publications, which will, I hope, satisfy you that, on the whole, we have reasons to congratulate ourselves upon the result, that the tendency towards rustication has been checked, and India under British Rule has been gathering up its forces, and marshalling them in order to ward off the evil effects of the first surrender that it had to make by way of homage to British skill, capital and enterprise.

Dr. Watts has in his Memorandum noticed one side of this counter-movement, which has become clearly visible during the last twenty years. A careful analysis of the Trade Returns of British India for, 1892-93 discloses the fact that, out of a total of one hundred and sixty four Crores' worth of Exports and Imports, excluding Treasure and Government Transactions, we imported nearly sixteen Crores of Raw Produce against nearly thirty-six Crores of Manufactured Produce while we exported eighty-five Crores of Raw Produce against sixteen Crores, worth of Manufactured Articles. In a word, our Exports to Foreign Countries showed that eighty-five per cent. of them were represented by the bulky agricultural produce, which gave no employment to local skill and capital, except such as was represented by the rude methods of Agriculture, while in the Imports we did not know how to supply our wants in regard to seventy-two per cent. of the articles we received from foreign Countries. These proportions of seventy-two per cent. Imports and eighty-five per cent. Exports are sufficiently expressive of the present condition of things. In 1892, we exported twenty and a half Crores of Cotton and Jute Fibre, another twenty and a half Crores of Grain, eleven and a half Crores of Seeds, ten Crores of Opium and Tobacco, about nine Crores' worth of Tea, Coffee, and Indigo, nearly three

Crores of Hides and Skins, Horns, etc., three-fourths of a Crore of Dye Stuffs and Spices, about two-thirds of a Crore of Raw Silk, two-thirds of a Crore of Timber, a quarter of a Crore of Manure, three-fourths of a Crore of Lac, and one-third of a Crore of Catechu or Cutch. These articles make up in all eighty Crores. The principal raw materials which India imported in large quantities in the same year, were the Metals,—Iron and Steel of about three and a half Crores, Copper two Crores, and the rest about a Crore,—one and three-eighth Crores' worth of Coal, other Minerals three-fourths of a Crore, one-third of a Crore of Stone, Marble and precious Jewellery. The rest of the imported articles were all more or less the products of skill and capital engaged in manufactures, including from twenty-five to thirty-one Crores of Rupees' worth of Cotton Goods, three Crores of Silk and Woollen Apparel, two and a half Crores of Sugar, one and a half Crores of Wines, six and two-thirds Crores of Machinery and manufactured Metals, three Crores of Dyes, two Crores' worth of Oil, and about a Crore of Tea, Coffee, and Sundries. This state of things was the growth of the last half Century. In 1853 Cotton Goods and Yarn imported to India were worth less than sixty Lakhs of Rupees, and in forty years they swelled to the enormous amount of twenty-five Crores. Silk and Woollen Goods imported in 1853 were worth only five Lakhs, and they rose to two and one-third

Crores in forty years. Similarly, raw Jute and Grain exported from India were about four Lakhs each in value in 1853, and were respectively worth five Crores and six Crores in 1892.

About twenty-two years ago, I had occasion to notice this collapse of domestic Industries, and the gradual rustication of our chief occupations, in a series of Lectures which have been published, and it was about this time that a welcome change took place, whose effects are now perceptibly visible. Things were as bad as could be about 1870-75; since then the tide has turned, and India has shown signs of a revival which marks its first step in the transition from a purely agricultural into a partly manufacturing and trading Country. Dr. Watts has in his Memorandum clearly brought out into prominence the chief features of this change. Of course, no change has taken place in the absolute disproportion between the Exports and Imports of raw and manufactured produce, but their relative proportions have changed in a way which marks the beginning of this new departure from the old traditions. The chief features of this change may be thus described. Firstly, our Exports of manufactured or partly manufactured goods have risen from five and a quarter Crores to sixteen and a half Crores in the past fourteen years, 1879-1893, the increase being thus two hundred and eleven per cent. in fourteen years. There is a steady annual increment of fifteen per cent.

with only two exceptional years, during that whole period. Secondly, our Exports of raw produce have also risen absolutely, but the relative rise is measured by the difference between sixty Crores and eighty-five and a half Crores, which means an increase of forty-two per cent. in fourteen years, or an annual increment of three per cent. per year, against an annual increment of fifteen per cent. in the export of manufactured produce. Thirdly, the increase of manufactured articles imported into India, has only been thirty per cent. in fourteen years, rising from twenty Crores to thirty-six Crores, which gives an annual increment of two per cent. per year. Fourthly, the increase in the imports of raw produce has been about a hundred per cent., rising from thirteen and three-fourths Crores to twenty-six and a half Crores' worth in fourteen years. This gives an average increment of six and a half per cent. The following Table sets forth the several points noticed above in a very clear manner.

	1879.	1892.	Percentage increased.	
			Total.	Annual.
Manufactured Imports ...	Rs. 25,98,65,872	36,22,31,827	39	2·8
Raw Imports ...	Rs. 13,75,55,837	26,38,18,431	91	6·5
Manufactured Exports ...	Rs. 5,27,80,340	16,42,47,566	211	15
Raw Exports ...	Rs. 59,67,27,991	85,52,09,499	43	3

It will be seen from this Table that while the absolute disproportion still continues to be very marked, there is a very healthy change in their relative proportions. Fifthly, while the Imports of manufactured articles were sixty-five per cent. of the total Imports in 1879, this proportion has fallen to fifty-seven per cent. in 1892; similarly, while the proportion of manufactured Exports was only eight per cent. of the total Exports in 1879. they were in 1892 nearly sixteen per cent. This change is a steady tendency which characterises the returns of most of the years included within the period noted above. Sixthly, the above conclusions are based on the Official Trade Returns. Dr. Watts, however, questions the principle of the official classification which relegates such Goods as Spirits, Flour, Sugar, Oils, etc., to the head of Raw Produce; while Coir, Cordage, Oil-cakes, Hides and Skins, Lac, are shown as manufactured. The growth of the Industries concerned in the production of Indigo, Tea, Coffee, Oils, Sugar, Beer, Tobacco, Cigars, etc., marks the first step in the progress of India from a purely agricultural into a partly manufacturing Country,— which is quite as important as the actual multiplication of Jute, Cotton, Silk, Woollen, Paper, Flour, and Oil-Mills, and Leather and Sugar Factories. By reclassifying the details of the Official Returns on this more correct basis, it is shown that our Manufactured Exports bear to our Raw Exports the proportion of thirty to seventy, instead of sixteen to eighty-four per cent.

The question naturally arises,—how has this change for the better been brought about? It has been brought about silently and surely by the efforts of the Indian people, assisted to a large extent by the influx of British capital and enterprise. A few illustrations will best explain the working of this double Agency. Taking Cotton Goods in the first instance, it will be noted that the Imports of Cotton Goods and Yarn were valued at nineteen and a half Crores in 1875, and though they rose as high as thirty-one Crores in one or two years, they have been almost steady during the last fifteen years at a figure which averages twenty-five Crores. Exports in the meanwhile have risen from less than two Crores, to nearly ten Crores, during the same period of eighteen years. The export of Raw Cotton stood at five and a half Crores, in 1860, rose to thirty-five Crores in 1865-1866, and has since fallen to about sixteen Crores in 1868, fourteen Crores in 1878, seven and a half in 1882, and was thirteen Crores in 1892. These changes in the Exports and Imports of raw and manufactured Cotton have been contemporaneous with the development of the Cotton Mills in India, which have risen from fifty-eight Mills with 12,983 Looms and 14,36,464 Spindles in 1878, to 130 Mills with 26,347 Looms and 33,78,903 Spindles, giving employment to one hundred and fifty

8

thousand hands. The capital sunk in these Mills was less than two Crores in 1875, and is now estimated to be nearly ten Crores. This vast Industry has all grown within the last forty years, and the Bombay Presidency takes the lion's share of the benefits secured thereby, inasmuch as no less than 88 Mills are in this Presidency, besides 380 Presses, and a still large number of Ginning Factories.

The place which the Cotton industry occupies in this Presidency, is taken up in Bengal by the Jute industry. There are twenty-seven Jute Mills, and twenty-three Presses, and many private concerns, with a capital of six and a half Crores, with 9,000 Looms and 1,80,172 Spindles, giving employment to over seventy-seven thousand men. The Exports were over ten Crores of Bags, and the home consumption is equal to the foreign demand. The export of raw Jute still amounts to fifty-two Lakhs of hundredweights.

There are eighty-one Silk filature concerns in Bengal, which give employment to 8,000 hands permanently, and an equal number temporarily, and produce five Lakhs of pounds of Silk. There are two Mills, one in Calcutta, and another in Bombay, which supply chiefly the Burmese markets. There are other factories which produce Tasar, and Chora silk for the local market. The Silk Mill in Calcutta exported sixteen Lakhs of Rupees' worth of Silk goods to

England and France. The exports of raw Silk were worth sixty Lakhs of Rupees.

There are five Woollen Mills with 532 Looms and 17,210 Spindles, and they give employment to over three thousand hands. The capital employed is thirty Lakhs, and the annual out-turn of goods is worth twenty-one Lakhs of Rupees, chiefly for the supply of local and departmental wants. The Woollen and Silk Piece-goods imported were of the value of nearly three Crores of Rupees, which shows what scope there is still left for further expansion. The exports of Cashmere Shawls, which at one time were nearly thirty Lakhs of Rupees in value in 1868, dwindled down to two and a quarter Lakhs in 1890-91.

There are ten Paper Mills with a capital of nearly twenty-five Lakhs of Rupees. The out-turn had quadrupled in ten years, and was twenty-six Million pounds in 1892. There is considerable scope for extension here also, since the value of imported Paper of all kinds averages about fifty Lakhs of Rupees.

There are forty-seven Tanneries, thirty-three out of which are in the Madras Presidency, nine in Sind, two in Calcutta, two in Cawnpore, and one in Agra. The Export trade in tanned Hides has increased from three Crores to five and a half Crores in eighteen years. In tanned Leather manufactures, these Indian Tanneries compete with the imports from Europe.

There are in India twenty-three Breweries, all started since 1850. The capital employed is seventeen Lakhs, the out-turn is fifty Lakhs of Gallons, out of which nearly twenty-seven Lakhs were purchased by Government for the use of soldiers. The remaining twenty-two Lakhs are consumed by the civil population. Till within the last three or four years, there was practically no import of beer for the use of the Army. Latterly, since 1891, this monopoly has been destroyed, and imported Beer is again coming in large quantities. Altogether one Crore's worth of Wines and Spirits is imported into India, and about half a Crore's worth of Beer and Cider was imported in 1892.

There are, besides, two Soap Factories and ten Rope Factories at work in this Country, chiefly supplying local and departmental wants.

There are fourteen Sugar Factories and Refineries, five in Madras, seven in Bengal, and two in the North West Provinces. The Capital of two of the more important Factories, that of Casipore near Calcutta, and the Rosa Factory in Shahjahanpur, is twenty-six Lakhs of Rupees. The Imports of Sugar are, however, seven times as large as the Exports. The competition of Beet Sugar has checked the local production for export markets, as also for home consumption. The wants of local consumption are chiefly satisfied by the use of the Jaggery. The value of imported refined Sugar was two and two-third of Croress in 1892, and its quantity two Million Tons. Raw Jaggery exported was worth forty-five Lakhs.

Next in order come the Flour Mills, of which we have forty-six at work in India, nineteen being in the Bombay Presidency. The capital employed by five of these, which are Joint Stock concerns, is sixteen Lakhs of Rupees, and the total capital of all the Mills might come up to thirty Lakhs. There are, besides, several Tobacco Curing Factories, Bone-crushing Factories, Iron and Brass Foundries, Oil Mills, Saltpetre Refineries, Saw Mills, Potteries and other Companies. In the words of Sir Edward Buck, they all indicate that "India is entering upon an important period of manufacturing activity. Already a substantial commencement has been made in Cotton and Jute Goods, followed by manufactories of Wool, Paper, Leather, Sugar, Oil and Tobacco."

Side by side with this expansion of Indian manufacturing Industries, we have to note the great development of the Tea, Coffee, Indigo, and Cinchona Plantations. The capital sunk in these industries is chiefly European, and the management is also in European hands. The total area under Tea cultivation in 1892-93 was 3,34,825 acres, out of which half the area is cultivated by Private Concerns, and one Lakh of acres belongs to Companies started in England, while half a Lakh of acres belongs to Companies started in Calcutta. The total exports were one hundred and twenty million of pounds in weight worth six Crores of Rupees in all.

The total capital employed by the registered Tea Companies in these concerns exceed eight Crores. The Capital of the Private Tea Concerns may be assumed to be as much. This Industry gives employment to ten Lakhs of people. The land occupied was waste land, which yielded nothing before European enterprise turned it to account.

The Indigo Concerns at work in India in 1892 were represented by 2,702 Factories and 6,032 Vats, which gave employment to three and a half Lakhs of people, solely in the production of the manufactured article of commerce. The Agriculturists who produce the Raw material are not included in this number. The average exports are fifteen Million pounds, valued at nearly fifty Lakhs of Rupees.

Coffee Plantations cover 1,27,648 acres in British India, besides large areas in Mysore, Cochin, and Travancore. The total area under the Coffee crop may safely be put down at two lakhs of acres. The total export of Coffee is nearly three lakhs of hundred-weights. There are thirty-seven Coffee Works in the Madras Presidency, which give employment to 1,379 permanent and 5,433 temporary hands. There are besides numerous Lac Factories, many Native, and a few under European management, giving employment to 2,614 permanent hands, and 1,600 temporary labourers.

The Catechu or Cutch Trade is also considerable. The value of the exports in 1892 was nearly forty Lakhs.

Next to these Plantations and Mill Industries, an important development of the resources has taken place in the Mineral wealth of India, and notably in the use of Indian Coal. The value of the Import of Foreign Coal was as high as two Crores of Rupees in 1888, but has fallen to one and a quarter Crores in 1892. The Imports have not expanded with the increase in demand, and this is entirely due to the working of Indian Collieries. The Bengal Collieries alone have quadrupled their output, chiefly as Exports by sea to other Provinces, in five years, the Exports having risen from four Lakhs of Tons in 1888 to twenty Lakhs in 1892. In 1892 there were eighty-two Collieries at work in India, of which seventy-three were in Bengal, one in the Punjab, three in Assam, one in Central India, one in Deccan, Hyderabad, and one in Beluchistan. The output has doubled itself in ten years, and was two Million Tons in 1892, more than one Million Tons being made up by the Bengal Collieries alone. Out of these two Million Tons, one Million Tons were used by the Railway Companies. Burma also has large Coal deposits which are being brought into use. Bombay, Madras, and the North-Western Provinces have no Coal Mines.

Gold Mines have been re-opened by the help of British capital and enterprise in Mysore, and Wynaad and the out-turn in 1892 was nearly worth nine Lakhs. The average of the imports of Gold in five years was more than four Crores per year, being nearly twice the figures in 1872, and thrice the figures in 1852, which were respectively two and a half and one and one-third Crores. One hundred and fifty Crores' worth of Gold has been imported into India since 1835 for hoarding purposes.

The success which has attended the flow of English capital in respect of Coal Mines has not rewarded the efforts made to develop the Iron resources of India. Not that India is wanting in this natural source of Wealth, but it is not possible to work these resources in the face of European competition. The great difficulty in the way is to find Iron deposits near enough to Coal Mines which can produce cheap and good fuel. The Baragor Iron Company in Bengal is, however, progressing satisfactorily. The imports of Iron, and Iron-ware, including Railway materials and Mill machinery, in the meanwhile, have remained stationary at the high figure of nine or ten Crores, during the past five years.

The amount of salt produced in India was over nine Lakhs of tons in 1892, and the Imports were three and a half Lakhs of Tons. The total duty levied was eight and a half Crores. Saltpetre was an Indian monopoly in former times. Owing to the discoveries a substitute by artificial processes, the demand for

Indian Saltpetre has fallen off, and Saltpetre worth only five Lakhs was exported in 1892.

India imported from sixteen to twenty Lakhs of Pearls during the last five years, while its own Pearl Fisheries yielded but a poor return. Since the conquest of Burma, Ruby, Jade, Amber, Sapphire and other Precious Stones have become a new source of wealth, but as yet these resources show no great development.

I have thus passed in review all the principal Manufacturing, Planting, and Mineral Industries which have sprung up in India during the last forty years, and which have shown a very healthy development during the last twenty years. They represent an investment of nearly fifty Crores of Rupees, and afford new and varied employment to nearly twenty-five Lakhs of people all the year round. This is an humble beginning, but it is a very hopeful one, and its effects are plainly visible in the altered relations which have come to subsist between Indian Exports and Imports of Raw and Manufactured Goods.

It might appear to some that it is not very safe to rely upon Statistics of Trade or Industry of a general character, and to base conclusions thereon which might or might not hold good of particular parts of the Country, in the welfare of which we may be more intimately interested. It is with this view that I desire you to turn to some Local Statistics of this

Presidency, about the correctness of which we need have no misgivings, and which also point in the same direction as those I have already examined. In another place I have noted the proportion of Rural and Urban populations in this Presidency, as they are disclosed by the two Census enumerations of 1872 and 1891. The Census of 1872 disclosed one Hundred and seventy-nine Towns with a population of more than five Thousand inhabitants in the Bombay Presidency. This same number rose to two hundred and thirty-two in the Census of 1891. The population of one Hundred and seventy-nine Towns was in 1872 shown to be 27,78,822, or seventeen per cent., while the population of the two Hundred and thirty-two Towns was found to be 34,53,569, or nearly nineteen per cent. of the total population. The number of Towns had thus increased by thirty per cent. in twenty years, and the population of these Towns had increased twenty-five per cent. The total increase of population during the same period of twenty years was only sixteen per cent., and the Rural Areas showed an increase of fourteen per cent. in their population. The increase of Towns, and the higher rate of increase in the population of Towns, as also the slight increase in the relative proportions of Urban and Rural populations, show clearly that the tendency towards rustication had been checked, and that gradually but surely, the first signs of the new

Civic Life were manifesting themselves. The difference in the relative percentages of the Town and Country population shows slight and scarcely perceptible Progress, but that slight Progress was in the right direction.

The same fact is brought home to us by a careful study of the Census of Occupations. Unfortunately no fair comparison can be instituted between the results of the Census of 1872 and those of 1891, because of the different principles on which the Census Tables in each of these years were prepared.. However, taking the last Census enumeration as a basis, we find that in 1891, out of a total population of 1,88,84,704 enumerated, 1,10,08,233 were returned as Agriculturists, which gives a proportion of nearly fifty-nine per cent. The division of Town and Country is not sharply marked out in this land. The Town has a considerable Agricultural population, and the Country has its own Village Industries. It is, therefore, useful to note the relative proportions of the different Classes of Occupations in Town and Country.

The Agriculturists, who are fifty-nine per cent. of the whole population, were returned as forming fifteen per cent. of the Male, and nineteen per cent. of the Female population, in Towns, and sixty-seven per cent. of the Male and Female population in the Country. The Purveyors of Vegetable Food were five to seven per cent. and of animal food one to two per cent., of the entire population. The Dealers in Building Materials and Artificers engaged in Building were about two per cent. in Towns, and less than a half per cent. in the Country. The Cotton Industry engaged three per cent. of the entire population, being distributed, however, in the proportion of nine per cent. in Towns, to about two per cent. in the Country. The Woollen, as also the Hemp and Flax Fabrics, engaged less than a quarter per cent. of the population, both in Towns and Country. The Silk Industry had no representatives in the Country, but engaged in Towns one per cent. of Males, and one and a half per cent. of the Female population. The Dress-makers were one and a half per cent. of the entire population, but predominated in Towns, where they were four and a half per cent. as against less than one per cent. in the Country. Gold and Silver-smiths were nearly one per cent. of the entire population, being, however, two per cent. in Towns, and less than a half per cent. in the Country. Brass, Copper and Tin-smiths were found in Towns only, but the Iron workers or Blacksmiths were nearly equally distributed between Town and Country, with a slight preponderance in the Towns. Wood, Bamboo, and Cane Work engaged about two per cent. of the population, these classes being nearly three per cent. in Towns, and less than one per cent. in the Country. Leather-workers and Shoe-makers were almost equally distributed, both in Town and Country, their proportion ranging from one and a quarter per cent. to one and a half per cent. of the population. Money Lenders were a luxury of the Towns, being nearly one and a half per cent. there, against less than half per cent. in the Country. Merchants, Brokers, Contractors were exclusively confined to Towns, where they formed one and a half per cent. of the population. Lawyers, Doctors, Priests and Engineers, were conspicuous by their absence in the Country, and their comparative importance in Towns was not great, since they together made up less than a half per cent. of the population. Music was almost equally distributed over Town and Country, but Prostitution was a feature of it which belonged to Towns only, where it figured as high as half per cent. of the Female population. Retired Pensioners and Owners of property, who lived on interest, were also Town luxuries, being half per cent. there, and altogether absent in the Country. If we bear these relative percentages in mind, we shall find that there are a number of Industries, especially those concerned with the working of Metals, Leather, Dealers in Books, Paper and Stationery, and in Hard-ware of all kinds, also Lamps, Matches, Timber, Stone-workers, Watchmakers, Railway Employees, Cartmakers, Butchers, Toddy-drawers and Liquor-sellers, Jaggery and Sugarmakers, Contractors, Builders, Lawyers, Doctors,

Engineers, Factory hands, which show a tendency to increase, while men engaged in Oil-pressing, Weavers and Spinners of Cotton and Wool, Potters, Grocers, Pedlars, Wood-carvers, Embroiderers and Dealers in Gold and Silver, and jewels, Priests, Musicians, Military Classes, and Carriers, of all kinds, have a marked tendency the other way. Industries which flourished by the favour of Courts, and their dependents, have a tendency to disappear, while the Industries which concern themselves which the comforts and convenience of the Middle Classes, have a tendency, as indicated above, to develop in course of time. As regards the majority of the Lower Classes, they are generally unaffected by either of these changes. Whether we wish it or not, the transformation of Industries sketched out above is inevitable, and we must make the best of it. I have tried to study the question from all sides with the help of Trade Returns, Census Statistics, and the Official Publications bearing upon the general welfare of the Urban and Rural population. I have placed before you what appear to me to be good grounds for the hope I entertain that India has now fairly entered upon the path which, if pursued in the same spirit which has animated its Capitalists hitherto, cannot fail to work out its Industrial salvation. What we have to do in each case is to learn by organized co-operation to compete with the Foreigner, and take in as much Raw Produce from Abroad as we need, and work it up here, and to send in place of our Exports of Raw Produce, the same quantities in less bulky, but more valuable, forms, after they have undergone the operation of Art manipulation, and afforded occupation to our Industrial Classes. I might illustrate this by the following table.

In Place of Exporting	Convert them into & Export
Oil Seeds	Oils
Dye Stuffs	Dyes and Pigments
Wheat	Flour
Unhusked Rice	Husked Rice
Jaggery	Sugar
Raw Cotton	Cotton Goods.
Raw Wool	Woollen Goods and Shawls
Raw Silk	Silk Goods
Jute and Flax	Gunny Bags, Ropes
Hides and Skins	Prepared and Tanned Leather
Raw Tobacco	Tobacco Cured, and Cigars
Fish	Cured and Salted Fish
Rags	Paper
Wood and Timber	Carved Wood and Furniture

I might multiply this list without end. This is the practical work which Providence has set down for us to learn under the best of teachers. We have already made fair progress. We have to improve our Raw Materials, or Import them when our Soil is unsuited to their production. We have to organise Labour and Capital by co-operation, and Import freely Foreign Skill and Machinery, till we learn our lessons properly and need no help. We have rusticated too long; we have now to turn our apt hands to new work, and bend our muscles to sturdier and honester labour. This is the Civic Virtue we have to learn, and according as we learn it or spurn it we shall win or lose in the contest. We have to work against great odds, which are represented by our Old Traditions, our Poverty of Resources, and the hostile Competition of Advanced Races, whose industrial organization has been completed under more favourable conditions than our own. My object in reading this paper before you is chiefly to show you that, notwithstanding these disadvantages, and the Free-Trade Policy of the Government, we may win, if we will only persevere in our efforts, and direct them by co-operation on a large scale into the proper channels. We cannot afford to be dreamy and self-contained, and turn back from our present opportunities to a past which cannot be recalled.

Natural aptitudes, undeveloped but unlimited resources, peace and order, the whole World open to us, our marvellous situation as the Emporium of all Asia, these priceless advantages will secure success, if we endeavour to deserve it by striving for it. This is the creed for the propagation of which, by exhortation and example, the Industrial Association of Western India was started, and I feel sure it will soon become the creed of the whole Nation, and ensure the permanent triumph of the modern spirit in this Ancient Land.

V.

INDIAN FOREIGN EMIGRATION.*

NO object of National Economy is more directly practical in its bearings upon the prosperity of the people than the question of providing expansive and remunerative labour facilities commensurate with the natural growth of the population. The Report of the Famine Commission has emphatically drawn public attention to the fact that "at the root of much of the Poverty of the people of India, and the risks to which they are exposed in seasons of scarcity, lies the unfortunate circumstance that Agriculture forms almost the sole occupation of the mass of the population, and that no remedy for present evils can be complete which does not include the introduction of a diversity of occupation, through which the surplus population may be drawn from agricultural pursuits, and led to find their means of subsistence on Manufactures, or some such Employment." There can be no doubt that the permanent salvation of the Country depends upon the growth of Indian Manufactures and Commerce, and that all other remedies can only be temporary

* **Read at the Industrial Conference, Poona, in 1893.**

palliatives. At the same time, it is admitted that this diversity and change of occupation is a very arduous undertaking. It pre-supposes a change of habits, it postulates the previous growth of Culture and a spirit of enterprise, an alertness of mind, an elasticity of temper, a readiness to meet and conquer opposition, a facility of organization, social ambition and aspiration, a mobile and restless condition of Capital and Labour, all which qualities and changes are the slow growth of Centuries of Freedom and Progress. It is the object of Associations, like those under the auspices of which we meet here to-day, to promote and facilitate this change and diversity of occupation, but it is clear that, as a present remedy, there is but little hope of relief in this direction. A vast majority of the surplus poor population of an agricultural Country can only be naturally fitted to work as Agriculturist Labourers, and the slow development of our Manufactures, borne down as they are by the stress of Foreign Competition, cannot provide at present the much needed relief of work suited to their aptitudes. Inland and Overland Emigration, the overflow of the surplus population from the congested parts of the Country to Lands where Labour is dear and highly remunerative, can alone afford the sorely needed present relief.

As regards Inland Emigration, we are all more or less familiar with the migration of our surplus Agriculturist hands to the large Markets of Labour, especially to places like Bombay and Karachi. The last Census Reports have demonstrated the fact, that the disinclination of the Natives of this Country to leave their ancestral Homes has been much exaggerated, and that a much larger proportion of our population show migratory habits than we were disposed at first to believe. The Districts of Khandesh and Panch Mahals are being thus settled before our eyes. The same process is going on in the other Provinces of India, particularly in the Punjab and the Central Provinces. A further development of this same system is supplying Ceylon in the extreme South, and in the North-East Assam, Cachar, Sylhet, and latterly the Districts of Upper Burmah, with the overflowing population of this Country. The whole of the Tea and Coffee Industry of the Country depends for its prosperity on the success of this Inland Emigration. Male and Female Recruiting Agents are employed to secure the services of Indentured Coolies, and Special Laws have been passed for their protection. There is, besides, a considerable flow of Free Emigrants also to these parts. From the congested Districts of Bengal, Behar and Orissa, as many as forty Thousand Coolies migrated in 1890, and thirty Thousand people emigrated in 1891, to Assam, the proportion of Free Emigrants showing a large increase over the Indentured and Sirdari Labourers. Of course, all who emigrate do not abandon their Native Homes. Three-fourths return back to India, but about one-fourth become permanent residents in their new Settlements.

Inland Emigration, however, cannot be, in any way, compared in its volume, or in its immediate and remote bearings on national prosperity, with Foreign Emigration to the British and French and Dutch Colonies beyond the Seas. I propose in this paper briefly to give a summary of the History and Progress of Indian Foreign Emigration. Few people are aware of the comparative magnitude of this relief, thus afforded to our surplus population, and of the magnificent field for extension which is opening before our vision in the possibilities of the future. In this respect, the expansion of the British Empire in Africa is a direct gain to the mass of the population of this Country. The permanent opening up of the heart of Africa and of the Central Regions of Australia would not be possible or advantageous even to the indomitable resources of British Skill and Capital, if it did not secure the help of the unlimited and intelligent Labour and Skill of Indian Emigrants. Of course, there are difficulties in the way, as there will be difficulties in the way of all great enterprises. But the certainties of the future are too imperative to be much interfered with by these present dangers and inconveniences. The tastes, habits, temperaments, and prejudices of our people have acquired an inveterate force which makes it no easy task to adapt themselves to new surroundings, and yet if the old thraldom of prejudice and easy self-satisfaction and patient resignation is ever to be loosened, and new aspirations and hopes created in their place, a change of home surroundings is a standing necessity and a preparatory discipline, whose material and moral benefits can never be too highly estimated. Mr. Draper, the American Philosopher, in his History of the Intellectual Development of Europe, went so far as to say that the Dotage and Death, which had paralysed Oriental Races, could only be cured by the Free Transplantation of these people into Foreign Lands, or by Free Intermixture in blood with more Energetic Races. We are ourselves witnesses of the undesirability and hopelessness of the second Remedy proposed. The other remedy is more hopeful, and it is on this account that I have ventured to take up this subject for discussion at the present Conference.

The First Question we have, therefore, to consider in this connection, is the extent of this Foreign Emigration and the Localities to which it has spread. The Localities where Indian Coolies emigrate are Mauritius, Natal, Jamaica, Trinidad, St. Lucia, Grenada, St. Vincent, St. Kitts, the Fiji Islands, British Guiana, French and Dutch Guiana, the

French Possessions of Martinique, Guadeloupe, Reunion, the Danish Island of St. Croix, Ceylon, and the Straits Settlements. In 1874, the Government of India appointed a Special Officer to report upon the question of Coolie Emigration from India. That Report gives a detailed account of the condition of these Settlements, and I shall first try to summarize its leading features, and then bring down the information to more recent times, with the help of such Official Publications as were made available to me.

MAURITIUS.

Mauritius is the largest, I am speaking advisedly, of our Indian Colonial Settlements. It is an Island, which lies on the East Coast of Africa, about 20° South Latitude and 57° East Longitude, and has a total Area of seven Hundred miles, thirty-seven miles long, by thirty-four miles broad. The Temperature of this Island ranges from 70° to 80° Fahrenheit. It has the closest affinities to India in its Climate and its Seasons. Out of a total Population of 3,10,000, nearly two Lakhs were Indian Coolies in 1861, and the rest partly Europeans, Negroes, Arabs, and Creoles. The number had increased to 3,16,000 in 1871, the addition being due chiefly to the increase of the Indian Population, while the non-Indian Population actually diminished by nearly 18,000 Souls. The latest Returns for 1881 show, comparatively, still better figures. The Indians were 1,50,000 Males, and about 1,00,000 Females, out of a total Population of 3,60,000 Souls. More than two-thirds of the Population of the Island is thus of Indian Origin. The Males naturally preponderate over the Females, being in the proportion of nearly one and a half to one. Of the two Lakhs and more Indian Residents in 1871, a Lakh and a half were Indentured Emigrants from India, about two Thousand had gone of their own accord, and fifty Thousand were the children born to these Emigrants in the Colony itself. The Indian Emigrants have no competitors in the Island in the matter of Agricultural pursuits, and they also find considerable employment in Domestic Service and in the Docks and in Trade, the latter chiefly Retail Trade. There are also eleven Indian Planters, and one Manager of a Plantation. The Chief Industry of the Colony is the production of Sugarcane, and the Manufacture of Sugar. The Indentured Indian adult Coolies get, besides their rations and houses free of rent, five to seven Rupees a month, and have to work six days in the week, and nine hours each day. Medical care is free of charge, and there is a free return Passage provided at the end of the Term of Five Years. There were about two hundred and fifty Sugar Estates in 1871 in the Island, which gave employment to 1,20,000 Labourers, Chiefly Indians. Of this number, nearly 50,000 had emigrated from the Calcutta side, about 27,000 from Madras, and about 7,000 from Bombay. Since 1871, Emigration from Bombay has apparently fallen off, owing to the rise of the Mill Industry in this Presidency.

The History of Emigration to Mauritius commences with 1834. Between 1834 and 1838, as many as 25,000 Indians emigrated to that Island. From 1838 to 1844, there was a prohibition in consequence of some well-founded complaints of abuses. In 1842, Act XV. of 1842 was passed, which re-opened Mauritius to Indian Emigration. In 1884, the Government of the Island took up the work of the protection of Indian Emigrants in their own hands. A bounty was paid out of Colonial Revenues for each labourer imported, and the Government received the orders of the Planters, and sent them to their appointed Agents in India. The Government of India appointed, besides, a Protector of its own to check the abuses of the Colonial Agents.

These arrangements lasted from 1844 to 1859, when, owing to the accounts of fearful mortality on board the Ships which took the Emigrants to Mauritius, Government enforced a temporary prohibition, which was subsequently removed on satisfactory assurances being given that the abuses complained of would not be again permitted. In 1859, there was a Commission appointed under the Presidency of Dr. Mouat, to frame Regulations for the convenience of

Emigrants on board the Ships, and fresh Regulations were enforced for the protection of the Indians. There was another Commission of Inquiry in 1866-67, which inquired into the Causes of an Epidemic in Mauritius, which proved fatal to a large number of the Indian Settlers. Notwithstanding, the beneficent interference of the Government of India. the Official Report for 1871 states that the tendency of Mauritius Legislation has been towards securing a complete dependence of the Indian Labourers upon the Planters who employ them, for Free Labour is both directly and indirectly discouraged, while the Indenture System is more and more extended. The condition of affairs in 1883 is thus described: "While the Government of India have taken great care to secure the satisfactory regulation of the Emigrant Ships, the Laws of the Island have been so unjust to the Coloured People, and so much to the advantage of the Planters, that gross evils and abuses have arisen from time to time. In 1871, a Royal Commission was appointed to inquire into the abuses complained of. Various Reforms were recommended and some improvements have been effected. But the Planters are not remarkable for their respect of the rights of the Coloured People, and the system is liable to gross abuse, unless kept under vigilant control by higher Authority."

The total number of Schools—Government and Aided—in the Island, was ninety-two, attended by about nine thousand and five hundred Scholars. Out of this number, fourteen per cent. were Hindus, five per cent. Mahomedans, seventy-three per cent. Roman Catholics, and eight per cent. Protestant Christians. There were seven hundred and twenty-five Scholars in all, of Indian parentage in 1871, attending twenty-five Schools. Much, therefore, remains yet to be done for the Education of the Hindu Population of the Island. The Labour Ordinances are very stringent, and are strictly enforced. The Indian Population on the Island follow, besides Agricultural Labour on the farms, the occupation of Carpenters, whose wages are on an average £3 a month, of Blacksmiths, Washermen and Tailors, who earn half that rate, of Sugar-Makers whose wages are £2, and of Mill-drivers who earn £2-10s. There are also Masons, Gardeners, Cooks, Coachmen and Grooms with wages ranging from fifteen to twenty-eight shillings. The Deposits to the credit of the Indian Immigrants in 1871, were nearly £83,000, and their Remittances to India amounted to Rs. 20,000 in 1871.

The Laws of the Island, as shown above, place some restraints on the liberty of Indians to settle down as Free Citizens. A considerable number, about twenty thousand in all, have, however, settled down as Free Men, and earn their living as market Gardeners, Artizans, Tradesmen and Job Contractors, and a few have even attained the position of Managers and Owners of Plantations.

The latest Report of Immigration in Mauritius, furnished by the Government Protector in that Island, which I could secure, is for 1890. It shows that about two thousand Emigrants came to Mauritius in 1890, from Calcutta, Madras, and Bombay, and about one thousand and fifty-four returned back to India. The Females were about thirty-six per cent. of the Males. The number of those who returned to India during the past five years has ranged from one thousand and fifty-four to two thousand three hundred and fifty, giving an average of sixteen hundred per year. Among those who returned in 1890, three hundred and seventy-seven went to Calcutta, three hundred and forty-seven to Madras, and three hundred and twenty-one to Bombay. The total amount of Savings brought by the returned Coolies was Rs. 32,394 in 1890. In some previous years, this total was as high as Rs. 1.40,000, Rs. 1,03,000 and Rs. 1,23,000 in 1886, 1887, and 1888 respectively. The Savings in Deposit Banks to the credit of the Indian Coolies resident in the Colony show an average of Rs. 16,50,000 during the three years 1888-1890. Out of the one and a quarter Lakh of the Indian population residing on Sugar Estates, more than half do not work on the Plantations, while less than half are employed on the Plantations, which numbered about one hundred and twenty-seven in 1890. This completes our review of the Indian Settlement in Mauritius.

BRITISH GUIANA (DEMERARA).

This Colony lies along the North Coast of South America between 7° and 8° North Latitude and 57° to 60 West Longitude, and has a rich alluvial soil. As in Mauritius, the cultivation is confined chiefly to Sugarcane. The Seasons are, as in India on the Coast, only two, the Rainy and the Hot Season. The Temperature is seldom below 75°, and rises to 90° Fahrenheit, and the average Rainfall is 100 inches. Out of a total population of one and a quarter Lakh in 1851, there were only 7,682 Coolies from India, and about 2,100 Europeans, the rest were Natives of the Country, and Negroes. When Negro Slavery was abolished in the West Indian Islands, it was proposed to transplant the free Negroes to British Guiana, but the attempt failed, and in 1838, the first importation of 400 Indian Coolies took place. In 1844-45, the number of Indian Coolies imported was 4,616. Between 1850 and 1870, about 65,000 Indian Coolies were imported, out of whom 7,000 returned to India during the same period. In 1871, the total population of the Colony was two Lakhs, out of whom 43,000 were Indians, half of them working on the Plantations under Indentures, about 9,000 were Free Labourers, and the rest, about 10,000, were otherwise employed in Towns and Villages. The Labour Laws in Guiana are as stringent and one-sided as those of Mauritius. The Labourers have no summary remedy for the recovery of their wages except by a civil suit, while the Planters' remedies in case of the absence or desertion of the Coolies are most ample and strict. The Coolies are employed in one hundred and twenty-three Plantations, out of which number, eighty-five are either owned by Absentee Landlords in London, Liverpool, and Bristol, or are mortgaged with Absentee Creditors. This is a peculiar feature of the Sugar Industry in British Guiana, which distinguishes it from the Mauritius estates, which are generally owned by resident French and Creole Owners. Owing to this peculiarity, task work is much preferred, and is rigidly enforced in preference to day-work. The Task Masters employ Overseers, and below them are Head-men who are called Drivers, who supervise the gangs of Labourers. The Drivers in charge of Indian gangs are chiefly Madrasees. The Indian Coolie does not get through the same task as the Negro Labourer, but the latter never works continuously. The Indian Coolie is more regular in his habits, and he is thrifty by nature, and saves money. The Guiana Coolies are independent in their bearing. The Chinese Labourers, however, surpass both Indian Coolies and Negroes in their several excellences. There were on the Plantation in 1871, about 44,000 Indian Coolies, 1,250 Africans, 6,600 Chinese, and about 1,700 Portuguese and West Indies men. Out of the 44,000 Indian Coolies about 9,000 men were not indentured. The Wages earned by an adult Coolie range from seven to ten Annas per day, and the cost of living was six Annas a day. More recent Legislation enforces the payment of twenty-five Cents, or ten Annas per day, as minimum Wages, of an adult Male over sixteen years, and twenty Cents for each Female labourer. Notwithstanding the hardships of the Labour Laws, the high wages earned have induced nearly fifty per cent. of the Labourers to re-indenture themselves on the expiration of their first Term. About 18,000 Labourers out of 40,000 so indentured themselves on receipt of fifty Dollars as bounty. There are besides, 8,000 or 9,000 Free Coolies who have saved money, and earn their own wages. The agriculturist Labourers have, as in Mauritius, free lodgings and medicine, and free rations in their first year of settlement. The fact that there are thousands of Indians who do not care to return to India, even after a stay of fifteen or twenty years, goes to show that, on the whole, these Indian Settlers are well-off in the Colony. While the majority of the Indian Settlers are employed on the Farms, a few keep Cows and ply Carts, and there are Lodging Houses and Shops owned and managed by the Indians. A few have also enlisted in the Police, and in the Army. About 2,820 Immigrants who returned between 1839 and 1869 brought with them 95,000 Dollars to India. The men are to women in the proportion of three to one. The Mahomedans and the Hindus settled in the Colony observe Mohoram, and the Hindus have built two Temples. As might be expected, the marriage tie sits loose with these men, and they also indulge in excessive drink.

The Report of British Guiana for 1890, shows that there were in all 1,07,424 Indian Coolies—62,000 Males, 23,000 Females, and 17,000 Children. About 73,000 of the number were indentured, and the rest not residing on estates were about 35,000. Out of 72,000 on the estates, 46,000 were Males, and 26,000 Females. These Indian Settlers owned 21,000 Cattle and 5,200 Sheep. About 2,125 Coolies returned to India in 1890, and brought with them 25,000 Dollars, worth of jewellery, and 1,17,000 Dollars, worth of Savings. The Deposits of 6,323 Indian Depositors were 1,16,000 Dollars in Savings Banks, and 259 Depositors had 10,283 Dollars in Post Office Banks.

TRINIDAD.

This Island lies off the Coast of Venezuela in 10° to 11° North Latitude and 61° to 62° West Longitude, and has an area of two thousand square miles. The Temperature ranges from 71° to 85° Fahrenheit and there are only two Seasons—the Rainy and the Dry season, and the heat is considerable. Sugar, Coffee, and Cocoa are the chief articles produced in the Plains, which intervene between the three high chains of hills that traverse the length of the Island. Cotton, Tobacco, and Indigo are also produced in large quantities. Sugar is the Chief Export, and its value rose from nearly fifty Lakhs to seventy-five Lakhs between 1856 and 1867. The total population of the Island in 1856 was 68,000, of whom 4,000 were Natives, and about 2,000 Africans, and 4,000 Indian Coolies. In 1871, the Indian Immigrants had increased to nearly 23,000 Souls, besides 454 Indian Children born in the Island. There is, as usual a Government Agent who inspects the estates, and reports to the Government of the Colony the condition of the Coolie Employees. He allots the Coolie labourers to the estates and cancels the Indenture of any Immigrant whose employer disobeys the law, and abuses his power. The contracts for service are generally, for a term of five years, and the work days in the year are 280, and the hours of work nine hours a day. As in British Guiana, the task work system finds most favour with the employer. The prescribed minimum rate of wages is twenty-five Cents, or ten Annas per day, for an adult Male Labourer. Wages are paid fortnightly, and may be summarily recovered by an application to a Justice of the Peace. The laws against vagrancy and absence and desertion are very stringent, and strictly enforced. Free rations are paid in the first two years of the Indenture, and afterwards they are paid in money. On completion of the five years' term, a certificate of industrial residence is given, and after ten years, a man is allowed free passage back to India, or he may in lieu thereof, claim a Ten Acre Grant of Crown Land. In this respect, the condition of the Trinidad Coolies compares favourably with those of Mauritius and British Guiana. Children under ten are not indentured. Out of 18,556 men employed on the Estates in 1871, 10,616 were indentured, and 7,949 were unindentured. The average arrivals for each year between 1867 and 1871, were 2,000 Coolies per year. There were 12,000 Male against 6,500 Female Indians in the Island in 1871. The general rate of Wages is considerably over the minimum of twenty-five Cents, and ranges from thirty-five to forty-three Cents, or fourteen to sixteen Annas per day. The number of Coolies who returned to India in 1869, was 372, and they brought with them 16,000 Dollars as Savings. In 1870, about 408 men returned, and brought back nearly 13,000 Dollars. Up to 1871 about 285 Indians commuted their back passage by claiming Grants of Land, and 253 purchased exemption from compulsory work under the Indenture for the last two years of their term. In one Province, 357 adult Males, 199 Females, and 246 Children are now settled on their own farms. Besides the 18,000 people employed on the Estates, there are 9,000 Indians absorbed in the general population. About 7,000 people have foregone their privilege of a back passage. About 131 Indian children attended the schools in Trinidad in 1871.

In 1884, the Trinidad Indian Coolies celebrated their Mohoram festival and a riot took place, which was punished with such severity that it formed the subject of an Official Inquiry. The dispute arose from the rivalry of the partizans of opposite bands of Tabut processionists, and more than twelve thousand Coolies took part in the riots, and the Police had to fire with a view to disperse the rioters. Twelve Coolies were killed, and four hundred injured in the tumult. Sir Henry Norman, a retired Anglo-Indian, once Governor of Jamaica, was appointed to report upon these disturbances. His Report shows that of the total number of Indians in Trinidad, less than one-fifth are Mahomedans, and the rest are Hindus. The Hindu Coolies took the chief part in the Tabut processions, and some of the Mahomedans had actually asked the Government to put a stop to the disorderly conduct of the Hindu processionists on religious grounds. The Tabut procession is turned to account by the Hindus as a day of National demonstration. The Indians in Trinidad formed two-thirds of the entire population. In one district where the riots occurred the Indian Coolies were four-sevenths of the population. Sir

Henry Norman officially reported that residence for some years made the Coolies independent, and even overbearing. A large portion elect to remain in Trinidad when they are entitled to Free Passage back to India. Those who go to India take large sums of money with them, and not a few return back to Trinidad. Occasional cases of ill-treatment might occur, but in the opinion of Sir Henry Norman, the Coolies are very well treated. In 1890-91, Coolies numbering about 3,800 landed in Trinidad. Men about 2,400 and Women about 1,400. About 685 returned back to India, taking with them nearly 11,000 Dollars as Savings. Between 1851 and 1891, about 12,000 Coolies returned, and brought twenty-four and a half Lakhs of Rupees as their Savings. The annual remittances to India by Trinidad Coolies range from £15,000 to £23,000. Between 1871 and 1881, about 24,000 Coolies went to Trinidad, and about 3,500 returned to India. About 600 Coolies commuted their Free Passage, and settled in the Island. Since 1869, about 1,168 Coolies have received their land allotments of ten Acres each, 1,475 have each received a five Acre allotment, and about 3,100 took their £5 bounty in lieu of Return Passage. The total population in Trinidad in 1891 was 71,533 of whom nearly 55,000 were Coolies. There were 2,750 Coolies who had deposits in Savings Banks, and this amount was in all 31,000 Dollars. The number in 1881 was 1,500, who had 24,000 Dollars in deposits. There were fifty-three Schools attended by about 2,900 Coolie-children—both boys and girls—in the Island.

FIJI.

Fiji is an Island in the South Pacific, where Emigration appears to have commenced within very recent times, since 1874. In the first year, 480 Indian Settlers landed on the Island. Since then, nearly 10,000 Indian Coolies have been imported into Fiji. The actual number resident in 1891 in the Island was 8,000. The number who went to Fiji in 1891 was 1,050 in all. Out of the total number about 3,000 were Indentured Labourers, and the rest had completed their term. The Births in the Island were about 151, and the Deaths 229 in the Indian population, and there were four Marriages. A Special Law for the Registration of Indian Marriages was passed in 1891. The Chief Industry in the Island is the cultivation of Sugarcane. The working days are six and a half in the week. The term of Indenture is five years. The minimum rate of wages is one Shilling for adult Male, and ninepence for Female Labourers. Rations are provided at the rate of five-pence for each person above ten years of age, for six months after arrival. Lodgings and medical relief are provided free. Free Return Passage is given after five years' service. In 1891, there were

343 Coolies who had deposited 10,638 Dollars in the Savings Banks in Fiji. The number of depositors and the amount deposited have both steadily risen, since 1885, when there were 106 depositors with 3,470 Dollars to their credit. Similarly, as against ten Coolies who remitted £84 to India, there were in 1891 as many as 102 Coolies who remitted £546 to India.

ST. VINCENT.

St. Vincent is a small Island in the Antilles Group, and lies in 13° North Latitude and 61° West Longitude. Its area is 130 square miles. It produces Sugarcane, Arrowroot, Cocoa and Cotton. The term of Indenture is for three years, though it may be extended for two years more, and at the end of eight years, the Indian Immigrant Coolie is entitled to a Free Passage. For re-Indenturing, bounty is given at a rate fixed on a sliding scale, according to the number of years of residence. The minimum rates of wages are fixed by law at ten-pence a day for adult males, with lower rates for women and children. Free rations are only given in the first month, and by special arrangement for two months more, and after that period, the wages earned cover all payments. The work-days and working-hours are the same as in the other Colonies. The Owners of the Estates are required to provide convenient lodgings and free medicines for their Indian Labourers. In the year 1891 about 1,273 Indian Labourers earned 8,821 Dollars in the first six months, and during the next half year 1,442 Indians earned 18,000 Dollars. This gives an average of eight to twelve Dollars per man per month. The Indian Coolies numbered 552 in 1864, and rose to 1,442 in 1871, out of whom 792 were adult Males, 338 were Females, and about 300 Children. Since 1871 St. Vincent is not much favoured by Indian Coolies, and Emigration has fallen off in this Colony.

GRENADA.

Grenada is the Southernmost Island of the Antilles Group, and lies 12° 20′ North Latitude and 61° 20′ West Longitude. It has an area of 133 square miles. Coffee, Cocoa, Cotton, Sugar, Indigo, and Tobacco are the chief products of the Island. The provisions of the Immigrant Legislation are the same as those of the Colony of St. Vincent. Indentured Immigrants agree to work for five years. Free Passage is earned by five years' industrial or ten years' total residence. In 1871, there were 1,863 Indians in this Island, nearly 1,000 being adult Males, about 400 adult Females, and 450 Children. These were settled on forty-six Estates. There were, besides, some free Settlers, but their number was not large. The able-bodied men earn one Shilling and three-pence per day, but the minimum rate of wages fixed by Law is eight-pence.

In the Census of 1881, the number of Indian Immigrants was shown to be 1,052, and in 1891, this number was reduced to 1,013. The Coolies are, for the most part, engaged in agricultural operations. Many of them, however, are Proprietors of small Holdings of Land, and some of tolerably large ones, and a good many are engaged in business. About 500 of the Indian Coolies were shown to be Hindus by Religion, 72 were Mussalmans, and the rest were Native Christians. The Missionary Schools are largely attended by the children of the Indian Settlers, and this circumstance accounts for the large percentage of Native Christians. Most of those who are now living in the Island were born there, or have come from other neighbouring Islands.

ST. LUCIA.

St. Lucia is an Island in the Windward Group and lies in 13° 50′ North Latitude and 61° West Longitude, and has an area of 245 square miles. The Temperature ranges from 71° to 83° Fahrenheit, and the average Rainfall is about 94 inches. It had a population of 24,123 Souls in 1854, out of whom 947 were Whites and the rest persons of Colour. Sugar-cane cultivation is the chief industry of the Island. The laws regulating Labour are clearer and more stringent than the laws of any other Colony. The Immigration Agent, who is a paid Government Officer, inspects the Ships on their arrival, and assigns the Immigrants to the Planters. The wages are required to be not less than those paid to free labourers, and as far as possible, the allotments are made so as to keep husband and wife, child and parent, together. The Indenture is then drawn up and signed before a Magistrate, and the Agent visits the Estates to see that the laws passed for the Protection of the Coolies are strictly enforced, and that the Labourers are fairly treated. The contracts are for five years, but the Immigrant may redeem the last two years by payment of a fixed sum of money. After five years of industrial service, he obtains a Certificate of Discharge, and after eight years, he is entitled to a Free Passage, which he may commute into money, or he may accept a Grant of Land instead. The rate of wages ranges from one Shilling to one Shilling and four-pence per day, for adult Males, and ten-pence a day for Females. The Employer is required to provide proper lodgings for the labourers, and each house has an acre of Provision Ground. For the first three months free rations are allowed, according to a fixed scale. The Penal provisions against absence from work and desertion are stringent and strictly enforced. Up to 1862, in all 1,535 Immigrants were imported into this Island. After 1862, no Immigrants were imported for many years. In 1864, the number of

Indian Immigrants in this Island was 1,316, and they were reduced to 1,079 in 1868. Though all had become entitled to free passage back to India, only 460 accepted the boon. The rest chose to take the bounty and become permanent Residents on the Island. Immigration to this Island has been resumed in recent years, since 1881. In 1891, there were on the Island in all 2,500 Indians, out of whom 1,640 were employed on twenty-two Estates and 225 of these Indians possessed twenty Horses, four hundred and eighty Cattle, and two hundred Sheep and Goats. Some of the more enterprising of these Immigrants had begun to purchase land with the object of forming a purely Indian Settlement of Peasant Proprietors on the Island. There were five Schools attended by the children of the Indian Coolies, which received Grants-in-aid from Government.

JAMAICA.

Jamaica is an Island in the West Indies, and lies between 17° 40′ and 18° 50′ North Latitude, and 76° 10′ to 78° 30′ West Longitude. It has a surface area of 6,400 square miles. There is a mountain range of considerable height which runs right through the middle of the Island, and the plains gradually slope down its sides to the sea. Its chief products are Sugar, Rum, and Coffee. Cotton and Indigo were formerly produced in large quantities, but these industries have either much declined or disappeared in recent years. The Indian Coolies are employed chiefly in Sugar and Coffee Plantations and in the Breeding Pens on the hills, where excellent Cattle and Horses are reared on the rich grazing grounds that cap these hills. The Indian Immigrants were first introduced in 1845. In the first three years, about 4,000 Indians were imported into the Colony. For the next twelve years Immigration was stopped by reason of internal troubles in the Colony. It was resumed in 1859, and during the next twelve years, about 9,000 Indian Coolies were imported. The Immigration Agent allots the Immigrants to the Estates according to their wants, after satisfying himself that the conveniences of the Coolies will be duly looked after. The period of Indenture is five years. As elsewhere, the Agent is required by law to see that wives and husbands, and parents and children, shall not be separated. Before the allotment, the Immigration Agent feeds and supports the Coolies at Government expense. The Planters contribute to this Fund, and the Government assigns the yield of certain taxes to the same purpose. The Agent has also the power of cancelling the Indenture in case the Employer ill-uses his work-people, or abuses his powers. In 1871 the number of Indian Coolies was nearly 10,000. Free rations, clothes and lodgings have to be provided by the Employer, according to a scale laid down by the Government. Rations are stopped after the Immigrant has been for some time on the Island, and the Agent is satisfied that he can easily procure within his earnings his own supplies. In this case, money wages are paid to the Immigrants. The usual rate of wages is one Shilling a day for each adult Male, and nine-pence for a Female adult labourer. There are six working days in the week, and the hours of work are nine per day. Special arrangements for Task-Work are permitted with the sanction of the Agent. The laws against absence and desertion are, as in the other Colonies, severe, and strictly enforced. In case of sickness, Medical Officers of Government attend upon the sick person and look to his wants. Out of the whole number of Indian Coolies in the Colony in 1871, about fifty per cent. *i.e.*, 4,608, were indentured Labourers, and worked on eighty-seven Estates. After the indentured term of five years is over, the Indian Coolie is free to follow any calling he likes. A few become Shop-keepers, but many continue their employment as free labourers on the Estates. After ten years' residence, the Immigrant becomes entitled to a Free Passage, which he may commute by accepting a Grant of ten Acres of Crown Land. Out of 2,140, who became entitled to a return passage in 1872, 925 returned to India, but 1,215 commuted their privilege, and settled permanently in Jamaica as Residents. Up to 1871, as many as 14,400 Indian Coolies came to Jamaica, and only about 2,773 returned during the same period. About 925 Coolies returned to India in 1870, and they carried with them Savings estimated at 17,000 Dollars. If a labourer becomes permanently disabled or sick during the term of his Indenture, free Return Passage is given to him. The conditions of employment are thus, on the whole, very satisfactory. Between 1860 and 1877, a period of seventeen years, about 16,000 Coolies have been imported, sixty per cent. Males, and forty per cent. Females. Out of the whole number, 1,952 have returned during the same period, and 12,600 were in the Colony in 1877, and worked on 103 Plantations. The total number of Indians in the Colony in 1892 was 14,000, of whom 4,100 were working under Indentures, and 10,000 had completed their ten years, and were working as Free Labourers. There were 667 Indian Depositors in the Savings Banks, and the amount to their credit was 14,054 Dollars, against 145 Depositors who had 16,758 Dollars in 1871. Among the new arrivals in 1892 was one Chandra Kumari, who claimed to be of the Jung Bahadur Family, and she stated that she had run away with one of the Palace servants. About 450 Coolies returned to India in 1892, and brought with them £1,748 worth of cash, and £500 worth of Jewellery.

NATAL.

Natal is a tract on the South-East Coast of Africa, 200 miles long and 100 miles broad, with a total area of 17,000 square miles. There are three Zones or Strips; the Coast Strip, about 15 miles broad, is sub-Tropical, and Sugarcane, Coffee, and Indigo are grown there largely, as also Mulberry, Vine, Olives, Oats, Beans and Potatoes. Maize is, however, the chief grain crop. The second Zone is more Temperate, and Cereals grow there. The third Zone is hilly, and on its Western Side the range of mountains rises to 8,000 feet above the level of the sea. This portion is best fitted for pasturing Sheep and Cattle, and is also suited for the Growth of Cereals and Fruits of Temperate Regions. In the Coast Strip the Temperature ranges from 77° to 85° Fahrenheit in the Summer Season, and from 85° to 70° in Winter. The Temperature in the Central Region is more mild. From 1842 to 1856, Natal was administered as a Dependency of the Cape Colony, but in the latter year a separate Administration was formed. In 1860, the total population was 1,25,000, out of whom 8,000 were Whites, and of these last one-third were Dutch Boers, who occupied the Territory before the British invaded it, in 1842. In 1872, the Indian Immigrants were estimated to be 5,700 adults, and they had all served out their term of Indenture. Nearly one-half of this number were employed on Sugar and Coffee Estates. The other half were Traders, Shopkeepers, Gardeners, Fishermen, and Domestic Servants. Some of the Coolies had also become Land-Holders themselves, and cultivated Sugarcane and Maize. Some 400 Indians had gone further west to seek their fortunes in the diamond fields of the Transvaal. Ordinary workmen get 15*s*. a month, skilled workmen earn from 30*s*. to £2. One Indian earned as much as £4 a month. On the Railway, Indian Coolies get 20*s*. to 30*s*. a month. In all cases rations are given in addition to money wages. About 6,445 Indians were imported as Coolies in Natal up to 1866. The children of the Coolies live and thrive better in Natal than in India. The death rate is lower, and the general state of health is better. The Coolies build their own houses out of materials supplied by their Employers, and a small garden grounds are attached to the houses in which Tobacco is grown. There are four Schools for Coolie children, which are aided by Government Grants. In recent years very few Coolies go to Natal under Indentures. The general Law of Master and Servant is found to be sufficiently protective of their interests. The percentage of Women is low, Males being sixty-seven per cent. against thirty-three per cent. Females. There were 231 Indian Coolie Depositors in the Savings Bank in 1871, who had deposited £6,000. A large portion of the Savings has been invested in the Colony in Vegetable and Tobacco Farms, and many Coolies earn their living as Boat-owners and Fishermen. After retiring from the position of labourers, many Indians take up Crown land, and grow Sugarcane on their own farms. In 1891, as many as 3,183 Indian Immigrants landed in the Ports of this Colony, and about 774 Immigrants returned to India, bringing with them in all £13,387 worth of cash and jewellery. Indian labourers are now employed throughout the length of the Colony, and no complaints are made in respect of them. The Indians introduced in recent years compare very favourably in physique and general health with those who were formerly imported. The Indian population has increased from 10,625 in 1876 to 38,365 in 1892. The births in this Community in 1892 were 966, and the deaths 617. Out of the total of 38,365 Indians in Natal, 24,010 were free Indians, and 14,325 were Indentured Labourers. There were nearly 19,000 Male adults, 8,500 Female adults, and about 11,071 Children. Immigration into Natal first commenced in 1860. Since that date 50,101 Indian Immigrants entered Natal. Out of this total number, 5,172 died, 7,115 returned to India, and 4,552 left the Colony otherwise, in thirty-two years. Out of 10,150 children born in the Colony, about 2,300 returned to India, about 2,000 died, and about 700 left the Colony otherwise. There were 130 Indian Marriages registered in 1891, but no case of divorce was instituted in the Courts. In 1891, about 641 Immigrants completed their indentured term, and obtained the Certificate of Industrial residence. A considerable number of them have taken to Farming and Gardening on their own account. They are also Hawkers, Traders, Fishermen and Fruit-sellers. Many have left the Colony for the Transvaal Gold Fields. They generally form a prosperous and orderly section of the population of Natal. The relations between the Employers and the Employees are reported to be very satisfactory. In the Up-country Districts, the Indians have the exclusive charge of ploughing, stock and agriculture entrusted to them by the farmers, and they are allowed to sell Potatoes, and Vegetables, Mutton and Milk in as large quantities as they need, in addition to their wages. Their reputation for reliability and Industry is thoroughly established, and without them the Industry of the Colony could not be carried on. In the Savings Bank 225 Depositors had nearly Rs. 50,000 to their credit, and a few more prosperous Indians remitted Rupees 5,000 besides to India.

This account extracted from the latest official Reports would go to show that the alleged misunderstanding between the Whites and the Indian settlers, of which we hear so much, is of recent growth. As might be expected, there must be, in the nature of things, considerable conflict of interests between the Indian Traders and the White population, and things apparently have gone from bad to worse during the last few years.

NON-BRITISH COLONIES.

Of the non-British Colonies, Dutch Guiana appears to attract a large number of Indian Emigrants. Indian Emigration appears to have commenced soon after the Abolition of Slavery. It was not till 1870, however, that a Convention was made between England and Holland, and a Dutch Government Agent for Surinam, the Capital of Dutch Guiana, was appointed at Calcutta. In 1873, 2,448 Emigrants were imported into this Colony. In 1874, 1,405 Coolies were imported. In December 1875, there were about 3,000 Indian Coolies in this Colony. During the last four years for which information is available about 3,200 Indian Coolies were despatched from Calcutta to this Colony. The Indenture term is for five years, the working year being of 313 days, and the minimum hours for work are seven hours in the fields, and ten hours in Building work. The minimum rate of wages is twenty-five Cents for Male adults and sixteen Cents for Females and Children. Rations are provided on a fixed scale for three months after arrival; provision for free lodging and medical relief is also enforced, and free Return Passage can be claimed at the end of five years. In 1891 about 570 Coolies returned to India bringing with them aggregate Savings of the value of Rs. 81,461. In 1889, the number returned was 587, and they brought with them aggregate Savings of the value Rs. 1,10,000.

The Colony of French Guiana also imports Indian Coolies, so also do the French Islands of Guadeloupe and Martinique, but detailed information about these settlements is not available. The only French Colony about which information is available is the island of Reunion, which lies 90 miles to the South-west of Mauritius. The Island is 40 miles long and 27 miles broad. Cotton, Coffee, Cloves, and Sugarcane are the chief products of the Island. In 1861, the number of Indian Immigrants was about 40,000, of whom 33,000, were adult Males, 4,300 adult Females and 2,000 Children. In 1863, the number of Indian Settlers had risen to 46,411. The Employers have to supply free rations, clothing, lodging, and medicines, and pay besides Rs. 5 a month as wages to each adult Male; Rs. 3 to each Female, and Rs. 2 to each Child. After completing five years, Free Passage is allowed back to India. The Coolie Emigrants are well off, and some own small Holdings and Gardens of their own, and others manage Shops. The working hours are nine and a half per day. In recent years Emigration from British Indian Ports has been stopped on account of complaints about mismanagement and abuse of powers. A few Coolies still emigrate from the French port of Pondicherry. Negotiations have been opened by the French Government with the Government of India to allow the resumption of Coolie Emigration from the British Ports to this Island, and Mr. MacKenzie was sent by the

Government of India to arrange the terms on which this concession could be granted with safety.

CEYLON.

Nearer home, the Island of Ceylon attracts a considerable body of Indian Coolies from the Madras Presidency. As many as 75,000 Coolies leave Indian Ports for Ceylon each year. Three-fourths of them return back to India, and the rest stay permanently in Ceylon. It has been estimated that between 1843 and 1867, nearly fourteen and a half Lakhs of Coolies went to Ceylon, out of whom eight and one-third Lakhs returned to India. The rest remained in the Island as permanent Settlers. Out of the total population of Ceylon, estimated in 1871 at twenty-four Lakhs, as many as six Lakhs, or twenty-five per cent., were Indian Coolies, and others settled in that Island during the previous forty years. The Straits Settlements, Singapoor, Penang, and Malacca also attract a considerable number of Coolies from India. About 40,000 Indians are found in these Settlements, employed chiefly as agricultural labourers, though a considerable number of them also follow other pursuits.

This completes our review of the British, French, and Dutch Colonies and Possessions to which, during the past fifty years and more, the surplus labour of India has been exported. Taking a general view of the question, it will be seen that Foreign Emigration from India represents a large and most important interest. As the result of the past fifty years of protected Emigration, as many as 12,00,000 of people are to be found scattered throughout these Settlements. The popularity of Foreign Emigration is evidenced by the following facts which can be gathered from the Reports:—(1) The number of Emigrants has been steadily increasing. (2) The proportion of Women to Men is also more favourable in recent years than it was in the first half of this period of fifty years, 1842-1892. (3) The number of those who return back to India has always been smaller than those who left each year. (4) Among those who return to India, a good many re-Emigrate with their families. (5) Of those who go out of India as Indentured Labourers under contract, nearly one half settle in these Colonies as Free Labourers. (6) Of those who so settle, a small proportion acquire land of their own, or become traders, or pursue other callings, indicative of their attainment of a higher social status. (7) Notwithstanding the severity of the laws against desertion and absence from work, the Indian Coolies thrive remarkably well, and acquire habits of thrift and independence for which they are not much noted during their residence in India. (8) The Wages earned are from two to three times those obtained in India, and the climate appears generally to agree with the Indian Settlers and their Families. (9) Their general prosperity is fully attested to by the large remittances they make to this Country, and the

Savings they bring with them when they return, as also by the increase of their Deposit accounts in the local Savings Bank. Of course, there are difficulties and obstructions in the way. Without a strict enforcement of the Protection Laws in their interest by the Government of India, the Coolie Emigrants would not be able to hold their own against the greed of their Employers, the Planters, who are not generally noted for their humanity. The Magistracy and the Government machinery in these Colonies, being entirely in the hands of the White population, are not very impartial in their treatment of the Indian Settlers, and there is not much scope allowed for the independent growth of the Coloured Races. Notwithstanding these disadvantages, there can be no doubt that the system of Protected Emigration has, on the whole, been very beneficial, and that it will, in course of time, lead to further developments in the interest of the Indian Settlers in those Colonies, at least, where, as in Natal, Trinidad, Mauritius and British Guiana, the Indians already represent a considerable proportion of the population.

The most hopeful feature of this stream of Foreign Emigration is represented by the fact that the Higher Castes of Hindus occupy no small place among those who emigrate. The Emigration Report for 1889 showed that, out of 11,000 Emigrants who left the

Port of Calcutta in that year, 1,315 were Brahmins and men of the Higher Castes, 3,356 were Agriculturists, 958 Artizans, and the Low Caste Emigrants were 4,152. The Hindus in all made up nearly 9,800, while the Mussalmans were 1,154 and the Christians 15. The Emigration Report for 1890 shows that, out of some 13,000 persons who left the Calcutta Port in that year, as many as 1,234, or ten per cent., were Brahmins and men of the Higher Castes, about 4,100 were Agriculturists, about 800 were Artizans and the Low Caste Emigrants were 5,200, in all. The Hindu Emigrants were 11,345, while the Mussalmans were 1,623, and the Christians 89. Similarly, out of nearly 16,000 Emigrants who left Calcutta in 1891, 1,170 were Brahmins and men of the Higher Castes, 6,000 were Agriculturists, and about 900 Artizans, while the Low Caste Emigrants were 6,200. The Hindu Emigrants were in all 14,000; the Mussalmans were 1,558 and Christians nine. This feature of Hindu Emigration is the most hopeful, seeing that it is not the Low Castes alone who emigrate. Out of nearly 47,000 people who emigrated from the Port of Calcutta during the three years, 1889 to 1891, about eleven per cent. were Mahomedans, and eighty nine per cent. were Hindus; and out of this eighty-nine per cent. less than forty-five per cent. were Low Caste people, and the rest were Artizans, Agriculturists and Brahmins and men of the Higher Castes.

It only remains now for me to indicate briefly the lines on which Associations like those under the auspices of which we meet here to-day, can make themselves practically useful. In connection with these twelve Lakhs of people settled in Foreign Parts, if people in Bombay, or Madras, or Calcutta would venture to go out of their usual track, they could easily establish thriving Agencies in all these ten or fifteen Colonies, where such a large number of Indians are settled, and are presumably well off. The Bombay Mill Owners, for instance, could not find a better market for their Native made cloth than in the outlying possessions. The Emigration business is one which Native Shippers could well undertake with advantage, especially with Mauritius and Natal on the African Coast. It should be the business of Associations like these to obtain the latest information from, and keep up communication with, these distant Settlements. The School-master, the Doctor and the Lawyer, the Artizans of all classes, and even the Priests of different Sects, have here a most favourable field for their operations and enterprize among people who are their kith and skin, and on whom sympathy would never be wasted. The Government of the Queen-Empress extends its common protection to us and to them, and the Government of India is most conscientiously alive to its duty of protecting the interests of these Indian Settlers. If we could send out our young men to these Possessions of the Crown, they will surely be able to earn their living, and do a great deal of practical good. A little organization and some enterprize are alone needed for utilizing this vast force which lies scattered about in distant Possessions. It is with a view to rouse interest in the welfare of these people, and enable us to do our duty by them, that I took up this subject for this year's Conference, and I shall be amply rewarded, if among those who hear me, the Merchants, Manufacturers, Traders, and Representatives of different Provinces, any one or more feels himself moved by the spirit of enterprize and sympathy, and is led in consequence to cultivate better relations of Trade and Industry with these twelve Lakhs of people established in Foreign Parts.

VI.

IRON INDUSTRY—PIONEER ATTEMPTS.*

I HAVE in my Essay on Indian Political Economy endeavoured to lay down a few general principles which should regulate the action of the State, in respect of the development of Industrial Enterprise in India. I propose on the present occasion to illustrate these principles by an historical review of the efforts made to develop the production of a particular Indian Product, which is closely associated with the revival of Indian Manufactures, and which may well be described as typifying the Resources of Wealth, on which our future prosperity mainly depends. The history of the successive attempts made by Private and State Agencies to develop the Iron Industry in India has a mournful interest, and yet it is full of instruction. As Captain Townsend of the Ordnance Department has observed in his work on the Mineral Wealth of India, nothing strikes the stranger who studies Indian Economy so much as the contrast between the bounty of Nature and the poverty of Man in the matter of this Iron Industry. Endowed

* Read at the Industrial Conference, Poona, 1892.

more richly in Iron ore than almost any other country in the world, India has in a commercial sense, no Iron Industry at all. There are only forty-two Iron and Brass Foundries in the Country, working chiefly on Foreign Imports, and employing twelve thousand men. Mr. Ball, Deputy Superintendent of the Geological Survey, in his work on Economic Geology, and Dr. Watt, in his Dictionary of Indian Economic Products, have described, the extent and richness of the Iron ores which occur in all formations, in the metamorphic rocks, semi-metamorphic or transition rocks, in the conglomerates, in the cretaceous rocks, in the Deccan trapp, in the sand-beds of rivers, and in the detrital ores of sub-recent Age. In respect of Geographical distribution, there is absolutely not a Province or even a large District in all India, which is not favoured with rich Iron ore deposits of one kind or another, and in which there are not traces of Iron manufactured by Native methods down to very recent times.

The Iron Industry not only supplied all local wants, but it also enabled India to export its finished products to Foreign Countries. The quality of the material turned out had also a world-wide fame. The famous Iron Pillar near Delhi, which is at least fifteen hundred years old, indicates an amount of skill in the manufacture of Wrought Iron, which has been the marvel of all who have endeavoured to account for it. Mr. Ball admits that it is not many years since the production of such a Pillar would have been an impossibility in the largest Factories in the world, and even now, there are comparatively very few Factories where such a mass of metal could be turned out. Cannons were manufactured in Assam of the largest calibre. Indian Wootz or Steel furnished the materials out of which Damascus Blades with a world-wide reputation were made, and it paid Persian Merchants in those old times to travel all the way to India to obtain these materials, and export them to Asia. The Indian Steel found once considerable demand for Cutlery even in England. This manufacture of Steel and Wrought Iron had reached a high perfection at least two thousand years ago.

All this is now changed. The Native Furnaces all over the Country have stopped work. The Domestic Manufacture has been, in most places, crushed out by foreign competition, and complete extinction in the near future is the fate with which it has been cursed. This fate has overtaken it contemporaneously with an enormous increase in the demand for Iron Goods. The measure of this increase will be gathered from the fact that in 1888-89 India imported nearly four million hundredweight of Iron, worth two and a half Crores of Rupees. The Imports of Steel were a quarter of a million hundredweight, worth thirty-four Lakhs of Rupees. Hardware and Cutlery Imports exceeded one Crore of Rupees. Railway Plant and Stock were worth two and a half Crores of Rupees, and Mill Work and Machinery two and one-third Crores of Rupees, while Government Imports came to one Crore. In all, about eleven Crores' worth of Iron Goods were imported in 1888-89. The Imports twenty years ago, under all these heads, were about two and a half Crores only, and the difference between the two totals to a large extent measures the displacement of Home Manufactures.

Of course, it is but fair to note that, besides the effects of Foreign Competition, the collapse of the Iron Industry has been brought about by the increasing scarcity of Fuel. The Native Furnaces have all along used Charcoal fuel, and their processes involve great waste of power and resources, as much as fourteen tons of fuel being required to produce one ton of Iron. As a consequence, the production of Iron by the old Native Methods cannot be continued, except at a cost which is prohibitive. This question of cheap fuel lies at the bottom of the success of any organized attempt to revive the Industry under modern conditions. In this respect, Nature has not been equally munificent in her gifts. While the Iron ore is to be found all over the Country, the only cheap fuel which can enable India to compete with England, namely, Indian Coal, is not so widely distributed, but in the region where it is found, the resources of India are by no means stinted or poor. The Coal-bearing area is estimated to exceed thirty-five thousand square miles. The regions of the Wardha-Godavari Valleys, the Valleys of the Soane and its Tributaries, and the Valleys of the Damuda and its Tributaries, and the Lower Range of the Vindhya and the Himalaya Mountains represent the Coal Region of India, and these Coal resources, thanks to the action of Government, and the Railway Companies, have been largely utilized. It was estimated in 1879-80 in Official Reports, that out of a total consumption of some one and a half Million tons, one Million tons were raised in India, and about five Lakhs of tons were imported. During the last fourteen years the consumption and Home production have nearly doubled. More than two Million tons of Indian Coal were produced and consumed in India, and the Foreign Imports were about eight or nine Lakhs of tons in 1888-89. Besides the convenient vicinity of cheap Fuel, another equally essential requisite for the successful manufacture of Iron is, abundance of Lime-stone to serve as Flux, and of Fire Clay for the Furnaces. This resource generally accompanies Coal Formations. At least, this has been the case in India. The need of proximity to Sea or Railway, and abundance of Coal and Lime-stone, limit the possibilities of successful Indian Manufacture of Iron to a few favoured regions. Mr. Ball has with some hesitation expressed his opinion as follows:— By adopting improved processes of manufacture in the Raniganj Field, Iron and Steel of high quality might be manufactured under proper management at a probable cost which would admit of their underselling the English Iron in the Bengal Markets. With improved communications, this same result may be predicated of the Palamow Field in the Hajaribag District. The Chanda field with improved process of reduction will be in a position to supply the Central Provinces and Bombay with Iron at an average rate lower than that paid for English Iron, and this remark holds true of some of the localities in the Narbada Valley and in Upper Assam. As regards the rest of India, there does not appear any solid ground of hope, under existing conditions, of manufacturing cheap Iron, which will compete in price and quality with the English imported article. Captain Townsend is equally, or if possible more, discriminating in his forecast. According to him the Raniganj Field possesses all the auxiliary advantages, though its Iron ore is not of the best. The Wardha Valley, in the proximity of the Warora Coal Mines has superior Iron ore, but its Coal supply is not equally good. He mentions the Hazaribag Field as in every way eligible, as its Coal is richer than Raniganj and Warora. The Southern Indian Iron Field near Salem is the richest in all India, and though it does not enjoy the advantage of Coal deposits in the vicinity, Captain Townsend thinks that this difficulty is not insuperable, especially, if the manufacture is limited to the higher classes of Iron, while the Raniganj and Wardha Fields might confine themselves with advantage to the cheaper and inferior classes. Mr. Ball also suggests, that when there are extensive jungles, the absence of Coal Mines does not matter much, since the unrestrained annual jungle-fires consume a much greater amount of timber than any number of Charcoal Burners could do, and with a judicious system of Forest Conservancy, it should be possible to allow Native Furnaces near such jungles. Sir George Molesworth, writing in 1882, gave it as his opinion "that Charcoal-made Iron will never be able to compete with English Iron, but a well-organized system of forest Conservancy ought to be able to secure Charcoal Fuel at a low price for smelting purposes, and within close proximity to the Iron Works." Such a Conservancy is not easy to secure, and there is no great prospect of help in this assurance. Dr. Watt, after a careful examination of all existing sources, arrived at the conclusion that the Bengal and Jabalpore and Chanda Fields offer, under existing circumstances, the only possible opening for large Iron Works.

Dr. Watt, in his Dictionary, quotes the testimony of an Official Expert, from which it appears that the price of Iron is increased fifty per cent. by reason of Freight and Landing Charges, about one mile of Iron Railway Sleepers costing in England £2,000 and in

India Rs. 31,000. The difference is due to £1,000 charge for Freight and Landing. The railway carriage charge and during recent years the heavy loss by Exchange raise this difference fully fifty per cent. more. It has been estimated that about one hundred and fifty Crores' worth of Iron has been imported into India during the last thirty years, and fifty Crores of Rupees at least have thus been paid for Freight and Landing Charges alone, which would have been saved if the Industry had been started here. Mr. Ball observes, that if the Government had started the manufacture of Iron on an extended scale at the time of the first opening of the Railways, great benefits would have accrued to the State. If the State was justified in undertaking the construction of its own Railways, there was nothing inconsistent with principle in its undertaking the manufacture of its own Iron any more than in its manufacture of Salt or Opium. The effect of its establishing factories for Iron manufacture throughout India would have, in Mr. Ball's opinion, enabled the State to keep vast sums of money in circulation, and would have given employment to large numbers of people who now resort to Agriculture as their only resource. This golden opportunity was allowed to pass, and we find ourselves in the anomalous situation that after one hundred and fifty years of British Rule, the Iron resources of India remain undeveloped, and the

Country pays about ten Crores of Rupees yearly for its Iron Supply, while the old race of Iron Smelters find their occupation gone.

It must be admitted at the same time, that the Government of India has not been altogether oblivious of its duties in this connection. The Government, through its Geological Survey Department has carefully, and at considerable expense, surveyed the Regions which abound in Iron Ores. The value of this service can never be overestimated. Next to these Surveying operations, it has also from time to time, spent considerable sums on experimental trials, it has subsidized Companies to whom concessions more or less favourable have been granted, and lastly, it has directed its various Departments to obtain their supplies from Local sources, and thus helped the efforts of these Companies. There is thus no question of principle involved in the matter. The principle of State-help and guidance in pioneering new enterprize has thus been accepted and acted upon by the Government here. The only fault one can lay at its door, is that this Policy has been followed with half-heartedness and oscillations of purpose, the result of which has been that as a rule most of the private attempts made on various occasions have proved more or less failures, serving only to discourage all enterprize in this direction.

The object of this paper is to give a brief History of these attempts, and to ascertain the cause or causes why they turned out failures :—1. I shall first take up the Salem Iron Field. In 1825 Mr. Heath obtained a Government advance for the purpose, and he succeeded in 1833 in forming a Company called the Indian Steel, Iron, and Chrome Company. The Leasehold rights of this Company extended over four Districts of South Arcot, Coimbatore, Malabar, and South Canara, and it established three Factories, at Porto Novo in South Arcot, at Beypore in Malabar, and at Palampetti near Salem. The Steel manufactured by this Company was very highly thought of, and it established a depôt at Chelsea. through which the Steel was tested and passed before being sold. The business of Mr. Heath's Company was after some years taken over by another Company, who continued to work the Porto Novo and Beypore Factories till 1859. The Company had in those days great difficulties to encounter. They consumed Charcoal Fuel, which had to be brought from a distance of more than twenty-five miles, and the Flux used was Sea-Shells, and both Fuel and Flux had to be taken to long distances. Notwithstanding these difficulties, the Pig Iron produced was pronounced by Sheffield Iron Workers to be superior to any produced in England and Sweden; and it commanded a good price, £6 10s. per ton, in London for conversion into Steel, and two

Bridges, the Britannia Tubular and Menai Bridges were built with this material. Next to the difficulties about Fuel and Carriage, there were in those days difficulties about Shipping. The Furnaces were seldom at work for more than four months, and stocks accumulated. The hold on the English Market could not be retained by reason of this irregularity of supply and the cost of management increased proportionately to the stoppages. As a consequence of these drawbacks, the Company never declared a dividend, and the Sheffield Ironmonger's prophecy that India would ultimately become one of the largest sources from whence Sheffield would draw her supply of Raw Materials, remained unfulfilled. The Company appears to have stopped work about 1860-61, so far as the Porto Novo Factory is concerned.

2. The Beypore Factory of this same concern was started in 1833, but it changed hands frequently. The Factory was working in 1857, and the Gun Carriage Department pronounced favourably upon the Iron turned out, as being suitable for their purposes. Ultimately, owing chiefly to deficiency of Fuel and the bad roads, the Company had to bring wood Fuel from Ceylon by sea. The German employees left service in 1859, and though improved processes were introduced in 1861 the resuscitation was only temporary, and the Works were shortly after abandoned. It will be seen from this account that the quality of the Iron turned

out was in every way satisfactory, and the attempts of the Company failed chiefly by reason of the smallness of their capital, which did not permit of their insuring a regular supply, and the difficulty about Fuel.

As far as the difficulty about Communication is concerned, the last thirty years have effected great changes, and this difficulty may almost be said to be minimized. The difficulty about Fuel is also likely to be overcome. Captain Townsend suggests that the distance between the Singareni Coal Field and Salem is not so great that a Light Coal Tramway would not pay a really large Firm consuming its hundreds of tons a day. He, indeed, cautions any new Company against limiting its ambition to the manufacture of Pig Iron only. He would insist upon a really large undertaking, complete with all the necessary Plant on the spot, the Puddling Furnaces the Rolling Mills, the Steam Hammers, and all the other appliances of a First Class Factory and Foundry able to turn out finished Bars, and even finished Steel. This means a very large undertaking, and as no dividend can be expected for the first few experimental years, no Capitalists would venture, unless the concessions are liberal, and a subsidy promised on the plan which helped the Guaranteed Railway Companies to obtain their capital.

3. In 1874 a fresh attempt was made to form a Company in Madras to work the Iron ores of Chin-

gelput. The difficulty in the way of that Company was chiefly that of obtaining Fuel which they expected to secure from the Godavari District. Nothing came of the venture, as apparently, the necessary capital could not be secured, though, as far as local consumption was concerned, there was an ample field, as more than eighteen Lakhs of Iron was imported annually into Madras City alone.

4. We next turn to the Bengal Presidency. The Districts of Beerbhum and Hazaribag and Raniganj are the chief places where rich Iron ore is found in close proximity to Coal deposits. In Beerbhum, so far back as 1774, one Native Trader, Indra Narayan Sharma, asked for a concession covering the Beerbhum Iron sources, and he agreed to pay five thousand Rupees as rent. The offer was accepted but no lease was taken out.

5. In 1777 Messrs. Motte and Farquar and Messrs. Summer and Heatly obtained concessions, the former of the Districts to the West of Burdwan and the latter in parts of Beerbhum and Pachete, to produce Iron and sell it free of Duty. Messrs. Motte and Farquar undertook to cast Shot and Shells for the Government at three-fourths of the cost in Calcutta of imported goods. Mr. Farquar obtained the concession, and entered upon the possession of his Districts. He also obtained an advance of fifteen thousand Rupees from Government to complete his Furnaces. The Factory

was carried on from 1779 to 1789, in which last year the concession about Gunpowder Works was resigned, and the lease was allowed to expire in 1795. While the Works were open, Mr. Farquar's Iron was sold for five Rupees a Maund against ten Rupees a Maund of imported Iron in Calcutta.

6. Dr. Oldham was appointed by the Court of Directors in 1854 to inquire into the Iron resources of Beerbhum, and he pronounced an adverse opinion, chiefly on the ground of the scanty supply of Economic Fuel. But notwithstanding this pronouncement, Messrs. Mackay and Co. of Calcutta started in 1855 the Beerbhum Iron Works Company. It was very favourably reported upon in 1856. Mr. Sowerby in 1858 made an adverse Report, and Messrs. Mackay and Co. replied to Mr. Sowerby's criticisms. They stated that they turned out two tons a day, and they were able to sell Iron at thirty-seven Rupees a ton. Notwithstanding this favourable account the Work was frequently interrupted, and in 1860, Mr. Blanford was appointed to report upon the Factory. His Report showed that, though the Factory was carried on at present at some loss, the cost would be considerably diminished, if production was increased by the employment of additional Capital. He also reported that the estimated prices were lower than those of imported Iron and the quality of the Iron turned out was superior to that of ordinary English Pig Iron. He also

stated that the supplies of Iron, Coal, and Flux were sufficient for works of moderate size, but not for large Works.

7. Notwithstanding this Report, the Works appear to have been abandoned, and their place was taken up by Messrs. Burn and Co.'s Factory, which commenced operations in 1875, but this new Company soon found it necessary to abandon all idea of enlarging the Works, and ultimately gave them up. The chief difficulty in the way of these Beerbhum attempts was that of Fuel, and this difficulty has since increased. This difficulty makes it impossible to work the Iron ores, which are richer than those of Raniganj, with the same advantage as that of the inferior material supplied by Raniganj, because of the abundance of Coal Fuel in that locality.

8. We next come to the Raniganj Field. The Bengal Iron Company was formed in 1874, and it continued to work till it stopped business in 1879. The Company committed the initial error of starting with an insufficient capital of ten Lakhs, out of which it had to pay a large sum for the land taken up. The Company asked Government to help them to raise additional Capital from the public on moderate terms, but these arrangements fell through, and the money had to be raised on Debentures at high rates of interest. Government, indeed, gave a large order for Castings, but owing to financial difficulties, the work had to be stopped, and the men employed were thrown out of work, and

the Shareholders lost their money. The Iron ore worked was of the best quality, and the Flux and Coal were conveniently to hand. As many as twelve thousand and seven hundred tons of Pig Iron were turned out by this Company before it stopped business. Its daily out-turn of twenty tons was secured by a charge of thirty-seven tons Iron ore, twenty-seven tons Coke, and twenty-three tons Lime-stone, the yield of Pig Iron being thus twenty-three per cent. The average cost was forty Rupees per ton, and it might have been reduced to thirty-three Rupees. In Mr. Ball's opinion, if the Company had been helped through its early financial difficulties, Iron cheaper and better in quality than is imported from abroad would have been turned out. Captain Townsend states that the failure of this Company proves nothing except that success in the enterprise is not possible with small Capital.

9. Three years later, this concern, since called the Barakor Works, was taken up by Government, and placed under the management of Ritter Von Schwartz. One Blast Furnace was started in 1884, and produced down to 1889 more than thirty thousand tons. A second Blast Furnace has been since added, and arrangements made to smelt from fifteen thousand to twenty thousand tons a year. Pipes, Sleepers, Bridge Piles, Ornamental Work, and Railway Axle Boxes, and Agricultural Implements, are made in large quantities here. The success of this Work has demonstrated the fact

that Iron could be smelted in large quantities on European principles in India.

10. Since 1889, these Works have been again made over to a New Company by the Government of India.

11. In the Jabalpore District, one Mr. Olpherts has obtained a concession, and is making experiments with a view to the production of Charcoal Iron by the use of European methods. The Umaria Colliery has been recently opened in this vicinity, and the rich Iron Ore to the North-East of Jabalpore will soon be taken in hand.

12. The Narbada Iron and Coal Company has obtained a concession of a lease of the Tendarkhera and Omarpani Iron Mines, together with the Coal Mines of Mopani. The Company has not yet worked the Iron Mines, though the conditions of its lease made it obligatory upon the Company to produce five thousand tons within five years from the time the Railway reached Jabalpore. It may be noted here that this ore also is very rich, and a Suspension Bridge over the Bias near Sagar was built so far back as 1830, with metal prepared after Native methods from this Mine.

13. The Chanda District surpasses all others in the richness of its Iron ores. Their superiority consists in their total freedom from Phosphorus. Government appointed Mr. Nees to make an experimental trial of the Iron Ores. In 1875 he made the first trial, but it did not succeed owing to the large quantity of Coal Ashes which prevented liquefaction. The second trial

proved a better success. While the Iron ore is of the best quality, the Warora Coal is not so suitable as Raniganj, as the percentage of Carbon is less, and of Ashes is unusually large. Captain Townsend believes that there are certain superior varieties of Coal in the Wardha Valley, and that they would enable the work to be carried on under favourable conditions.

14. In Central India in the Narbada Valley near Barwai Station, Colonel Keatings arranged with the sanction of the Government of India to start an Iron Factory. Colonel Keatings was deputed by the Secretary of State to go to Sweden, and study the processes there, and he engaged a Swedish Engineer named Mitandar, and brought him over with him to India in 1861. The Fuel used was Charcoal, and the Flux was conveniently near. A Blast Furnace, Rolling Mills, Charcoal Ovens, Calcining Kilns, were all set up, and after two and a half Lakhs of Rupees had been spent, the Government refused to incur further expenditure, and declined to give the help of more European hands to Mr. Mitandar, who consequently left India in 1864, and the Works could find no purchaser even for five Thousand Pounds.

15. In the Punjab the Native Ruler of the Nahun State has incurred considerable expenditure in starting at Sirmur a Factory supplied with European appliances, and in 1880 the Works were opened with great *Eclat* by His Excellency the Viceroy.

16. We shall next turn to the History of the Kammaon Iron Mines. In 1855 the Court of Directors sent one John Henwood to report on the Iron and Copper ores of Kammaon, but nothing came of this deputation. Mr. Sowerby was, at the same time, employed by the East India Railway Company to explore the resources of the Country in Upper India. General Strachey in 1856 framed a Scheme estimated to cost fifteen and three-quarter Lakhs of Rupees, on which it was expected that six and a half per cent. interest would be earned by the manufacture of thirteen hundred tons of Cast Iron, and three thousand five hundred tons of Wrought Iron per year. Mr. Sowerby was appointed by Government in 1857 to take charge of this work. About the same time, a Company was formed which took over the Government Works at cost price in 1860. It did not work satisfactorily, and Dr. Oldham was appointed to report on the cause of the failure, and he ascribed the failure to the extravagance and incompetency of the men employed. In 1862 two Private Companies, Messrs. Davies and Co., and Drummond and Co., which had been working separately before, were amalgamated and called the Kammaon Iron Work Company. A License was promised by Government, but two years elapsed before it was issued, and in the meanwhile the Company had come to grief, as they were unable to raise the capital required, by reason of the delay in granting the License.

In 1877 the Government again took up the question of Iron manufacture in Kammaon, and spent money considerably, but there was no great improvement.

17. The latest attempt in the way of direct Government manufacture of Steel for Shell and Shot purposes was made at the Cossipore Factory, and the *Pioneer* reports that it was in every way a success. In the interests of Military Defence, the necessity of the Indian Government being provided with its own Arms and Ammunition, is so obvious, that it is not likely to be disputed. The same justification exists for the manufacture of the Rolling Stock and other Materials likely to be required for State Railways. For commercial success the extension of the Works, so as to meet private demand, will be soon forced upon Government.

We have thus passed in review the History of seventeen attempts made by Private and State Agencies to start Iron Manufactures on a large, and this brief survey of previous attempts leads one to the conclusion that the failures were due:—

1. To the smallness of the Capital employed, and the poverty of the financial Resources of the Private Companies.

2. To the scarcity and heavy cost of good Fuel.

3. To the inaccessibility of some of the places chosen, in respect of Railway and Sea Communication.

4. To the oscillations of purpose shown by the Government which made them impatient of results.

5. To the want of skill and good management on the part of the persons employed to conduct the Experiment.

6. To the delays caused by Red Tape, and the unwillingness of Government to Subsidize or Guarantee Interest during the experimental period of the concern. The failures are due to causes which can all more or less be provided against by proper care and prudence, and some of them have obviously ceased to be the obstacles they once appeared to be, by reason of improved Sea and Land communications.

The *Pioneer*, in some of its recent issues, has spoken in strong terms about the illiberal character of the Concessions offered in the way of Prospective and Mining Leases. Leases for Short Terms confined to very small areas will never answer the purpose. If the Manufacture is to be carried on, on a large scale, the Term must be a long one, exceeding fifty years or so. Such a concession may well be given to Companies which undertake to raise at least twenty-five Lakhs of Rupees of Capital. In the case of such Companies the detailed Surveying and Prospecting work must be completed by the Government, associating its own trained Officer with the private Expert. This plan was to some extent followed with success in the case of Gold Mining Wynaad a few years ago. The necessary Capital being raised, Government should, when satisfied of the *bona fide* character and skilled management of such concerns, guarantee a secure minimum interest rate during the first trial periods, on the plan so freely and advantageously resorted to in the case of Railway Companies, and Government should reserve its right to share in the Companies' profits when they exceed a fixed minimum.

On the security of their Property and Machinery, Government should help the Company to float its own Debentures when necessary, or lend the money itself. The Companies should get their Lands free of cost, on condition that *bona fide* work is done within a given period. No Royalties and Fines should be charged till after the Company begins to earn a definite minimum of profits. The Factories should also be guaranteed continuous and certain demand for their produce at fixed prices, which should include not only the English prices in England, but Ship Freight, Landing and Railway Charges, and Insurance and Exchange. A separate Department of Commerce and Manufactures can alone devote itself to this work without frequent oscillations of purpose. These rules can only apply to large Concerns, which must be limited to places selected by Government Experts, as possessing all the advantages of good Ore, cheap Fuel and Flux, and easy Communication and near Markets. Smaller Concerns, to be worked with Charcoal Fuel near dense Forests in out-of-the-way Regions, will require separate treatment. The Lessees here may have a portion of Reserved Forest area handed over to their charge, on condition of their being required to replant fourteen times the area cleared in one year, or the Department may undertake to supply good Fuel at cheap rates on the spot. In all these various ways, Government may well help this new Enterprise on the development of which the Industrial Revival of the Country so largely depends. Government owns the Lands, the Mines and the Forests. It is also the largest Consumer, and the largest Capitalist and Manufacturer in the Country. There is no question of Protective Duties here. The Natural Resources are in unmeasured abundance, and the natural Demand is increasing every day in volume and urgency. Organized skill and direction are the only needs of the Country, and these the Government possesses or can command in a way which makes it their duty to step in, and assist the development of Local Enterprise, for which the necessary Capital will be forthcoming in this Country, if the early risks of such employment are reasonably assured against. In the words of Captain Townsend, where there is no Private Enterprise to interfere with, it is not only wisdom but a duty for the State to start the required Works. State Help and State Direction are required in India, when new lines of Industry are to be opened up, and if given freely, the expenditure will not only pay itself, but will enormously develop the Wealth of the Country.

VII.

INDUSTRIAL CONFERENCE *

AT the desire of the Chairman, and on behalf of the promoters of this movement, I wish to bespeak your favourable attention to a few observations on the objects of this Conference. We are met here to-day, for a purpose which is eminently catholic and acceptable to all. The programme of the Congress gatherings is avowedly Political. Here we eschew Politics altogether, for there is really no conflict of interests between the Rulers and the Ruled, who all alike desire to promote the Industrial and Economic Progress of this Country. The object of the Social Conference, similarly, sets the Reformers and the Orthodox majority in apparent opposition. Here, on the Economical platform, all shades of opinion, all differences of views on Social, Political, and Religious subjects, may unite and co-operate. This is a point on which it is needless to dilate much. Our people in times of old set to themselves only one question, and all our Works on Philosophy and Science commence and end with the Problem of

---

* **Inaugural Address at the first Industrial Conference, Poona, 1890.**

13

Deliverance from Evil—which is described to be three-fold—the Weakness and Sinfulness of our internal Nature, the Evils we suffer from others, whether Gods or men, and lastly, the Evils we suffer by reason of our Physical Surroundings. People will not easily agree as to the method of Deliverance from the first set of Evils—hence the diversity of Creeds. In their advocacy of their own particular Creed, they will not even admit the right of others to cross-question them about their Faith, and they are too often disposed to deny the existence of any Sin or weakness when challenged by others. In respect of the Second class of Evils, different classes of men will necessarily disagree to some extent, and proposals for co-operation are not always welcome. In regard to the Third class of Evils, however, presented by the poverty of our resources, and our physical weakness, all men are agreed, and all have a common interest in co-operating together for the common good. In this Country especially, there is no room for a difference of opinion. Hindus and Mahomedans, Parsees and Christians, the Rulers and the Ruled, the Privileged and the Unprivileged Classes, all stand on a common platform, and, as the constitution of the present meeting itself demonstrates, are prepared to work together. The work of this Conference thus possesses certain advantages which are denied to similar gatherings, for other more or less Sectarian and Party purposes.

The Problem we have met here to consider is one of Ways and Means. About the existence of the Evil, there is no difference of opinion among us. The highest Official authorities, like Sir Evelyn Baring,* Sir William Hunter, and others, with the highest Non-official authorities such as Professor Dadabhai Naoroji and Mr. Hyndman, are agreed in admitting that the Poverty of this Country is phenomenal. The existence of this Poverty needs no demonstration. We need only walk through our streets, and study the most superficial aspects of our Economic situation, and the fact forces itself upon us that we are a people of little resources. Many millions among us scarcely earn a couple of annas a day, many millions more are always underfed, and live on the borderland of Famine and slow Death, into which the failure of a single Monsoon precipitates them. Of course, this condition of things is not of yesterday, and is not the result Solely of Foreign Conquest and Competition. It is an old, a very old Inheritance. If we feel it more keenly now, we feel it because we are being roused from the Sleep of Ages, and our eyes have learnt to see, and our ears have learnt to hear.

The question of our comparative improvement or decline under Foreign Rule is similarly a question of Antiquarian History. The practical question for us all to lay to heart is not the relative, but the absolute

* Now Lord Cromer.

Poverty and the present helplessness of the Country generally. To a certain extent, the historical discussion of the situation is instructive. There can be no doubt that, whatever may have been our improvement in other respects, we have in recent times become more than ever dependent upon the single resource of Agriculture, precarious and contingent as that resource is, upon influences we cannot control or count upon with certainty. The co-ordination of Industries, which regulates the due proportions of men who plough the soil and raise raw produce, with those who manufacture this raw produce, and others still, who exchange and distribute it, and the interplay of whose three-fold activities makes a Nation thrive, was never a very strong factor of our collective Social Polity. We have been all along like most Ancient Nations, more or less exclusively agricultural. But our contact with the world outside, and the freedom of Exchange which has resulted in consequence, have produced one most undesirable result. They have aggravated the situation by making us more than ever dependent upon a single and precarious resource. The Industry and Commerce of the Country, such as it was, is passing out of our hands, and, except in the large Presidency Towns, the Country is fed, clothed, warmed, washed, lighted, helped, and comforted generally, by a thousand Arts and Industries in the manipulation of which its Sons have every day a decreasing share. Foreign Competition, not because it is foreign, but because it is the competition of Nature's powers against man's Labour,—it is the competition of organised Skill and Science against Ignorance and Idleness,—is transferring the monopoly not only of wealth, but what is more important, of skill, talent, and activity to others.

The increases of our Exports and Imports should not dazzle our vision. The increase is good so far as it goes; but it is not unmixed good, when that increase shows that we are only perfecting ourselves in the faculty of growing Raw Produce, and are forgetting by disuse, the skill and the wealth of resources which manufacturing and industrial activity brings in its train. Last year, we exported sixteen Crores of Rupees' worth of Wheat, Rice and Pulse, fifteen Crores Raw Cotton, ten and a half Crores Opium, nine and a half Crores Oil-Seeds, eight Crores Raw Jute, nearly five Crores of Hides and Skins, one Crore of Raw Wool, three-fourths of a Crore's worth of Dye Stuffs, half a Crore of Spices, half a Crore of Raw Silk, and a Crore of Miscellaneous Produce. Out of a total of nearly one hundred Crores of Produce exported, seventy-five Crores were thus raw Goods, while of manufactured or half manufactured Goods, Cotton six and one-third Crores, Jute nearly two Crores, Sugar half a Crore, Tea five and a quarter Crores, Indigo four Crores, and Coffee two Crores, making a total of only twenty Crores. were exported, and of these twenty Crores nearly twelve Crores were again the product of Foreign skill and capital. While we exported raw Cotton, worth fifteen Crores of Rupees and six and three-quarter Crores' worth of Cotton Goods, we imported twenty-seven Crores of Cotton Goods, and nearly four Crores' worth of Twist and Yarn. This single Export and Import represent the change in our condition typically, and in fact sums up the situation. India, fifty years ago, clothed herself with her own Manufatures, and now she is clothed by her distant masters. The same is the case with Wool, Silk and other Textiles, with Oils and Hides. In 1888-89 we imported forty-one Lakhs of Rupees' worth Umbrellas, fifteen Lakhs' worth of Children's Toys and Games, twenty-two Lakhs of Stationery, forty-one Lakhs' worth of Paper, ten Lakhs of Soap, twenty Lakhs of Matches, sixty-six Lakhs' worth of Glass, ten Lakhs' worth of Clocks and Watches. Carriages worth seven Lakhs of Rupees, eight Lakhs Candles, ten Lakhs Furniture, fifteen Lakhs' worth of Arms and Ammunition, twenty-one and a half Lakhs of Books, sixteen Lakhs of Leather and Leather Goods, thirty-one Lakhs of Paints, nearly two Crores' worth of Oils, both Kerosine and Seed Oils, nearly two and a half Crores of Railway Materials, two and one-third Crores of Machinery and Mill-work, and Iron, Steel, and Metals of all sorts worth five Crores in all. We imported even Flour, Salt, and Salted Fish, and lastly Grain and Pulse. This is our condition, and when the whole situation is thus taken in at one view, we feel that we are standing on the edge of a precipice, and the slightest push down will drive us into the abyss below of unmixed and absolute helplessness. Our Shipping is not ours; not even the Coasting Trade is carried on in our Bottoms. The proportion of Native Craft to the total tonnage is two and a third per cent., and it is a stationary percentage. Our Banking is not ours, though to a large extent we find the money which finances the Exchange Banks. The Insurance and the Freight and the Commission Business are all Foreign Monopolies, and the Foreign Merchant's hand is seen trafficking direct with our producers in the remotest and smallest Villages. The Railways are admittedly foreign Monopolies. We have, of course, no legitimate ground to complain about these Foreign Agencies. They do very useful work and they are our masters, and helpful masters too, if we are apt pupils. They all indicate one fact which our people should lay to heart, but which they are too often tempted to lose sight of. Political ascendancy is not the only particular vantage ground which we have lost. Commercial and Manufacturing predominance naturally transfers. Political ascendancy, and in this our collapse has been even far more complete. Of course, the situation is not hopeless, for no situation is ever hopeless to those who master its real significance, and resolve to do their best to improve it. As stated above, the question at issue is one of Ways and Means, and it is this question which we have met to consider.

There are some people who think that, as long as we have a heavy tribute to pay to England, which takes away nearly twenty Crores of our surplus Exports, we are doomed and can do nothing to help ourselves. This is, however, hardly a fair or manly position to take up. A portion of the burden represents interest on moneys advanced to, or investel in, our Country, and so far from complaining, we have reason to be thankful that we have a Creditor who supplies our needs at such a low rate of interest. Another portion represents the value of Stores supplied to us, the like of which we cannot produce here. The remainder is alleged to be more or less necessary for the purposes of Administration, Defence and payment of Pensions, and though there is good cause for complaint that it is not all necessary, we should not forget the fact that we are enabled by reason of this British connection to levy an equivalent tribute from China by our Opium Monopoly. I would not, therefore, desire you to divert and waste your energies in the fruitless discussion of this question of tribute, which had better be left to our Politicians.

Secondly, in certain quarters. it is feared that till we find in India Coal and Iron in abundance, our struggle with the present situation is hopeless. The answer to this is, that the resources of Iron and Coal that have been discovered are not utilised by us to the full extent. It will be time enough to complain when we have done our best with the existing Coal and Iron Fields. There can be no question that the success of foreign Competition is greatly helped by the abundance of these materials, but far more helpful than these materials is the spirit and skill which work them, and which conquered India long before Steam Power came into use, and which turned the balance of Trade against India. If we but acquire the spirit and the skill, the resources will be discovered in yet unexplored situations all over the Country.

Thirdly, people are also heard to ask in despair the question, Where is the Capital to come from which will enable us to buy the Coal, Iron, and Machinery, and hire Foreigners' skill, and make them do service for us here? Our resources are no doubt scanty, but they are abundant enough, in all conscience, if we would only use them as such, and not throw them away into the sea, as we do year after year, in deference to old traditions, and antiquated fears and mistrust. Every year we import in Treasure Bullion, Gold and Silver of the value of twelve Crores' worth, *i.e.*, three Crores of Gold and nine Crores of Silver. The whole of the Gold disappears, and is absorbed by the soil, and of the Silver seven Crores are sent by us to the Mint every year, and the rest is absorbed like Gold. Since 1834, this absorbing process has secured the virtual destruction of nearly four hundred and fifty Crores of Wealth, which might have been turned to better account. The saving of four hundred and fifty Crores in fifty years by twenty-five Crores of people is not a sign of great prosperity, but we have made our position worse by burying it or using it unproductively. This hoarding, at least, proves that nearly eight Crores of Rupees may be each year turned to capital account, if we were only resolved so to use it.

Fourthly, of course, in the choice of Ways and Means, it is not open to us to adopt certain plans of operation, which, however much they might be condemned on abstract grounds, have been followed with practical success in many of the most enlightened Countries of Europe and America. We cannot, as with the Government of these Countries, rely upon Differential Tariffs to protect Home Industries during their experimental trial. We cannot expect the Government here, to do what France or Germany does for their Shipping Trade, and their Sugar Industry, and ask Government Bounties, and subsidies to be paid out of general Taxes. These are heresies according to English Political Economy, such as is taught to us, and whether they be really so or not, it is useless to divert our energies in fruitless discussion, and seek to achieve victory over Free Trade. We may, however, fairly expect Government to try as an experiment the Policy of the Culture System which the Dutch Government actually worked for thirty years in its own Possessions in the East Indies with signal success, and the principle of which is acknowledged by the Government of India in its Policy of *Tagai* advances, and its Railway development. If the Government borrows Crores of Rupees every year and constructs Railways and Canals out of these loans, it can as well encourage the growth of new Industries, by guaranteeing or subsidising such Enterprises in their pioneering stage. It has done so successfully in pioneering Tea, Cinchona, and Cotton Enterprise in certain parts, and it can well extend the scope of its operations in other and more fruitful directions. It can also very well be asked to produce its own Stores here, just as it produces certain minor articles required by its Military and Postal Department. It can also undertake to buy Leather, Woollen Goods, &c., from the Indian Producer, and thus secure the benefit of a sure custom at remunerative rates to new undertakings. It can, finally, help people to join their Capital together under such Guarantees and Official supervision and afford such special facilities as the Governments of Europe have extended to Land Improvement Banks.

After all, Government help can do but little, save pioneering work. The Government of India is anxious to help us. It is prepared to encourage Emigration abroad, and Immigration from densely crowded to sparsely inhabited tracts. But, where are the men who are prepared to take advantage of this extended field of Colonization both in India, Burmah, and elsewhere? We have yet to realise the situation. We have to resolve to work earnestly and perseveringly with a purpose and an organization which will conquer all obstacles. The Evil is too great, and of too long a standing, to be brought under control by private individual efforts. We have to work with a will, to pull long, and pull all, and to pull till we succeed. It is on this account that we are met together. This is only a Preliminary Meeting. We have to move the other Provinces, and arrange for a General Conference of those who think with us on this matter, and when the men of light and leading from different parts meet together, we may hope to set the ball rolling. The Promoters of the movement have not hit upon this Conference on the spur of the moment, or as an agreeable distraction. The idea has been slowly developing itself. It first found expression in a speech made two years ago at Ahmednagar. Since then friends have worked, and tried to educate Public Opinion. A very thoughtful article covering the entire range of the Indian Economical situation, and suggesting Ways and Means, appeared in one of our Journals, and it has attracted extensive notice. The particular positions taken up in that article may be controverted, and have in fact been controverted, but its general accuracy as a description of the existing state of things has not been questioned, and if it promotes discussion, it may yet serve most important purposes. I think, I have placed before you the whole situation, and have also given you an idea of the lines on which I desire that the entire question should be discussed, now or hereafter. We have to keep in mind the following almost axiomatic Truths in all our deliberations.

1. The work of the Conference should be conducted, and its Constitution framed on Non-Sectarian and Non-Party lines, so that all Classes of people may take part in it.

2. What we have chiefly to avoid is the pursuit of impracticable objects. We should husband our little resources to the best of our power, and not exhaust them by vain complaints against the drain of the Indian Tribute, or by giving battle with Free Trade.

3. We must realize clearly our exact situation, *i.e.*, first, our phenomenal Poverty, and secondly, our growing dependence on the single and precarious resources of Agriculture.

4. Having realised this situation, we must strive to correct it with a full sense that we cannot do all that we wish in a single year or a decade, and that we can at the most create the spirit and the tendency, and initiate the movement of Change and set it afloat.

5. The proper scope of the work to be done is to correct the disproportion between our engrossing production of Raw Agricultural Produce, and our backwardness

in the production and distribution of Manufactured Produce.

6. In the accomplishment of this aim, we should not forget that there are permanent advantages and disadvantages enjoyed by certain Countries and Races, which regulate distribution and choice of Labour, and that we cannot hope to accomplish impossibilities. And yet, within these limits, there is ample scope for good and honest work, for many a decade to come, in the utilization of our existing,—relatively to us ample, though as compared with other Countries scanty,—resources of natural Agents and Capital, with our limitless Supply of Labour. The skill and patience of our Industrial Classes are a rich inheritance which cannot fail to help us, if we but provide a larger sphere for its growth and training.

7. Bearing these limitations and advantages in mind, our more immediate efforts should be directed to the improvement by Art and Industry of our raw wealth of Agricultural Produce, and of the articles which we send away as Raw Produce, and import as Manufactured Produce.

8. No Hand-made Industry can hope to thrive in competition with Industry moved by cheap Natural Agents. The free use of Natural Agents, moreover, makes large investments of Capital a necessity, and thus handicaps all individual efforts beyond rivalry. What we have to bear in mind is, therefore, the orga-

nization for Industry and Capital on the Joint Stock principle for collective and large undertakings.

9. The superior skill of the Foreigner must be availed of freely by importing it from other Countries, till we train up our own people for the work, first, in Technical Institutes here and in Foreign Countries, and further, in the far more practical discipline of Factories and Mills at work.

10. Our Resources of Capital are scanty, but if we only knew how to use such resources as we have, and brought them together, we have more Wealth and Capital than we can at present properly handle.

11. While we put forth our energies in these directions, we can well count upon the assistance of the State in regulating our Co-operative efforts by helping us to form Deposit and Finance Banks, and facilitating recoveries of advances made by them, by encouraging New Industries with Guarantees or Subsidies, or Loans at low interest, by pioneering the way to new Enterprises, and by affording facilities for Emigration and Immigration, and establishing Technical Institutes, and buying more largely the Stores they require here, and in many cases by producing their own Stores.

12. State help is, after all, a subordinate factor in the Problem. Our own exertion and our own resolutions must conquer the difficulties, which are chiefly of our own creation.

These are a few of the thoughts which occur to me at this moment. You are most of you far better and more practically versed in these matters than I can well hope to be, and if I were called upon to justify this presumption on my part, I can only appeal to the fact that it has been the Brahmin's Hereditary Privilege to formulate the Nation's Wants and suggest Remedies. With these observations, I shall, with your permission, conclude the speech and resume my seat.

VIII.

TWENTY YEARS' REVIEW OF CENSUS STATISTICS.*

THE Decennial Census Report for 1891, for the Bombay Presidency, loses much of its interest by reason of the great delay that has taken place in its publication. This defect, however, sinks into insignificance by the side of another and more serious omission, for which apparently there was less excuse,—we refer to the disappointment caused by the total and studied neglect to bring together the facts and figures of the past three Censuses, in a way to illustrate the Social and Economical History of this Presidency, during the last twenty years. Attempts, indeed, have been here and there made to compare and contrast the Census figures of 1891 with those of 1881; but these attempts, being only half-hearted and unsystematic, lead to very inconclusive results. In the first place, India is not America, and a period of ten years is too short a term to measure any real or permanent changes

* **Published in the *Poona Quarterly Journal, 1893.***

in the condition of Indian Society. The figured results of 1881, moreover, had the additional disadvantage of recording the losses sustained, in consequence of the great Famine of 1876-78, and thus furnished no safe basis for a comparison of the normal conditions of life in this Country, and of its progress or otherwise in ordinary circumstances. Thirdly, the Census figures of 1881 were arranged and classified in many respects upon lines not observed in 1871, and these lines have been again abandoned in enumerating the results of the last Census. For these reasons, the Census Report of 1891 appears to us to be useful chiefly in its Appendices, and we propose, in the following pages, to make an attempt to present a connected view of the progress of this Presidency during the last twenty years, as far as it may be gathered from a comparison of the results of 1891, with those of the Census of 1871, only occasionally referring to the intermediate Census of 1881. Mere figured Statements, however detailed and numerous, have no suggestiveness about them, and it is necessary to study them in the lights and shades of contrasts and comparisons to obtain practical lessons for the guidance of the Administration, and for the studies of the Political Economist. We shall confine our observations for the present to the purely British Districts of this Presidency, reserving our remarks upon the figured results for the Feudatory States to a future issue of this Journal.

The area of the British Districts has continued con stant, being about 125,000 square miles. The Populations Statistics, however, do not present stationary figures. The total Population, according to the Census of February, 1871, was 16,228,774. The numbers were almost stationary in 1881, being 16,454,414, or an increase of only two and a half Lakhs—1·5 per cent. in ten years. In February 1891, the numbers returned were 18,857,004, the increase being over twenty-five Lakhs, or 16 per cent. in twenty years, or about 88 per cent. per year. The Density of the Population, which was 130 per square mile in 1871, and 135 in 1881, has increased to nearly 151 per square mile. A comparison of these figures with those of England and Wales cannot fail to be very instructive. The area of England and Wales is 58,186 square miles, and its Population, which was 22,712,266, in 1871, rose to 29,001,048 in 1891, showing an increase of 6,278,782, or nearly 30 per cent. in twenty years, being nearly double our rate. This high rate of increase was, it must be noted, maintained notwithstanding the great relief given to the Population of England by an extensive system of Emigration, the like of which relief, we do not enjoy here. The actual density of the English Population increased from 389 per square mile in 1871, to nearly 500 per square mile in 1891. The rate of increase in this Presidency was only 8 per cent. against the English rate of 1·5 per cent per year, and the increase in our rate of Density is only 20 per cent against the English figure of 110 per cent. In other words, the rate of Density in England, which was three times our rate in 1871, has now increased to three and a half times the average Density in this Presidency

We have next, to examine the details for the several Divisions of the Presidency. For enumeration purposes, the Census Report of 1872 recognised chiefly four Divisions based on the principle of distinctive physical and climatic peculiarities, namely, the Deccan, Konkan Guzerath, and Sind. In the Census of 1881 this principle was not followed, and the grouping was made on the basis of five Divisions (Deccan, Konkan, Guzerath, Karnatic, and Sind) based partly on physical and partly on Language peculiarities. In 1891, the same principle was followed with this further change, that the Kanara District, which was classed under Karnatic in 1881, has been classed under Konkan this time. These changes make it impossible to compare the totals of one Census with another, and introduce a needless element of variation which should always be avoided in such enumerations. We have found it necessary in consequence of these changes, to take up the District figures separately, and then group them together, and the following Statement presents the comparative results of the ascertained totals of Population by Districts and Divisions in 1881 and 1891.

Division.	Population. 1871	Population 1891	Increase or Decrease in 20 years.	Pecentage Increase.	Remarks.
1 **GUZERATH**					
Ahmedabad	829,637	871,589	41,952	5·0	
Panch Mahals	240,743	313,417	72,674	30·0	
Kaira	782,733	871,589	88,856	11·0	
Broach	350,322	341,490	—8,832	—2·5	
Surat	607,087	649,989	42,902	7·0	
Total Guzerath ...	2,810,522	3;048,074	246,384	10·0	
Area in square miles ...	10,082	10,296	...	...	
2 **KONKAN.**					
Kanara	398,406	446,357	47,945	12·0	
Ratnagiri	1,019,136	1,105,926	86,790	8·6	
Kolaba	350,405 }	509,584 }	159,179 }	4·0	Due partly to transfer of Talukas.
Thana	847,414 }	904,868 }	57,444 }	16·0	
Total Konkan ...	2,615,371	2,966,735	351,358	13·5	
Area in squire miles ...	13,558	13,639	...	...	
3 **DECCAN.**					
Kandesh	1,028,642	1,460,851	432,209	42·0	
Nasik	734,386	843,582	109,196	14·0	
Nagar	773,938	888,755	114,817	15·0	
Satara	1,116,050	1,225,989	109,939	9·5	
Poona	907,235	1,067,800	160,565	18·0	
Sholapur	662,986	750,689	87,693	13·5	
Total Deccan ...	5,223,237	6,237,666	1,014,419	20·0	
Area in square miles.	39,355	38,390	...	...	

Division.	Population 1871	Population 1891	Increase or Decrease in 20 years.	Percentage Increase.	Remarks.
4 **SIND**					
Karachi	423,495	564,880	141,385	33·0	
Hyderabad	721,947	918,646	196,299	28·0	
Thur-Parkar	180,761	298,203	117,442	65·0	
Shikarpur	776,227	915,497	139,270	18·0	
Upper Sind Frontier ...	89,985	174,548	84,563	90·0	
Total Sind ...	2,192,415	2,871,774	678,959	34·0	
Area in square miles ...	46,598	47,789	...	...	
5 **KARNATIC.**					
Belgaum	938,750	1,013,261	74,511	8·0	
Dharwar	988,037	1,051,314	63,277	6·5	
Kaladgi } Bijapur }	816,037	796,332	—19,698	2·4	Due partly to transfer of Talukas.
Total Karnatic ...	2,742,824	2,860,907	118,090	4.0	
Area in square miles ...	14,853	14,928	...	...	
6 Town and Island of Bombay ...	644,405	821,764	177,359	26·0	

It will be seen from this Statement that the increase of Population in Sind has been nearly twice the average for the Presidency,it has been a little over the average in the Deccan, sensibly below the average in Guzerath and Konkon, and much below the average in the Karnatic. The surplus Population of Guzerath finds a convenient out-let in the Panch Mahals, that of the Deccan in Khandesh, that of the Konkon in Bombay, while in Sind the expense of arable but unoccupied lands is almost limitless, being dependent upon the extension of Irrigation and not on Rainfall, and there is apparently no out-let for such expansion in the Karnatic Districts. The relative densities of the several Divisions disclose the following variations in the proportion of increased Density during the last twenty years.

DENSITY.

Divisions.	Years.		REMARKS.
	1871,	1891,	
Guzerath	279	300	The largest absolute increase in Density occurs in the Deccan, and the least, in Karnatic.
Deccan	134	162	
Konkon, excluding City of Bombay	193	217	
Karnatic	185	191	
Sind	47	60	

If the Panch Mahal figures be excluded from those of the Guzerath Divisions, the increase of Population in twenty years in the older and settled Districts of Guzerath, has been only eight per cent., and in Broach, there has been an actual decrease which requires to be accounted for. Excluding Khandesh, the increase of Population in the Deccan Districts has been about 14·0 per cent. in twenty years. The Sind rate of increase is nearly equal to that of England. The Konkon Districts show a rate of increase which is nearly equal to that of the Deccan, excluding Kandesh, and the Karnatic Districts fare the worst of all—the increase being almost nominal—only 4·0 per cent. in twenty years. It is obvious that the small proportion of increase in these Districts is due to the after effects of the Famine, from which apparently, these parts of the Country have not yet recovered. The Population of Belgaum, Dharwar and Kaladgi or Bijapur in the years 1871, 1881, and 1891, will be seen from the following Statement.

Districts.	1871.	1881.	1891.
Belgaum	944,985	864,014	1,013,261
Dharwar	989,671	882,909	1,057,314
Kaladgi or Bijapur ...	816,273	638,493	796,339
Total........	2,750,929	2,385,416	2,866,914

It will be thus seen, that these three Districts lost nearly three and a half Lakhs of their Population or 3·0 per cent. in the famine, and they have been just able to make up that deficit during the last ten years. The actual loss of Population was, of course, more than three and a half Lakhs, for, the normal increase in ten years must be added to this figure of registered deficiency. This ciscumstance accounts for the small rate of increase in these Districts. Compared with the totals of 1881, the increase in the Karnatic Districts has exceeded 20·0 per cent. in ten years, the rate of increase being 2·0 per cent. per year. In the Deccan Districts, Khandesh and Nasik did not suffer a shrinkage of Population, in consequence of the Famine, and Khandesh showed an increase of over two Lakhs, and Nasik of 143,000 people. The other four Districts showed a falling off, of 27,109 in Nagar 20,732 in Poona, 229 in Satara, and 136,888 in Sholapur, the deficiency being in all one and four-fifths of Lakhs between the totals of 1871 and 1881. The actual increase in these four Districts between 1881 and 1891 is about seven Lakhs, which raises the proportion of increase in ten years to nearly 20·0 per cent. In other words, the Deccan Districts, having suffered less severely, have rallied more rapidly than the Karnatic Districts— which now stand very much where they stood twenty years ago, in point of Population. The Guzerath Districts, excluding Panch Mahals, did not suffer in any way from the Famine, and the slow progress of Population there, appears to be due partly to external checks, such as Cholera and Fever mortality, and partly, to the operation of prudential and preventive influences. The advantages of a fertile Soil and industrious Population are fully utilized by the existing Population of three hundred Souls per square mile. and the available area for extension is so limited that the *Ryots* have no other resource but to emigrate to the Panch Mahals. There is a similar escape for the congested parts of the Deccan in Khandesh, and for the Konkan Districts apparently in Bombay.

Excluding Sind, whose climatic conditions are so entirely different from the rest of the Presidency, there are only four Districts where the extent of available arable land per one hundred of the Population exceeds ten Acres, and in two only, Khandesh and Panch Mahals, this provision exceeds twenty-five Acres per one hundred of the Population. In all the remaining Districts, the proportions are below ten Acres per one hundred of the Population. which, as everybody will admit, is a very nominal figure. These proportions will perhaps, not be quite intelligible without further amplification. As the chief dependence of our increasing agricultural Population is on the land still available for cultivation, the following Statement has been prepared to show, what area of culturable unoccupied land is still available for further expansion of cultivation, to keep pace with the increase of Population.

District.	Population.	Acres of Cultivated Land.	Land still Available for Cultivation.
Ahmedabad ...	871,589	1,870,717	87,872
Kaira... ...	871,589	747,565	74,132
Panch Mahals ...	313,417	480,716	177,800
Broach ...	341,490	649,477	25,868
Surat... ...	649,989	740,266	65,260
GUJERATH...Total.	3,048,074	4,488,741	430,932
Thana	847,424	953,993	115,046
Kolaba	350,405	704,786	57,914
Ratnagiri	1,019,136	395,877	5,403
Kanara	398,406	324,746	61,743
KONKAN ... Total...	2,615,371	2,379,402	240,106
Kandesh	1,406,851	3,187,064	779,864
Nasik...	843,582	2,316,207	134,076
Nagar	888,755	3,079,555	123,263
Poona	1,067,800	2,451,806	18,188
Sholapur... ...	750,689	2,456,513	23,031
Satara	1,225,989	2,123,870	35,245
DECCAN ... Total.	6,283,666	15,615,015	1,113,667
Belgaum	938,750	2,087,353	105,157
Dharwar	988,037	3,113,655	103,899
Bijapur	816,037	2,314,014	72,953
KARNATIC Total.	2,742,824	7,515,022	282,009
Karachi	423,495	850,476	1,139,634
Hyderabad ...	721,947	2,198,200	2,300,263
Shikarpur	776,227	1,490,961	1,722,414
Upper Sind Frontier	89,995	522,390	154,781
Thur and Parkar...	180,761	5,278,623	443,203
SIND ... Total.	2,192,425	10,340,650	5,760,295
Grand Total ...	16,882,360	40,338,830	7,827,009

The average per head of the Population of cultivated area is one and a half Acres in Guzerath, one and four-fifths Acres in Konkan, two and a half Acres in the Deccan, two and three-fourths Acres in Karnatic, and two and one-third Acres in Sind. These figures give for the Presidency, an average of two Acres of cultivated land per head of the Population, or ten Acres per head of each Peasant Proprietor's family. As regards arable land available for cultivation, it is about five per cent. of the cultivated area in Ahmedabad, ten per cent. in Kaira, about thirty-seven per cent. in Panch Mahals, four per cent. in Broach, and nine per cent. in Surat, the average for the Division being nine per cent. of the cultivated area. In the Konkan, this margin is one and a half per cent. in Ratnagiri, twelve per cent. in Thana, eight per cent. in Kolaba, and nearly twenty per cent. in Kanara ; this last figure brings up the average for the whole Division to nearly ten per cent. In the Deccan, this proportion of arable to cultivated land is twenty-four per cent. in Khandesh, five per cent. in Nasik, four per cent. in Nagar, less than one per cent. in Poona and Sholapur, and about one per cent. in Satara. The average for the whole Deccan is seven per cent. These same proportions are five per cent. in Belgaum, and three per cent. in Dharwar and Bijapur. The average for the whole Division is four per cent. In Sind the uncultivated arable land largely exceeds the cultivated land in Karachi, Hyderabad and Shikarpur. The average for the whole Division is nearly ninety per cent. It will be seen from these details that, excluding Sind, there is not much room left for extended cultivation except in Panch Mahals and Khandesh, and to a small extent in Kanara and Nasik. In Sind these conditions are reversed. In all the older and settled Districts of the Presidency, the Agricultural Classes must, henceforth, resort chiefly to intensive cultivation or improvements. As it is, about one Crore of the agricultural Population manage barely to support themselves upon the yield of about four Crores of Acres, including fallow and twice cropped lands, and have, except in Sind, Khandesh and Panch Mahals, less than fifteen Lakhs of arable land to fall back upon for extended cultivation. These figure results present a very dark future as looming before our vision, if our chief dependence were placed on extended cultivation, as the only resource for supplying the wants of our increasing Population.

The only escape from this danger lies in the direction of the gradual transformation of the chief means of our livelihood, and the growth of an Urban and Industrial Population, in other words the rise of Towns or Cities. A careful examination of the statistical results furnished by these Census Reports satisfies us, that there are indications which prove that such a change is operating strongly in our favour. Defining a Town, as a collection of over five thousand inhabitants, it appears (1) that there has been a large increase in the number of our Towns, and (2) that the increase of the Town population has been greater than the increase of the Rural population. In 1871, there were in the twenty-three Districts one hundred and seventy-eight Towns, excluding the City of Bombay, with a total population of 2,134,419. In 1881, a different principle was adopted, which did not accept the test of Population as the basis of distinction, and sixteen places below five thousand in Population were included, and twenty-eight places with a Population exceeding five thousand were excluded, from the definition of Towns, giving as the result one hundred and sixty-five as the number of Towns according to the Census of that year, with a Population of 2,925,190 inhabitants. This unnecessary refinement was dropped in the last Census enumeration, and applying the old test of Population, it was ascertained that there were in all two hundred and thirty-one places which had more than five thousand inhabitants, and which might, therefore, be regarded as Towns. Comparing the figures for 1871 with those of 1891, it will be seen from the following Statement that all the Divisions except Karnatic showed an increase under this head.

Names.	Number of Towns.		Population of Towns.	
	1871.	1891.	1871.	1891.
Guzerath ...	35	46	592,459	665,856
Konkan ...	26	30	218,397	283,292
Deccan ...	65	96	724,862	957,499
Karnatic ...	43	34	412,268	387,863
Sind ...	9	25	186,431	342,295
City of Bombay ...	1	1	644,405	821,764
Total ...	179	232	2,778,822	3,458,569

The number of Towns has thus increased nearly thirty per cent., while the Population of these Towns shows an increase of nearly twenty-five per cent. The total increase of the Population in twenty years has been shown above, to have been about sixteen per cent., and it is thus plain that there is a slight tendency inclining the scale in favour of Urban over Rural increase. This last appears to have been about fourteen per cent., the actual figures being 13,553,962 as against 15,398,445, as the Population of the Rural tracts in 1871 and 1891 respectively. So far, the figures are not unsatisfactory. The percentages of the Rural and Urban population for the several large Divisions, according to the Census Reports for 1871, 1881, and 1891 will be seen from the following Statement.

Names.	1872.		1881.		1891.	
	Urban.	Rural.	Urban.	Rural.	Urban.	Rural.
Guzerath...	21	79	19·9	80·1	21·5	78·5
Konkan ...	8	92	9	91	8·8	91·2
Deccan ...	13·8	87·2	14·3	85·7	15·4	84·6
Karnatic ...	15	85	12·2	87·8	13·5	86·5
Sind ...	9	91	10·7	89·3	12·6	87·4

The above Statement shows clearly that the progress is very slow and not very striking. Guzerath retains an easy command over the other Divisions, and no District in that Division comes up to the level of Ahmedabad, which has twenty-five per cent. Urban to seventy-five per cent. Rural population.

The Sind figures are more hopeful, and the Deccan also appears to be slowly but successfully struggling against ruralization. The Karnatic Districts, however, do not appear to have yet recovered from the shock they sustained during the Famine. Taking the several Districts in their order, while Poona, Dharwar and Karachi show large advances in the direction of urbanization, and Ahmedabad, Broach, Nasik, Bijapur and Belgaum show slight advances in the same direction, ten Districts, Ratnagiri, Surat, Thana, Kolaba, Kanara, Nagar, Satara, Thur and Parkar, the Upper Sind Frontier, and Hyderabad show slight decline, and Kaira, Panch Mahals, Khandesh, Sholapur, and Shikarpur, show decided decline in the Urban elements of their Population. Even in the Districts which show better results, the so-called Towns are only larger Villages, and are wanting in the essential element of industrial activity.

This partial and not very strongly marked tendency towards urbanization is also attested to by the figures which show the relative proportions of Villages of different sizes and Population. Excluding Sind and the City of Bombay, it appears from the Census Returns of 1881 and 1891 that, while the proportion of Villages inhabited by less than five hundred persons was 65·5 per cent. in 1881, this proportion fell to 60 per cent. in 1891. The proportion of the class of Villages next above it, with a population, ranging from five hundred to one thousand was 21 per cent. in 1881, and 23 per cent. in 1891; the proportion of the class next above it, with inhabitants ranging from one thousand to one thousand and five hundred, was 9·7 per cent. in 1881, and 11·3 per cent. in 1891; of the class next over it, with a Population ranging from two thousand to three thousand, the proportion was 2 per cent. in 1881, and 2·7 per cent. in 1891; and of the highest class of all, with Populations ranging from three thousand to five thousand, the proportion was 1·3 per cent. in 1881, and 2·6 per cent. in 1891. It is not generally known, but is none the less true, that the proportion of Urban to Rural population normally stands higher in this Presidency, than in most of the other Provinces of India.

Of course, it must be noted that the residents of Urban Towns, as defined above, are not all really Urban, in respect of their profession or source of livelihood, and on the other hand the residents of Rural areas do not all of them derive their livelihood from the land. It thus becomes necessary to examine the Statistics about the occupations of the people given in these Census Reports. The Census Classification of Occupations given in the Report of 1891 departs so materially from the principles adopted in the two previous Reports, that no fair comparison can properly be made between their results. Both in 1871 and 1881 there was a large class, nearly fifty per cent. of the total Population, who, being dependent on other persons, were returned as having no profession or occupation. This principle was not followed in 1891, when all these dependents were counted as forming a portion of the class to which the male or female bread-earner, on whom they depended, belonged. This appears to us to have been a perfectly wanton innovation, and even if there were some apparent advantages in the new classification, the Report ought to have furnished columns of Comparative Tables contrasting the results of 1891 with those of previous years on the old basis.

In the absence of such Comparative Tables, we can only present the results separately. In 1871, persons employed in Government and other Public Service were 184,332, and formed 1·1 per cent. of the whole. The Professions absorbed 135,340 persons, and were ·8 per cent. of the whole. Those, who engaged themselves in Personal Service, were 281,216, and were 1·7 per cent. of the whole. The Agricultural Industry, including the care and breed of Cattle and Sheep, was followed by forty Lakhs, who thus constituted 24·7 per cent. of the entire Population. Those who were engaged in Trade and Commerce were about four and a half Lakhs, and were 2·6 per cent. of the whole. Artizans and Handicraftsmen came to about twenty-two Lakhs, and were 13·5 per cent. of the entire number. All these classes made up forty-five per cent.; and the Unoccupied and dependent Classes came up to ninety Lakhs, being fifty-five per cent. of the total Population. In 1881 Government Public Servants and those who were employed in the Professions, made up 1·5 per cent., those rendering Personal Service were 1·1 per cent., and the Commercial and Trading Classes represented 1·2 per cent. The Agriculturists were thirty-two per cent., the Industrial and Artizan Classes were fifteen per cent., and the Unoccupied were forty-nine per cent. of the whole. In the Census of 1891 the heading of Unoccupied Classes was discontinued as a separate Class, and we find that sixty per cent. of the total, and sixy-nine per cent. of the Rural, populations are shown to be Agricultural. The Artizans and Handicraftsmen, or the Industrial Classes, are shown to be twenty-one per cent. Their proportion is slighty higher in Towns than in the Country. The two Classes between them absorb eighty per cent. of the Population. The Trading and Commercial Classes are shown to be 4·6 per cent. in Towns, and 3·5 per cent. in the Country. Those who rendered Personal and Domestic Service are shown to be 2·7 per cent. Those engaged in Public Service appear to be 3·8 per cent., and the Professionals 3·3 per cent. If we have these percentages, so as to exclude the dependent Population, mostly women and children, we shall arrive by a rough guess at what these proportions would be under the old plan of classification. The old proportions of those engaged in Agriculture and Handicrafts do not appear, thus, to have been sensibly altered in favour of the latter Classes; and the same remark holds good of the Commercial and Trading Classes. This seems to be the general impression left on the mind by a study of these figures—into the details of which, we cannot now afford to enter at greater length.

The Statistics relating to Occupied Houses are also vitiated by the innovations adopted at the last enumeration, of excluding Unoccupied Houses from the Census definition of a House, and the omission to classify Houses according to quality, which attempt was made in 1871 with some success.

The Census of 1871 showed that the tolal number of Houses in the Bombay Presidency was 3,254,540, out of which about 336,629 were of the Better Class, and were occupied by 1,885,910 persons. The rest, about ninety per cent., 2,917,911, were of the Inferior sort, and were occupied by 14,342,842 persons. These figures furnish a safe basis for fixing the relative number of our Classes and Masses, which are as eight to ninety-two of the Population. In the Deccan Division, including Karnatic, the average number of persons per House was 5·43, in the Konkan it was 5·7, in Guzerath it was 3·6, and in Sind it was 4·9 per house. The superiority of Guzerath, in this respect is further brought out by the fact that out of the Better Class of Houses fully fifty-eight per cent. are found in the Guzerath Division. The Deccan comes a long way behind, and Konkan and Sind follow at no great distance. The Census of 1881 showed the total number of Occupied Houses and other Buildings to have been 3,605,812, being an increase of two and a half Lakhs over the figure for 1871, but of these 2,822,731 Houses were occupied. Between 1881 and 1891 the several Divisions showed the following increases.

Name.	1881.		1891.		Increase Per Cent.	
	Houses in Towns.	Houses in Country.	Houses in Towns.	Houses in Country.	In Town.	In Country.
Guzerath ...	1,35,293	4,99,082	1,60,737	5,36,209	19	7½
Konkan ...	42,465	4,30,144	46,667	4,90,320	11	14
Deccan ...	1,28,001	6,37,867	1,87,468	8,61,770	47	23
Karnatic ...	54,488	3,75,847	69,475	4,46,611	27½	17
Sind ...	42,223	3,91,331	64,804	4,52,216	53	15
Bombay City	28,310	......	56,959	......	100	...

Here also, next to the Town and Island of Bombay, Sind heads the list; Guzerath, while it is absolutely at the head of the rest of the Presidency, shows no progress. The Deccan Districts take a high rank, and Karnatic and Konkan come last.

We have now passed under review all those points of the Census enumeration which have a bearing upon the Economical condition of the Country. The Statistics relating to Sex and Age and Civil Condition, Education, Religion, Languages, and Infirmities are interesting in themselves, but they have little or no direct bearing upon the Economical Well-being of the Population, and must, therefore, resist the temptation of entering upon a consideration of these matters. We hope, however, to take them up in a separate issue of the Journal.

IX.

LOCAL GOVERNMENT IN ENGLAND AND INDIA.

NOW that the subject of Local Self-Government has been raised from a mere speculative question to the position of the one great problem of the day, which absorbs general attention, and taxes the highest statesmanship of the Rulers, it cannot fail to be of interest to review the subject historically in its development in the Free and Self-governed Communities of Europe, where these Institutions have been long naturalized to the soil, and have influenced the political and economical arrangements in various forms and degrees, so as to serve at once as a warning and an example to this Country. The Cobden Club has published a series of essays on the subject of Local Government and Taxation in England, Scotland, Ireland, Holland, France, Russia, Spain, and Germany, and in the English Colonies of Australia and New Zealand, and we propose to summarize in the present and consecutive numbers the more important of these exhaustive reviews, and discuss the Indian bearings of the positions there laid down and the analogies suggested by our own Local Institutions of customary and legislative origin.

England deservedly enjoys the foremost rank in respect of the great historical antiquity, and the unbroken continuity of its Local Institutions. Mr. Rathborn, in a recent number of the *Nineteenth Century*, has stated on the highest authority that in England alone Local Taxation had reached the magnificent total of fifty-five Crores of Rupees a few years ago, a revenue almost as large as the whole of the net revenue of British India. In this Country our total Municipal and Local Funds expenditure does not represent one-tenth of the Imperial expenditure, while in England the proportion is as high as two-thirds of the grand total of the Imperial expenditure of Great Britain and Ireland, and if the English portion of this expenditure is alone taken into account, it may be fairly estimated that the English people spend as much on their Local Government as they raise for the public or general expenditure of the Empire. This single fact will clearly bring home to every one the enormous development of the powers and functions of Local Boards in English Boroughs and Counties. None of the other countries of Europe can present more magnificent totals of receipts and a more varied expenditure, or afford a more instructive field for the study of local responsibility and power. As the destinies of India are now indissolubly united with those of England, and that country furnishes the fountain source of brain power and initial energy of the Administrative

Body in India, we propose to select the Institutions of England for our more immediate study in the following observations.

It may be noted at the outset that, as far as the lowest unit of local power is concerned, no country in Europe could present a more self-contained and self-sufficient organization than the Village Community of India. The Russian *Mere*, the German *Gau*, the French *Commune*, the English *Parish*, though kindred in origin to the Indian Village, never possessed the full independence which the latter community enjoyed in times of old. The people of this Country, however, did not proceed further in the development of Civic and Communal life. The old Greek and Roman Communities developed their *Civitas* and *Demos* with a luxuriant fulness, which has been rarely equalled, except in some of the towns of Italy, the free towns of Germany, the Netherlands, and Switzerland, in the best days of European History. The Greeks and Romans, however, broke down lamentably when they tried their hands at large organizations, and it is in this direction of the organization of Local Boards, and the incorporation of Parishes into Hundreds and Cantons, and these latter into Counties and Departments, and the whole under one National State, that the countries of Europe have achieved their most remarkable success. Moreover, the more important of these

States, such as the British Isles, and the Colonies and Dependencies of Great Britain, the United States of America, and the German Empire, have successfully solved the great problem of a Federation of States under sovereign Congress Diet or Parliament, which forms, so to speak, the coping stone of the edifice. It will be thus seen, that there have been four distinct stages of growth in the history of these Local Institutions, and the different Nations of Asia, the old Mediterranean Republics, modern Europe, and the Colonial Empires of Europe and America, have each contributed in their own way to the symmetrical development of the little Parish unit into the great Confederacy of States, which appears to be evidently the destined form of the future Political Organization of the Human Family.

Guizot has well observed, that in the primitive condition of Society, when Status, and not Contract, governed the relations of private life, when Law was personal and not Local, when Tribes, Castes and Nationalities formed distinct groups, when intercommunication was difficult, and the central authority was limited to purposes of foreign war, none but the Local form of Government could have any practical existence. When these Local Groups are absorbed into a Central Organization, it may regarded as a distinct advance in Civilzation. In the history of Local Government in England, it is necessary to bear this point prominently in view. The Anglo-Saxon times present the old features of Local Government in their purest form, attended, however, with their great draw-back of a permanent tendency to disintegration. It was the strong pressure of the Norman Conquest, which first, though not without many centuries of struggle, checked this tendency, and by an infusion of races sowed the seeds of the great English Nationality. The old Saxon divisions of the country were based upon the Parish (the Indian *Moujê*) as the initial unit. A Group of Parishes made up the Hundred (the Indian Tarf or Tashil or Peta), and several of these Hundreds made up the Country, the equivalent of our Revenue Zilla or Prant or District. Rural Society in old England recognized only two distinctions, the Thane or Land-owners, and the Thralls or Slaves. The large Thanes were the Chief men of their Villages, with a body of Free Tenants, and a large number of Slave dependents. The leading Thanes met in "the Town-moot," and elected the Town *Reeve*, or Patel. The Town Reeve and the leading Thanes governed their little Village Republic in all local matters, repaired their roads and bridges, judged petty offences, settled their petty civil disputes, assessed their Holdings to pay judicial fines, and executed commissions of inquiry issued by the Central Authority. The leading Thanes sent their Representatives to "the Hundred-moot" or Local Boards, which consisted partly of such Representatives, and partly of the Parish Priests and other Functionaries, and this body had large fiscal, judicial, and executive powers. It levied Assessments imposed by themselves or by the Central Power, it dispensed Civil and Criminal Justice as Jurymen and Honorary Magistrates, under the presidency of the Sheriff of the Hundred, the Deshmukh or Desai of the old Indian Revenue System. A group of these Hundreds made up the County, which was the most influential corporate body, so far as local authority was concerned. It consisted of the Representatives of the Hundreds associated with the Bishop, Sheriff, and Earl who represented the Central Power. In its judicial character, the County Board, called "the Folk-moot," heard appeals from the Hundred Courts. This same body was referred to by the Earl or Lord-Lieutenant of the County to muster the land proprietors for war, by the Royal Sheriff (the Indian Collector) to assess and collect State dues, and by the Bishop to regulate Church matters. Water-courses, roads, and bridges in the whole County were subject to its authority, and it had the sole cognizance of the Registration of land transfers. On rare occasions, these Folk-moots sent representatives to the Grand Councils of the Nation, called the Witenagemotes or meetings of the wise Elders of the State. Taxes were but few in those days and not needed; men rendered and exacted personal services instead, both in war and peace.

There were large Cities, and these were governed or rather they governed themselves, on the analogy of the Hundred. The meeting of the Free Men in these cities combined the judicial and administrative functions of the Parish, the Town and the Hundred Moot. They sent, however, no representatives to the County-moot. The King's Sheriff for the County collected the assessed taxes in these Cities, and the first step taken in the direction of Civic Liberty was in obtaining Royal Charters, by which a fixed composition in commutation of the Sheriffs' uncertain dues was secured to them. When this payment was made, the King's Officer did not interfere with the local authority of the Town Guilds, which made their own Bye-laws, and regulated their trades in accordance with the exigencies of long settled customs.

Such, in brief, were the main features of the distribution of local authority and power before the Norman Conquest. The details given above present strange analogies and contrasts with the existing local bodies in India, which it is unnecessary to notice at length here, as they will easily be recognised by the most superficial observer. The Norman Conquest substituted at first a Foreign Court and Nobility for the old Saxon Kings and *Ceorls*, but left the territorial and local arrangements for the most part undisturbed. The growth of the Barons under the Feudal System, however, soon eclipsed the splendour of old traditions, and encroached upon the continuity of the Saxon order of things. The Barons obtained Fiefs and Grants over-riding all local powers and they soon took up the place of the old Sheriffs and Ealdormen, and discharged these duties by means of stewards or Deputies. The Towns gave up their independence to seek shelter under the protection of these powerful Barons. The old Parish and Hundred-Moots became the Barons' Courts, and the old Free-Holders, now reduced to the status of the Baron's tenants, discharged the functions of assessors. The long-continued struggle between the Crown and the Church in these early feudal times resulted in the enforced absence of the Bishops and Parish Priests from these new Courts. As these Barons and their deputies were too powerful subjects to be dealt with by the local authorities, the Kings, as they grew in power, appointed Commissions of Peace and Conservators to assist the Sheriffs; sent their Sheriffs on circuit to collect the fiscal burdens and administer criminal and civil Justice, directed the nomination of High Constables and Parish Constables for police regulation, and appointed Coroners to hold inquests. The later Plantagenet Kings, with a view to check the power of the Nobles, encouraged and legalized the growth of the Honorary Justices of the Peace, at the great centres of local authority in the Counties, and granted

Charters extending the liberties of the Municipal Burghs. The Justices of the Peace in course of time, monopolized to themselves the functions of the old Town and Hundred and County Moots, and the Barons' Courts and Sheriffs' Towns. They were mostly large land-owners, they sat as a Full Bench in the Quarterly General Sessions, and singly or in twos in Petty Sessions, and disposed of miscellaneous offences without the help of a Jury. They were the Guardians of Peace, and discharged the higher duties of an organized Police by helping the high and petty Constables and Conservators. They levied Taxes with the assent of local representatives for the repair of roads and bridges. They built their own gaols, and provided accommodation and discipline for vagrants and incarcerated prisoners, and appointed overseers to superintend the dispensing of charity to the poor. One of their body was appointed Lord Lieutenant of the County, and had the charge of the Militia, and this Officer was also entrusted with the charge of the County Records, and presided as Chairman at Quarter Sessions. The old elective principle of Saxon times thus gave way in the administration of Counties, to that of nomination by the Crown.

While this change was taking place in the Counties, the elective principle underwent a similar transformation in the larger Burghs or Municipal Towns, which had proved so useful allies to the Kings in their disputes with the Barons. The City of London took the lead in this new development. The larger Cities purchased their freedom by paying heavy fines to the King, Bishop or Baron who overlorded them. They obtained Charters securing to them the right of electing their own Mayor, and Justices or Magistrates. They further secured an immunity from the jurisdiction of Baronial, and even King's Courts for their Citizens. They purchased by a lump or commuted payment freedom from all liability to the Sheriff's jurisdiction in the matter of fiscal levies. They soon obtained the right of sending Representatives to Parliament. These great powers, so secured, were monopolized, however, by the leading Citizens in their Guilds and Town Councils, and the Free Citizens of Saxon times gradually lost their right of citizenship in their own borough administration. Self-elective Boards acting in the Counties as Justices of the Peace, and nominated by the King, and in the Towns as Town Councils, and nominated by the Liberties and Guilds, soon monopolized all local powers in England. These great changes were contemporaneous with the Wars of the Roses which destroyed the powers of the factious Nobles, and the Reformation which destroyed the powers of the Church, and paved the way for the Tudor Line of English Kings, who admittedly wielded more absolute powers than their old Saxon or even their great Plantagenet predecessors.

The next period witnessed under the Stuart Sovereigns the decline of the Sovereign's arbitrary powers, and the firm establishment of Parliamentary liberties. In respect of Local Government, however, this period is less eventful. The Kings of England, having succeeded in their struggle with the nobility, soon found that the city Burghers and the Protestant Knights of Shires, who had proved so useful to them, would not go any further length in exalting the prerogatives of the Crown, and in consequence of this discovery misunderstandings arose, and culminated in the attempts of the Kings to rule without Parliament by the help of Standing Armies. The Burghers and Knights proved stubborn in their resistance, and after the Restoration, especially under James II., it was deemed best to rescind their old liberties, and issue new Charters with more restricted powers. The Town Council Juntas were bribed into support, and new Commissions were issued to whom many of the duties of town conservancy and improvement were entrusted. These attempts were of course, facilitated by a decline of the public spirit and an increase of corruption in these close Boroughs. While the liberties of the Towns were being thus circumscribed, the authority of the Justices of the Peace in the Counties was, during the same period, still further strengthened. They were allowed statutory powers to levy rates for bridges and tolls, to build highways and public roads lunatic asylums, and gaols. Altogether, by the time that the Reform Bill of 1832 was passed, Local Self-Government had ceased to be popular in the old Saxon or early Plantagenet sense of the word, both in Towns and Counties. Power was centred in the hands of an oligarchy of rich land-owners in the County, and of rich merchants or traders in Towns, who exercised their functions not so much as the representatives of the tax-paying public, but as nominees of the State, or of their close Guilds.

There was thus complete justification for the radical change which has been inaugurated in the matter of Local Government during the last fifty years in England. The old traditional organizations had lost their touch, and had become oligarchical monopolies, wholly incapable of securing public confidence or undertaking the discharge of new and varied duties, which the necessities of a growing Civilization rendered indispensable. Since 1832, Local Government has been extended by numerous Acts of Parliament in various directions; new Bodies and Boards have been created with vast powers, half representative and half oligarchical in their constitution. The divisions of Parish, Hundred, and County, have lost to a great extent, though not wholly, their distinctive features, and in their place have been substituted Poor Law Unions, High Way Boards, Boards of Health, School Boards, and a host of other

Bodies, with jurisdictions overlapping and conflicting with each other. The Parishes, however, continue still, for some Ecclesiastical and School Board purposes, to be the lowest unit of organization. Each Parish has its own Church, its own School and Burial Ground, assesses its own rates in Vestry Meetings, and collects them through its own Overseers. The civil Parishes in England number 15,416, and consist generally of single Villages, but some large Parishes represent the wards of Cities, while others include several villages. The old powers of the Parish Vestry of maintaining its Watch or Police Constables, and of repairing its highways, roads and bridges, and maintaining its Poor, have been transferred to the superior Unions and Boards which often include many Parishes. Superior in authority to the Parish comes, as stated above, the Union of Poor Law Guardians, first organized by the Statute for the Relief of the Poor, but subsequently enlarged by the addition of other responsibilities. There are six hundred and forty-seven such Unions in England, mostly congergated together round some Market Town, with its neighbouring Hamlets or Villages, twenty-three of which on an average are included in every Union. Another superior centre of power is represented by the Petty Sessional Divisions of Counties, which divisions are about seven hundred in number exclusive of Boroughs, and each of these divisions has a separate Commission of the Peace.

This secondary division does not correspond with the Poor Law Union. The Counties still retain their old territorial limits, but many of the old powers of County Magistrates have been transferred to a great extent to other bodies exercising a partial or total independence.

As the law stands at present, the Local Government of each County, as such, is vested in a Lord Lieutenant (who is also a *Custos Rotularum*, or Keeper of the Records), a High Sheriff who is the representative of the superior Civil Power, a Commission of Justices nominated by the Sovereign, and a Clerk of the Peace appointed by the Keeper of the County Records. The Lord Lieutenant is supposed to be the head of the Militia, while the High Sheriff is the representative of civil functions, and superintends the election of Knights and Coroners, and executes the writs and processes of Judicial Courts. The Justices of the Peace are mostly Land-owners, and discharge honorary functions without expecting any payment. These functions are of various sorts. In their Judicial capacity, they hold Quarter or General Sessions to hear Appeals from the decisions of Magistrates, and appoint Committees of their body for various purposes. As single Magistrates in Petty Sessions, they dispose of petty cases, and commit the graver sort to the Quarter Sessions, which dispose of them with the help of a Jury. Certain of the more heinous offences are tried at the Assizes by the Westminster Court Judges on Circuit. As Civil Judges, the Justices of the Peace possess at present no power, as the duties of County Courts in this class of cases have been entrusted to the Stipendiary Judges who dispose of Small Causes cases. The Magistrates are also the visitors and supervisors of the Gaols and Lunatic Asylums. They still retain the charge of the Police of the County, and appoint the Chief Constables and District Superintendents. They levy the County Police rate, and the Jail and Lunatic Asylum rates, through their Finance Committee. The Magistrates sitting together, and in some cases acting singly, have the power of renewing and suspending Liquor Licenses, and of fixing the places and regulating the hours, where and when the shops might be opened. They have the power of prohibiting the movements of cattle in times of Cattle Plague. All these, and many other miscellaneous functions, have been entrusted to the Justices by various Statutes.

There are other duties in which the Justices, as nominees of Government, are made to share the power and responsibility with representatives of the Rate-payers. The most important of these functions is the regulation of highways. The Honorary Magistrates are ex-officio Members of the High Way Boards, which contain besides a majority of the repesentatives of Tax-payers. In a similar manner they are ex-officio Members of the Boards of Poor Law Guardians. The Poor Law Boards are in principle elected by the Rate-payers, but the Justices of the Peace, residing within the limits of the Union, are ex-officio Members of such Union or Boards. Appeals from the assessment of these Unions or Boards lie to the Magistrates in Petty and General Sessions. These same Poor Law Union Boards have been also constituted Boards of Public Health, and the Magistrates are ex-officio Members of the Boards, and act along with elected Representatives. The School Boards, on the other hand, are entirely composed of members elected by the Rate-payers. This multiplicity of Boards, whose jurisdictions overlap one another, is one of the most distinctive features of the existing local arrangements for the Government of Counties. Though they imply a considerable waste of power, and foster various other abuses, they are the outcome of a wise conservatism which seeks to retain its hold on the past, while making concessions to the needs of the present, and they suit the patch-work instinct of practical Englishmen, who have no admiration for theoretical symmetry. In the Poor Law Union Boards, as also in the Boards of Health and Improvement, the principle of proportioning votes to the value of rateable property is followed, while in School Boards, the practice of comulative voting is allowed to secure a fair representation of the minorities in large Constituencies. All these various Boards are kept under control by the Home Department, which possesses extensive powers of arranging and altering their limits from time to time, and in case of default the Law allows the absolute interposition of the Home Secretary, even to the extent of a temporary suspension, with a view to enforce obedience.

In the larger Towns and Boroughs, of which there are two hundred and twenty-seven in England, the Exercise of local power is vested in two different bodies. These are first, the Commissions of the Peace, which exercise judicial powers on the analogy of the County Magistrates in General or Petty Sessions. Where the City has outgrown the limits of effective control by voluntary agency, a Recorder, who is a paid Magistrate, is appointed by the Crown, and is paid by the Borough, and exercises large criminal powers like our own Presidency Town Magistrates. Besides their criminal work, these Magistrates grant Licenses for the Sale of Liquor, and they also supervise the Borough Jail. The larger Boroughs appoint and pay their own Police. The chief administrative body in these Boroughs consists of the Town Council, and is made up of the Mayor and Aldermen who are elected by the Town Council, and the Town Councillors who are elected by the resident Burgesses, and hold office for three years. The Mayor and Aldermen are ex-officio Justices and Magistrates, and thus form the connecting link with the Town Justices and Magistrates. The Town Council has the power to levy rates and appropriate them to the purposes of Local Government. Every large Town in England has to pay a variety of local rates, a Police rate, a Poor Law rate, a School Board rate, a Jail rate, a Lighting rate, a Water rate, a Conservancy rate, etc., and these rates are in some places, like Birmingham, consolidated into a general Borough rate. The Town Council maintains its own Magistracy, its Police force, its Gaols, Asylums, Schools, Poor Houses, Baths, Wash-houses, Libraries, Museums, Water Works, Hospitals, Parks, Cemeteries, builds and repairs, lights and waters its streets, takes care of its Sewers and Drains, and Slaughter Houses, Gas Supply, Offensive Trades, Smells, Markets, etc. The multiplicity and the burden of these charges will easily be understood from Mr. Rathbone's account of the local finances of Liverpool, which Borough raised from rates nearly fifty Lakhs of Rupees in 1871, and supplemented these receipts with the income of its own Corporate Property, to the extent of thirty Lakhs more. Excluding London, two hundred and twenty-three Boroughs in England and Wales spent a sum of thirty-three Crores of Rupees in 1872-73, derived from rates and the income of corporate property, and they had besides, raised loans to the extent of seventy-two Crores. The Poor Law Unions alone represent an expenditure of more than ten Crores all over England. The number of paupers, supported both by out-door and in-door relief, was one to twenty-six of the population, or in all nine Lakhs. The School Board rate also represents an expenditure of several Crores. The Revenue and Expenditure of the great Metropolitan Borough of London dwarfs even these magnificent totals. The gross Revenue of the London Corporation alone in 1871 was one and one-third Crores of Rupees, of which sum seventy-five Lakhs were the proceeds of Rates, Rent, Tolls, Duties, and Market Fees.

This brief summary of the leading features of the arrangements for Local Government and Taxation in the Counties and Boroughs of England will suggest to the thoughtful student many points of comparison, but more of contrast, with our own system of Municipal and Local Fund organizations, which cannot fail to prove very instructive. The great complexity of the arrangements in England is certainly not a point in its favour. In London alone, there is a multiplicity of governing bodies and a division of powers, which baffle enumeration. There is first, the Corporation of the City of London proper, whose jurisdiction extends over six hundred and forty acres within the City Walls, including a population of seventy-five thousand souls, and divided into twenty-six Wards and a hundred and five Parishes. This Corporation consists of the Lord Mayor and twenty-six Aldermen and two hundred and six common Councillors. two Sheriffs, a Recorder, a Common Serjeant Chamberlain, and a Town Clerk. The Mayor is chosen by the Aldermen annually, out of two names submitted to that body by the Members of the City Livery Companies, and the old Trade Guilds, whose constituency numbers seven thousand Free Men. The Aldermen are elected for life, one for each ward, by a body of twenty thousand Free Men. The Mayor and Aldermen are all Justices of the Peace, and as such the Aldermen preside each in his ward, and the Lord Mayor in the Common Council. The Mayor also presides as Chief Magistrate in the Mansion House Police Court, and the Aldermen sit by turns in the Guildhall Police Court. The Recorder, and in his absence the Common Serjeant, presides in the Chief Civil Court for the City. The Sheriff is elected by the Liveries, and the Sheriff's Court is the London Court for small debts. The Mayor and Aldermen sit with the Recorder at the General Sessions of London, held eight times in the year. These Civil and Criminal Courts have exclusive jurisdiction over the City, and are not subordinate to the Jurisdiction of the superior Courts at Westminster. The Police

Force for the City of London is separate from the Metropolitan Police, and the City Commissioner of Police is appointed by the Common Council. There is also a separate Commission of Sewers which regulates drainage, public health, and the repairs of streets, and a Thames Conservancy Board. Outside the City limits the London Metropolitan District includes seventy-five Parishes and nine Boroughs, and has a population of nearly forty Lakhs. This vast population is governed by thirty-eight Vestries or Local Boards, which have the charge of Drainage and improvement of Streets, Water Supply, and Lighting. A Central Metropolitan Board of Works, consisting of the nominees of the City and the Suburban Vestries, has charge of the general Drainage. This Board, through its various Committees, takes care of the Building arrangements, Fire Brigade, Parks, Common Sewers, Tramways, Infected Food Supply, &c. The Metropolitan Police is under the direct charge of the Home Secretary. For the administration of the Poor Law, London consists of fourteen Parishes and sixteen Unions. A Metropolitan Asylums Board has the charge of Infirmaries and Work Houses, the expenses of which are paid out of a common Poor Fund. In these Poor Law Boards, Government nominates one-fourth of the number of Members. while the remaining three-fourths are elected by the Rate-payers. Lastly, there is the Metropolitan School Board of forty-nine Members, elected separately by the Freemen in London, and outside the City limits by the Rate-payers generally, under the cumulative system of voting. This brief enumeration of the governing local bodies of London will furnish an accurate idea of the complexity of the arrangements. To a more or less extent, the same remark applies to all the other Boroughs and Counties. The best thing that can be said in its defence is that this complexity has grown in course of time, as every newly felt want had to be separately provided for. The efforts of Parliament have been directed for years to simplify this complexity by a more thorough-going and systematic arrangement for the common subordination and co-operation of the various Divisions under a Central Organization. Even now the Liberal Government has a Bill on hand for the incorporation of the whole Metropolitan area under a common Local Government. The division of power and responsibility is a correct principle in executive arrangements, but it has certainly no application in the case of deliberative bodies. The waste of energy involved, and the great cost of maintaining separate Boards for separate duties, are certainly great evils, which must be guarded against, and we cannot but think that in this respect our Municipal and Local Funds Boards are a great improvement on the English arrangements.

The next feature which attracts attention is the large provisions which Local Government Bodies in England,

(and in this respect Scotland and Ireland may also be included with England), have to make for the compulsory relief of the Poor. Nearly four per cent. of the population are thus relieved in England. while in Scotland the proportion is five per cent., and in Ireland it is four and a half per cent. The charge for the Poor Rate in England on the total rental of lands and houses. estimated to be one hundred and twenty Crores of Rupees, is 1*s.* 4*d.* per Pound, or nearly eight Crores of Rupees. In Scotland, the charge is 1*s.* 1½*d.* per Pound, which on a rental of fourteen Crores represents nearly eighty-five Lakhs of expenditure on Poor Relief. In Ireland the charge is nearly eighty Lakhs. In the whole of the United Kingdom of Great Britain and Ireland, the total charge was thus ten Crores in 1873, which is the latest year for which we have the available figures. In England and Ireland, the able-bodied Poor, as well as the infirm, are provided for, while in Scotland no relief is afforded to the able-bodied. The whole of this relief is defrayed voluntarily by the people of this Country, and in this respect also we think that India has little to borrow from English example. Not that we have no large class of persons who need relief at the hands of the well-to-do community. The Census Tables of 1872 show that out of a population of nearly seventeen millions in the Bombay Presidency, about four Lakhs were returned as Beggars and Paupers, and two Lakhs more may be added for Priests and religious people. This represents an average proportion of three and a half per cent. which, it should be borne in mind, is smaller than the proportions which obtain in England and Scotland. No people on earth take better care of their beggar population than the people of this Country. Charity with us is a sacred duty, an observance which symbolizes the essence of all Religion. It is this active sense of the obligation of riches which the compulsory system of Poor Law Relief, as administered in England, tends to destroy. Charity is in England a heavy burden to be shirked, not a loving duty to be rejoiced over. The effort of every Parish and District Poor Union in England is directed to shift its own responsibility, and saddle the charge of its Beggar population on to other Parishes and Districts, by proving that the poor man or woman had not obtained a settlement within its limits. Landlords and House-owners resent every such settlement as a direct encroachment on their rights, and this leads to a misery and hard-heartedness of which we in India can with difficulty form any adequate idea. The charges of management absorb from ten to fifteen per cent. of the Receipts, but what is far worse, the dispensation of charity, enforced as it is by Law, renders both the giver and the receiver callous to the misery and the humiliation. It has been observed that in Scotland, wherever the proportion of the Poor House Inmates is the largest, and in some Parishes it is as high as fifteen per cent. of the population, the proportion of illegitimate births is frightfully high. In some of the badly administered Parishes, the proportion of illegitimate to legitimate births is as high as one to two, and the average for the whole of Scotland was ten years ago one to ten. These evils are naturally aggravated in places where the out-door system of relief is largely adopted in preference to in-door relief. In this respect also, England compares favourably with the state of things which obtains in Scotland. Poor Law Relief may have prevented the spread of Socialist and Anarchist Revolutions in Great Britain, but there can be no doubt that the voluntary dispensation of relief, as it prevails in India, is in every way more healthy and humanizing than the compulsory system such as it is found in the United Kingdom.

While, in these two respects, the Local Government organizations in England have nothing to recommend their adoption here, at least for the present, there are other features in respect of which there can be no doubt that we have much to learn from the practical success of the experience of the English System of Local Government. We allude chiefly to the large powers which the Leaders of the landed and well-to-do classes possess as Honorary

Magistrates in the management of local affairs. Their functions, it will be noted, are not confined to merely Municipal and Conservancy duties. It is as Magistrates and Guardians of the Peace that this voluntary agency proves most useful. The Scheme of Local Self-Government, propounded by His Excellency the Viceroy in Council, while it enlarges and elevates the sphere of public-spirited activity in various ways, has one essential weakness at its root, which will surely result in rendering the reform nugatory, as a means of Political Education. It does not confide to the men of light and leading those functions of Government in which people feel most interest. If possible, it tends to sever the small connection which was hitherto recognized in the contributions to the Police Expenditure levied from Municipal Bodies. This severance has been justified for reasons which certainly appear plausible under present circumstances, but there can be no doubt that Local Government, limited to Conservancy and Charitable functions, is more or less a misnomer, and is doomed to inevitable failure. For, it will never secure the same enthusiastic support of the population which would have been enlisted, if Local Bodies had been organized on the English plan of appointing representatives of the Local gentry Conservators of Peace, and Guardians of the Law, and associating with them representative Rate-payers in every Local Board. It will be found that in no single self-governed Country of Europe or America, has this power and responsibility of Magisterial and Police functions been denied to the Local governing bodies. We have already described at length the English arrangements for the government of Boroughs and Counties. In Scotland, the Institution of Justices of the Peace is not of a very ancient date, and yet, even there these Honorary Officers are required to exert themselves to protect the Peace, to issue warrants against criminals, to try petty offences and breaches of Revenue Laws, and decide small civil suits not exceeding five Pounds in value. In this latter respect, the Institution of Village Munsiffs and of Conciliators in some of the Bombay Districts is a tardy recognition of their duty on the part of the Government. A few Honorary Magistrates have also of late been appointed in some of the large Towns, but they are too few to acquire the status of a recognized Local Authority, and cannot make head against the Officials. Commissioners of Supply, as they are called in Scotland, correspond with our Local Fund Members and are elected by the suffrages of properly qualified Landowners. They assess for each County the local rates, out of which are defrayed the charges of the Police, kept up for apprehending and punishing criminals, the salaries of Procurers Fiscal (who correspond with the Government Solicitors of the Presidency Towns in India), the expenses of maintaining Courts, Gaols, and the charges

17

of Lunatic Asylums. These Commissioners have the chief control, not only of roads and improvements and public conservancy and health, but of the County Police and the County Prisons. The connection of the Central Government with these and other bodies is maintained by the nomination of the Sheriff, who is ex-officio member of this Board of Commissioners, and of the Police and Prison Committees, and by a subsidy granted from the Treasury to the Local Funds. The Poor Law Boards, and the School Boards, and the Church Synods, are separate local authorities with distinctive functions, and are constituted chiefly on the basis of election. In Ireland the Baronial Presentment Sessions and the Grand Juries exercise similarly both judicial and fiscal functions. In the Netherlands and in France, as also in Norway and Switzerland, the Communal Authorities control, to a greater or less extent, their own Police arrangements, and the Officers presiding over them, called Burgo-Masters and Prefects, have petty criminal powers. In the Colonies of England, these powers are more exclusively enjoyed by the local organizations. The necessity and importance of localizing Police and Magisterial functions cannot be exaggerated in a bureaucratic country like India. The old Village Community, with its Panchayat of Elders, and its voluntary system of Night Watch by the citizens in turns, and its hereditary Police Officers, fulfilled the same purpose. The petty tyranny of the

French Prefect and Burgo-Masters in the Netherlands is aggravated with us by the difficulty of access to the District Authorities, who in India are the only source of local power. A petty Police Constable is thus more powerful for evil than the richest Sowcar, or the largest Landlord in the country. It is this evil of centralized government which enervates and demoralizes all the local springs of action. It will no doubt be said, that these local representatives are more likely to abuse their power than even the worst officials. We think Honorary Magistrates associated together and sitting as a Bench once a month or more, may safely be trusted never to go wrong, and they will certainly relieve the hands of overburdened Officials. Their functions may also be duly subordinated to the superior authority of the higher Civil and Criminal Courts. It is in this direction chiefly, that we think our efforts must be directed in the future development of the great reform which is being introduced at the present day all over the country. The people generally, and certainly those residing in the larger Towns, may well be expected to accept gladly even increased burdens, if the lower Magisterial powers, and the control of the Police, were freely bestowed on their Natural leaders. The Conservancy of Public Health, the charge of Education and Medical Charity, and even the making and repair of Roads and Buildings, are not in any real sense of the word the distinctive duties of Government. They essentially belong to the sphere of private effort, and are only undertaken by civilized Governments, because their organization affords a ready-made agency for corporate usefulness. It is the Magisterial and Police functions which represent the distinctive feature of sovereign authority, and these must be localized if Local Government is not to be a misnomer, and a certain failure. We are perfectly aware that the condition of Self-governed Countries is very different from the order of things which has been established in India, but this is no reason why no effort should be made to find room for local authority in these directions, as far as the safety of Foreign Rule permits such a concession. The experiment may safely be tried in the larger Towns, and gradually extended to the Country at large. The great principle underlying all these arrangements is, in the words of Mr. John Stuart Mill, that power must be localized, while knowledge, especially technical, is most useful when subordinated to a central control. The principal business of the Central Authority should be to give instructions, and to lay down fixed principles, and it should leave the local bodies to apply them in practice. Election by popular suffrage enlists public confidence in the acts of Government; and when a majority of elected Representatives are duly mixed with a minority possessed of educational and property qualifications, and these at present must be the nominees of the central authorities, the organization so secured can alone afford full scope for the development of the Political Education of the people, and the growth of that self-reliant energy which is the best support and the highest justification of coercive rule.

X.

EMANCIPATION OF SERFS IN RUSSIA.*

NOW that the Governments of England and India have seriously taken in hand the task of relieving the Agricultural Classes from their heavy depression, it cannot fail to be of use to note the progress of a similar Emancipation undertaken in European Russia about twenty years ago, and which, so far as one can judge from Official Reports, has been attended with great success. European Russia, including the Kingdom of Poland, the Grand Duchy of Finland, the Baltic Provinces, and the Trans-Caucasian Regions, covers an area of nearly 2,000,000 square miles of Territory, inhabited by a population of seventy-two millions, including the Cossacks and Kerghiz Hordes. The extent of Russia proper is about 100,000 square miles, and its population is sixty millions. Of this number, nearly eighty per cent. constitute the Rural population, and about ten per cent. are Urban, including the Nobility and the Clergy. About seven per cent. represent the Military element of the population, which gives to Russia its position as a First Class European Power. For administrative purposes, Euro-

* Published in 1883.

pean Russia proper is divided into forty-five Districts. One third of the whole cultivable area is Crown Land, one-fifth of the same area belongs to the great Landlords who number about a Hundred Thousand Families, one-fifth belongs to the Peasantry who number about forty-eight millions in all, and the rest belongs to the Church, Mines, Military Colonists, Royal Appanage Lands, etc. Of the total of forty-eight millions of Peasants, nearly one half, or twenty-five millions, were attached as serfs in 1861 to Crown and Appanage Lands. The great Emancipation Act of 1861 was not directly intended to apply to this large number, but the scope of relief was extended from time to time, till there is now no Serf left on Russian soil. They are at present, like the Survey Occupants of this Presidency, Peasant tenants at fixed rents called *Obrok*, payable to the Government, and revisable every twenty years, and may alienate their Holdings subject to this liability, at a fixed price, which represents the capitalized value of the rent at five per cent. As long as this *Obrok* is paid, the State Tenant's land cannot revert to the State.

The Emancipation Act of 1861, sought chiefly to elevate the condition of the Peasants who cultivated the private lands of the Nobility and Gentry, and made up a total of nearly twenty-two millions of Serfs. Serfdom, like Caste and Slavery, was originally founded on the great fact of Foreign Conquest. Serfdom, as a recognized Institution, was introduced in Russia about the end of the Sixteenth Century, by a Law of 1592, which prevented the Peasants from migrating from one estate to another, without their Lord's permission, and attached them to the soil in a way to secure their transfer with the land. Peter the Great introduced the Poll-tax in Russia, and made the Lords responsible for the tax due from the Peasants on their lands. The abuse of powers, so natural under these circumstances, soon degraded the Land Serfs to the still lower depth of landless Bondsmen and life Convicts working at the Mines. The landed Gentry owned in all, in 1861, about three hundred million acres, of which one-third was in the occupation of the Serfs, and of the two-third in the occupation of the Landlords, one half was mortgaged with the State or private Creditors. In consideration of their free occupation of one hnndred million acres, the Serfs were compelled to serve a fixed number of days, which was generally three days in the week, on the two-thirds in the occupation of their Landlords, or paid them rents or services instead. The Serf could hold no property of his own, and although remedial measures were introduced from time to time, since the commencement of this Century, it was not till 1847, that the Serf could buy his personal freedom from his Landlord, or buy even Waste Lands from his private savings, except in his Landlord's name. The Serf had no Civil Rights against his master, the latter could flog him at his pleasure, or banish him to distant Plantations, or send him into the Army. When the noble Landlord required a loan, he mortgaged his Serfs with his land and cattle. The Serfs on Crown and Appanage Lands were in much the same condition as private Serfs, in respect of the incapacity of free locomotion and Civil Rights, only their rents were lower and less variable. Such was the condition of the unprivileged Rural Classes throughout Russia proper scarcely twenty years ago. Of the forty-eight millions of Serf population, representing ten millions adult males, attached to Crown, Appanage, and private lands, seven millions of Serfs were in pawn with mortgagees, 7,50,000 Serfs were domestic servants or land-less Bondsmen, and 5,00,000 were employed in the Mines in 1861. These ten million serfs cultivated one hundred millions of acres of land. Each adult male Serf enjoyed thus the usufruct of ten acres of land, which agrees with the average holding of an Indian Ryot in this Presidency. It was in respect of this immense population that the late Emperor Alexander promulgated the great Charter of Russian Liberty, and completed their Emancipation between 1861 and 1869.

It will be interesting to note the chief features of this Reform, and to study the details of the method by which it was accomplished. The grant of Civil and Personal Liberty, and the assurance of this independence by securing to the free Peasant a minimum of property, represented by the allotment of a parcel of land in tenancy or free-hold purchased with Public Funds, and a recognized voice in the management of local affairs, these were the three-fold and principal features of this great Reform. Domestic Serfdom, the right of the master to the control of the person of the Serf, was first abolished without any reservation or compensation, except that the Poll-tax, which the master used to pay for his Serfs, was now transferred to the Emancipated Serf. Between 1861 and 1863, the Emancipated domestic Serf was required to pay to his master this Poll-tax, of five shillings for each male, and four shillings for each female. After 1863, the freed Serf paid his own Poll-tax direct to the State.

In regard to the allotment of land held by the Serfs on their master's estates, and the right of the latter to receive Quit Rents and Services from them, the question was not so easy of solution. As a rule, the allotments were one-third of the whole estate, and never exceeded one half. For allowing the Serfs to enjoy the usufruct of this land, with the right of pasture on the commons, and of cutting timber and fuel for building and burning purposes, the masters either received rent on this allotment, or more generally required the Serfs to cultivate three days in the week the unallotted or reserved portion. They seldom Paid Quit Rent in money. The personal labour which the Serfs gave on their master's land was the usual consideration received by the master from the Serfs attached to his land. In the Industrial Provinces, money rents were more common. It has been estimated that about twenty-five per cent. of the Land Serfs paid Quit Rent varying from 2*s.* 3*d.* to 2*s.* 9*d.* per acre ; the rest rendered services instead.

The Emancipation Committee had first to settle the maximum allotment of the land which was to be made over to the Serf as his private Holding discharged from all burdens, and they had next to determine the amount of compensation which the Serfs, or on their behalf the State, should pay to their masters for the loss of their rents and services. The money rents which ranged from Rupees four to Rupees fifty according to the quality of the land, and the necessities of the master, could be easily ascertained and valued, but the valuation of personal services was not so easy, as these services were of a most miscellaneous variety, and subordinated the Serf to the most ordinary necessities of his master's every-day life. Another source of complication was due to the fact that many of the estates belonging to the Privileged Classes were mortgaged, together with the Serf population on them, to the State, which had advanced about fifty millions Sterling on their security. This condition of affairs furnished, however, the working lever for the action of the State. After much discussion, the final plan adopted by the late Emperor Alexander's Government was a compromise of several more extreme proposals. An average allotment of ten acres was fixed as the size of a Serf Holding. This Holding, together with the Homestead, was ceded in Perpetual Tenancy by the Master to the Serf on terms settled by mutual arrangement, or failing that, on conditions fixed by law, which, however, limited the compulsory occupation of the tenant to nine years. Over and above this right of tenancy, the Serf could compulsorily demand the sale of this allotment with the Homestead on it at a prize fixed by mutual agreement, or failing that by the State Officials. The State undertook to provide the Serf with funds to enable him to buy off his master's rights over the allotment. The rights of Personal Service on his master's lands were commuted into a money payment equivalent to the Quit Rent which would have been received, if no service had been rendered, and this Quit Rent was capitalized at a fixed valuation. The Political Rights of the master, and his profits derived from the drudgery of the domestic Serfs, were abolished without compensation. While the Serf's interests were thus advanced, the master was absolved from all liability on account of Imperial and Rural Taxes due from the Serfs, and he had not to pay his Serf's fines, or defend his actions in Civil or Criminal Courts at his own cost as before. The State protected its own Finances by establishing, or rather reviving among the Serfs the Institution of Communal or Cantonal responsibility, *i. e.*, the joint liability of the *Mere* or Village Community. The Allotment and the Quit Rent were all fixed in a lump sum for the Communal units, and the individual Serf was made responsible to the Commune of which he formed part, and each local community of Serfs became in their turn jointly responsible to the State. To borrow an illustration from our Indian Revenue system, the Settlement was made with the collective body of Village Zamindars or Mirasdars, as in the Panjab and North-Western Provinces, and not with the individual Ryot as in this Presidency. The Russian word for Canton or Commune is *Mere*, which has an ethnical and lingual affinity with our Indian Miras.

At first, the change of condition in the Serf's lot was a transfer from the yoke of a private alien master to that of the collective Commune. The Serf, though emancipated, was not allowed to leave his native Village, or to detach himself from the land without the permission of the heads of the *Mere*, who received the redemption price from the Serf as a condition of his release. In the old Social Polity of Russia, the father, or the head of the family, under whose protection all the subordinate members lived together, had very large powers, and as these Village *Meres* or Communities were most of them settled by the descendants of one family, next to the Lord's power, the Patriarch's authority was all-potent for good or for evil. As may be easily imagined, this power was greatly abused, even to the extent of degrading the purity of family life. The financial interests of the State, as the mortgagee of all the redeemed estates, and the receiver of the Poll-tax, compelled it to lend its countenance to the maintenance of this Patriarchal and Communal system. As a counterpoise to these drawbacks, the new organization set up by the Emancipation Committee greatly strengthened the hands of this Peasant population by the constitution of elective Communal and Canton Councils with the broadest suffrage, and with very extensive powers of Local Self-government. The Serf, once freed from his Lord's control, and possessed of full Civil and Political Rights, was not likely to submit long and patiently to this Communal restraint, and the process of this second liberation may already be said to have commenced. The disintegration of the old Patriarchal System and domestic oppression may be safely regarded as by no means the least of the beneficial changes inaugurated by the great Emancipation. Between 1861 and 1869, the latest period for which information is available, it appears that about one-third of the adult male Serfs were converted into

Perpetual Tenants of their ten acre Allotments and Homesteads. The rental these free tenant Serfs pay for their land is fixed in the shape of a Poll-tax, which, when spread over the extent of their Holdings, represents a charge of two Shillings an acre. The State claims the right of reassessing the rentals after twenty years. As will have been seen from the summary given above, the Scheme of Emancipation presented two alternatives, compulsory Perpetual Tenancy, or compulsory Purchase of Free-Hold, as a qualification for elevating the Serf to the condition of a Freeman. A third alternative was also left open to the Serf by which he might accept a quarter of the maximum allotment from his master as a settlement, in compromise of all compulsory relationships. About six hundred thousand Peasants have accepted this alternative, which enables them to dispense with the aid of Government Funds, and the necessity of submitting to the restraints of Communal life upon free locomotion and residence. Out of a total of ten million Serf families, six millions have become purchasers of their allotments, thirty-one per cent. of this number became so by their own voluntary choice, and sixty-nine per cent. were obliged to purchase by the choice of their old masters, who elected to accept the redemption with State Funds. It appears from detailed statements that the State has advanced fifty-one million Pounds

Sterling for the compulsory redemption of thirty-five millions of acres, allotted to about three and a half millions of freed Serfs. The price paid for redemption by the State was about 20*s.* per acre. In the case of voluntary settlements accorded to nearly two millions of Serfs, the Landlords obtained twenty per cent. more from the Tenants than the State assignment. The money advanced by the State to redeem the Serfs, together with six per cent. interest, is made recoverable in forty-nine years by an annual payment of two shillings and a half per acre, which he pays to the officers of the Redemption Board. Peasants who have not elected the quarter allotment, or who have not been forced to redeem with State help, and have agreed to continue to be Perpetual Tenants, generally prefer Service rents to Money rents, and the Metayer form of Tenancy, which agrees best with the economical condition of the country, is coming extensively into vogue in respect of these properties.

The total extent of settled lands throughout Russia proper occupied by perpetual Tenants or proprietary Free-Holders, is about sixty million acres, while the Landlords occupy on their own account two hundred and forty millions. The Crown Peasants come under a different category, by their condition is being daily assimilated to that of the redeemed Free-Holders. The total sum advanced by the State, and secured on the lands of the Peasants, up to the end of 1869, was sixty-five million Pounds Sterling out of which the State had foreclosed mortgages to the extent of fifty-three millions. The whole of this money has been raised in the first instance by the issue of State Banks Bills and Government Stock at five or five and a half per cent. and the receipts from the Peasants, spread over forty-nine years at six per cent. per annum, are expected to clear off the whole of these heavy liabilities. The Capitation Tax, the Imperial Territorial Tax, and the Redemption payments, taken together, average from 27*s.* to 35*s.* per head of the Rural population, or 1*s.* 6*d.* to 3*s.* 3*d.* per acre.

We trust these details of the progress of the Emancipation of the Peasantry in European Russia will prove of interest for more reasons than one. There can be no doubt that, as a consequence of this Emancipation, the Russian people have thriven in material and commercial prosperity, notwithstanding the increase of taxation caused by Foreign Wars, and the responsibilities of an Empire which covers nearly a quater of the area of two great Continents. The Russian Exports of raw Agricultural Produce have vastly increased in value and amount during the last twenty years. The Cotton Spinning Industry has become a power in Western and Central Russia. The resources, material and moral, of Russia were severely

18

tried in the late Turko-Russian War, and she stood the test in a way to confirm her position as a First Class Military Power, which could at any moment send ten Lakhs of Soldiers to any portion of her vast territory for defensive and aggresssive purposes. The Nihilist Outrages and Siberian Exiles should not in any way be allowed to come in the way of our appreciation of the great strides which Russia has made both at home and abroad, in the arts of Peace and War, during the last twenty years, and although for the time Absolutism has triumphed, we may almost with safety prophesy that a Nation of Peasant Proprietors, with such Democratic Institutions as the Communal and Cantonal, and District and Territorial Assemblies, will not rest content till it establishes its control over national affairs to the displacement of arbitrary or Bureaucratic Power.

A few words more before we bring to an end this brief review of the revolution effected in Russian Agricultural Economy twenty years ago. One of the worst effects of Absolute Power is that it warps men's perceptions in regard to the innate dignity of human nature, and its Common identity under all manner of extraneous disguises. The representatives of a Ruling Class soon learn to lisp the shibboleth of the natural and inherent superiority of European over Asiatic Races. It is urged that heroic remedies like the Emancipation of Serfs in Russia, and the creation of Peasant Proprietors in France and Germany, can safely be undertaken by the State with Public Credit or Funds, but that out here in India, the State, while claiming a monopoly of Landlord's Rights, must not incur any such responsibility, because the Indian Ryot is an improvident, spiritless, and ignorant Peasant, whose condition has been wretched all along, and can never be improved. Our reply to this charge is that the French Peasant was not always the abstemious and prudent Citizen that he now is; there was a time when Arthur Young mourned over the condition of the Agricultural Classes of France. The magic of Property and of Free Institutions have worked all this wonderful change. The degradation from which the Russian Peasant has been freed by a National Government can scarcely be said to be realized in the case of the Indian Peasants. The Imperial Government there, ventured in a spirit of statesmanship and philanthropy to redeem its Serfs, and make them Free Men, regardless of cost. The Power of the Sowcar and of the State Landlord in this Country cannot be compared in the continuity and intensity of its abuse, for one moment, with the tyranny of the Nobility of Russia. The depression, however, such as it is, in this Country is real, and becoming worse every day. Let the State interfere not merely with a minimum piecemeal dose of Judicial Reform, but by the wholesale dispensation of a large administrative relief. If it subsidizes or guarantees Private Banks against risk during the first few experimental years, and enables them to rid the Peasantry of their ancestral debts, and if at the same time it allows the Land Revenue to be redeemed or permanently settled at a moderate figure once for all, it will provided an ample fund for Agricultural Relief Improvement without the necessity of borrowing a single rupee of fresh loans. The Ryot once emancipated, and set on his feet, and inspired with a sense that the land is as absolutely his as his home or clothes, there need never be any apprehension of his running into debt again and not practising thrift. The awakening of two hundred millions of the earth's most gifted Races will be a triumph of beneficent Government by the side of which the Abolition of Slavery in 1833 in England, or the Slave Emancipation War in America of 1860, and the contemporaneous Serf Emancipation of Russia, will be but child's play. It only needs a Statesman to grasp the full height of this argument, and to restore India to its proud position as the garden and granary of the world

XI.

PRUSSIAN LAND LEGISLATION AND THE BENGAL TENANCY BILL.*

IN one of our former numbers we presented an outline of the great Reform achieved by the Government of Russia about twenty-five years ago, which resulted in the emancipation of many millions of the prædial Serfs on Crown lands and the estates of the large proprietors in that country. A similar Economical Revolution was effected in the early part of the Century on an equally large scale, and with equally beneficial results, in the Social and Agricultural Economy of the Kingdom of Prussia. To us in India, which is now in the active throes of a great agricultural crisis in every portion of its widely scattered provinces, the origin and progress of this enfranchisement of the Prussian Peasantry possess a more than mere historical interest and teach us lessons which in the interests of this country we may not ignore without exposing ourselves to a great social cataclysm. The agitation in Bengal in connection with the great question of the Tenancy Bill will soon come to a head with the return

* Published in 1883.

of the Viceroy and his Council to Calcutta, and the strife of Class against Class, and of Labour against Capital, will be fought out to the bitter end. We feel persuaded that the Land Legislation of Prussia in the early part of this Century furnishes the most striking and historical parallel to this great impending crisis. There, as in Bengal, the Government of the Country sided with the cause of the enfranchised Labourers as against the all-powerful Landlord; there, as in Bengal, the tradition of a free Peasantry in a remote past, smothered but not killed outright by a long period of depression, furnished the stimulus for renewed efforts on a grander scale. This same Problem is equally prominent in Contemporary Politics in other parts of India, but the Classes representing the interests of Capital have not the cohesion and power which the Bengal Zemindars possess, and which establishes the closest resemblance between them and the great Feudal Aristrocracy of Prussia. Of course, there are deep underlying differences in the situation which we shall notice later on, but the resemblances are sufficiently great to warrant a careful study of the Prussian land question by Indian students. We propose, accordingly, to furnish a brief *resume* of this great revolution, which, in its distant consequences, has raised Prussia from a Second Class Power to be a leading State of Continental Europe, and enabled it, with a Confederated Germany at its back, to control the destinies of modern civilization in the latter half of this Century.

In the following observations, we have in view the Prussia of the first half of this Century, before the great victories of 1866 and 1870 raised it to its present towering position. The seeds of Prussia's present advancement were sown in the great humiliation which overtook the country on the battlefield of Jena, which annihilated for a time the power of the Hohenzollerns, and made Prussia the sport of Napoleon's victorious Armies. Alone of the Continental Powers, however, her Sovereigns and Generals took part with Great Britain in the great revenge on the battlefield of Waterloo. It was in this period of national humilitation that Prussia consigned her destinies to the great statesmanship of her Chancellors Stein and Hardenburg, who, more than Bismarck or Moltke, may claim the glory of having saved their country in the dark hour of her national humiliation. The Feudal System, and the Social Polity and Agricultural Economy based on its principles, were buried in the great overthrow at Jena, and when the national energy had its upheaval, it refused to be bound by the old trammels, and urgently called for a change. The Cycle of Reform commenced in 1807, when Municipal independence was conferred upon the Towns, invidious privileges regarding taxation were abolished, monopolies and restrictions gave place to a more liberal system of local and general management, and a more equitable Administration of Justice. The foundations of a system of Universal Conscription, and general if not compulsory, Education, had been laid in the last Century by Frederick the Great, and were vigorously pushed to completion at this time under the stress of a great necessity. These Agencies have contributed, along with other reforms, to be more particularly noticed hereafter, to develop the latent energies of the population in all directions. The eight Provinces of the Kingdom, Prussia proper, Posen, Silesia, Pomerania, Brandenburg, Saxony, Westphalia, and Rhineland, were about this time subdivided into districts; these last contained many Departments, which were either made up of Townships or Rural Communes. These Unions, Departments, and Provinces have each their representative Councils, consisting of privileged Landholders, representatives of the old Nobility, and of elected Representatives of the Departments and Town Communities. The holders of privileged estates, who exercised vast Judicial and Administrative Powers under the Fuedal System, have been allowed to retain a considerable predominance in these Provincial and Local Councils, as also in the Upper House of the Legislature, but their other powers were destroyed by the Agricultural Legislation in the commencement of this Century. These few remarks upon the general course of Prussian Reform will now prepare the reader to follow intelligently the great work of Liberation achieved in connection with the Agricultural Economy of the country, which falls within the more immediate scope of our present inquiry.

A brief survey must here be taken of the condition of landed Property, and its distribution between the different classes of the population interested in the ownership and cultivation of the soil. The Feudal conception of land was that it determined the status of the owner, and too often, the land became the unchanging subject of fixed ownership, and did not follow the changing lot of the Cultivator, or of the Proprietor. Land in large areas, and bounded by the Natural limits of rivers or mountains, was held in common by entire communities of settlers, and this common right was affirmed by an interchange of fallow with cultivated land after every five or six years. In course of time, the cultivated land was broken up into smaller lots for the larger sections of the Tribe, and these subsequently became subjects of individual rights, while the pastures and forests were held in common as before, and, when the Feudal System was organized, became the Demesne Lands of the Sovereign, or Manorial Lands of the Barons.

The Western Provinces of Prussia, lying to the West of the Weser river, being early colonised by more civilized Dutch and Flemish Settlers, gave more scope to the position and independence of individual Proprietors of farms, while Silesia, Posen, and Pomerania retained more exclusively the old organization of Village Lands, being owned in common by entire communities of Cultivators. In these Provinces, the land was divided periodically into lots, which were redistributed after intervals of seven years, while the pasture lands were used in common. On this condition of things, the Feudal System of the middle Ages impressed its stamp and effected great modifications. Its general effect was to destroy or subordinate the ancient rights of small farmers, as also of Village Communities, to the dominion of the Lords of Manors, who monopolized all the profits and privileges of the lands included in their domains, partly by gift of the Crown, partly by forcible dispossession, and partly by the imposition of hard conditions of military and personal Services, subsequently commuted into payments of tithes and other burdens of serfdom or slavery. The cultivating Peasant forefeited or surrendered his personal freedom, and became a fixture of the soil he cultivated, valuable only for the services he rendered. He could not rise superior to his low status, and the aristocratic Noble could never forfeit his high caste. Custom, as settled by general assent or judicial decree, was the only restraint to these exactions of the Barons, and gradually Rural Society crystallized under its force into disinct factors. The personal services were commuted into money payments, but the nobility continued to have the monopoly of the lands, which they let to the Peasantry to cultivate on most disadvantageous terms. The original distribution between the Eastern and Western Provinces thus reappeared under the steadying influence of custom. The powers of Landlords were less onerous, and the sense of property, at the best a more or less limited hereditary, or leasehold usufruct, and the rights of equal succession to the Peasants' farm, were more distinctly and freely recongnized in the Western than in the Eastern Districts. But as a general feature, the old Customary Law was nearly effaced by the growth and abuses of the Feudal System. So that about the middle of the last Century, when Prussia was blessed with a capable Ruler in the person of Frederick the Great, the largest proportion of Peasant-estates were subject to the crushing and unquestioned dominion of the Nobles, and their highest interest in these lands was a more or less limited usufruct. Only a very small proportion of estates were Free-holds, or customary copy-holds, but even here the owner's powers of alienation were very restricted. Such was the miserable condition of the Peasantry in the last century, and we have now to trace the gradual steps by which the Enfranchisement of many millions of the Peasants, and the bestowal upon them of full Proprietory Rights, were achieved by the genius of Stein and Hardenburg in the early part of this century.

With rare statesmanship, they grasped the fact that the essential condition of rescuing the Country from its miserable helplessness was to effect a radical change in the relationship of the soil with the person who cultivated it. They laid hold of the principle of Individual and Independent Property in the soil as the cardinal point of their Reform, and subordinated all other considerations to this main end. In the words of the first Edict issued by Stein, the great underlying principle all reform was "to remove whatever had hitherto hindered the individual from obtaining that degree of well-being which he was capable of reaching by exertions, according to the best of his ability." This Edict, for the first time in Prussian Legislation, recognised the fact that land was made for man, and promised to encourage all facilities for the acquisition of absolute ownership, and the free use of the land. As a commencement, it was resolved that all personal Servitude should be abolished before 1810, *i.e.*, within three years from the promulgation of the Edict. The shackles thus fell off from the bodies and spirits of many millions of human Beings, and this inspiration of new energy helped the subsequent work of Reform. In 1810, Stein, the author of the Edict of 1807, was banished by the Emperor Napoleon, and Hardenburg became Chancellor of the Kingdom and his Edicts moderated the sweeping force of the first Edict by the adoption of a more cautious

Policy, which effected the same end gradually, without the risk of disruption and violence. A gradual abolition of Services and Rights of Common was shown to be possible by these famous Edicts for the "Promotion of National Agriculture" and "for Regulating the Relations of Landlords and Peasants." This legislation of 1807 and 1810 was subsequently carried out by numerous supplementary Edicts, and by the inauguration of plans for subsidizing, with the help of State Funds, undertakings for the promotion of agricultural prosperity which were beyond the means of the Peasant Proprietors so freed from their Feudal Bondage.

We shall now address ourselves to a closer consideration of the methods followed out by the Prussian Government in giving effect to these great Edicts, which abolished Serfdom or personal Services, consolidated the Peasant's common Rights, and encouraged credit Organizations. The guiding principle in regard to the first of these changes was that all that is common is hurtful to the individual, and that perfect freedom of agricultural orgnanization constituted the strength of the Rural population, and of the Nation at large. To abolish all encroachments on personal freedom,—to remove restrictions on rights of property in land,—to relieve the Peasants from being the sole class liable to the payment of State charges,—to buy out the rights of the Lords of Manors over their

Peasant Serfs' services,—and turn these Serfs into free Proprietors,—to commute the Real charges and services,—to consolidate rights of common,—and to facilitate the improvement of farms and other landed properties—these were the manifold methods by which effect was given to the Edicts of 1807 and 1810. A brief notice of the Legislation in each of these directions will illustrate the greatness of the work done in Prussia.

Personal servitude was abolished in 1807, and all servitude attached to the land was made to cease from 1810. Real Charges, which constituted the conditions on which the Peasants held their lands, were not abolished at this early epoch. By the old customary law, the power of eviction was unhampered, except by the condition that the Landlord should find a new Peasant for the cultivation of the soil. When absolute freedom of alienation was allowed, there was a great danger that the Landlords would buy out or evict their old Tenants, and retain the vacated lands in their own hands. The Edict of 1807 accordingly restrained the freedom, with this condition in favour of all Peasants who had any hereditary or particular interest in the lands, that these lands could not be absorbed except by the free consent of the parties. If the Lord had satisfied all the claims of the Peasant possessors, he was permitted to convert such lands into large Peasant Farms. The Edict of

1811 introduced a further modification. In consequence of the operation of the former Edict, two parties, were recognized as having co-equal interest in land, the Lord entitled to the real charges and services, but burdened with an obligation not to absorb Peasant, properties, and the necessity of finding a cultivator for them, and the Hereditary or leasehold Peasant burdened with the charges and servitudes mentioned above. If the parties agreed to a mutual compromise, the State gave full liberty to the Landlords to carry out the agreement. The rights of Landlords to be compensated were (1) the right of property, (2) claim for services, (3) the dues in money and kind, (4) farm stock and (5) real services. The rights of the Peasant which had to be valued for compensation purposes were (1) claim for support in misfortune, (2) the claim for wood and forest produce, (3) obligation on the Lord to build and repair buildings, (4) obligations on the Lord to pay taxes, (5) and certain rights of grazing. As some of these rights were not capable of valuation, the parties were left to arrange their differences amicably, otherwise the State intervened. A balance was struck between these mutual rights and obligations, and as this balance was against the Peasant Proprietor, a commutation was effected by the Peasant's foregoing one-third of a Free or Copy-held Holding and one half of the other Holdings to his Lord, after which both parties were left free to act as their interests dictated. This commutation was also made payable in the shape of a rent charge. In valuing the interests of the Peasant, the farm buildings were not included. Money commutations were not thought of because the Peasants had no money to spare, while the land in their possession had little value. To check any sudden disturbance of properties, the liberty of commuting was at first, allowed to holders of hereditary and taxable properties, and was subsequently extended to smaller farms. In 1815, it was ordered that rents in kind and money rents should be extinguished, or made terminable by their possessors, who were permitted to receive twenty-five years' value by way of redemption. In 1849, a Commission, composed of Rent Receivers and Rent Payers in equal numbers, was appointed, who fixed the form of commutation, and the rates and prices so fixed were made obligatory on all parties. It was in these various ways that the benefits of personal freedom, free use and free transfer of land, the abolition of all personal distinctions of rank and status as regulating the capacity for holding lands, and the abolition of the rights of pre-emption, were secured, and restrictions on absorption of Peasant Properties were gradually lessened. It is to be noted that, as was the case later on in Russia, no compensation was allowed for the abolition of personal servitudes. The Serfs on Crown Lands were similarly set free by an Act of State. All restrictions in the interests of State Policy. such as the requisition of sanction for alienation upon the transfer of land were abolished by the Edict of 1861. Restrictions as to the use of Private Forests were similarly done away with. It was this last Edict of 1861 that sanctioned the formation of Agricultural Associations of which so much use has been made in subsequent years. Of course, it is not to be supposed, that there were no alternations of Policy in respect of this liberal and far-reaching Legislation. There were numerous examples of retrograde Amendments in 1815 and 1851, but on the whole the Policy of converting Peasant Holdings into Absolute Properties was honestly carried out, till in 1860 the final Legislation on the subject completed the work commenced sixty years before, and abolished all vestiges of Feudal Restraints upon the powers both of Landlords and Peasants.

The commutation of Real Charges was a more difficult problem, and the State had to intervene by appointing experts to act as arbitrators, and fixing official prices and rates of compensation when parties would not agree. When the Rent Charge so commuted did not exceed two-thirds of the value of the land, its payment was undertaken by the Rent Charge Banks. If it exceeded two-thirds the Bank authorities might refuse advances. The arrangements for the settlement undertaken in the early part of the century were carried out by an allotment of portions of Peasants' Holdings to the Landlords, varying from one-third to half of the lands in their possession. The Legislation of 1850 and subsequent years interposed the machinery of Courts and Arbitrators to determine money compensations for abolished Rent Charges, and provided the machinery of State-subsidized Rent Charge Banks to help the Peasant to liquidate his liabilities at his convenience, without any injustice to the Landlord. Of course, these great Reforms were not carried out all at once throughout the Country. Each Province was dealt with separately after due consideration of its circumstances.

The abolition of the Rights of Common and Forest Rights was secured on a principle similar to that which was applied so effectively in respect of Lands, Servitudes, and Rent Charges. The interest of every sharer in these Rights of Common was valued, and to the owner of the same an equivalent piece of land was allotted, and when the land was insufficient for such a purpose, a Rent Charge was created in his favour, and these Rent Charges were subsequently commuted at twenty or twenty-five years' purchase. In carrying out these arrangements, parties were encouraged to come to a settlement by which, as far as possible, their Holdings would be consolidated, and the views of a majority of the interested parties were allowed to prevail, in respect of such Consolidation or Exchange arrangements. This principle of subordinating individual to public rights and conveniences formed the basis of the compulsory Drainage and Irrigation Schemes of Improvement, as also of Forest growth and Conservancy which on a grand scale were at this time undertaken by Government, while smaller works were promoted by compulsory or voluntary Associations of interested Landowners. When the State did not undertake improvements, it, at first, subsidized them by handsome advances of Public Loans, and more than fifty Lakhs of Rupees were advanced in this way in seventeen years (1850—1867). The payments made in satisfaction of these demands as they came in, were again advanced by the Department of Agriculture, which had the charge of these Funds, for helping similar fresh undertakings. Besides these direct subsidies, more recently the Prussian Government has sought to create a spirit of self-help by securing to such advances, when made by private individuals for purposes of improvements, paramount rights even against mortgagees, for purposes of recovery, and has also empowered such Associations to issue mortgage Debentures, which were at first secured by a minimum State guarantee. This condition, however, has of late been dispensed with as no longer necessary. The Land Tax, which pressed heavily in former times, was also established on a fair and certain basis, being two to four per cent. on the value of the net yield, the incidence of the Tax on Land being made equal to the weight of taxation on other kinds of property. It is no wonder that, under such stimulus, real Credit Institutions, Mortgage Debenture Banks, Rent Charge Banks, and Self-help Associations of all sorts, were promoted all over the country, providing the machinery and the funds by which the great national aims of the Legislature were facilitated by a free exchange of Capital, with the least possible risk and the largest possible returns.

This brief summary of the Land Legislation of Prussia will not be complete without some reference to statistical figuers, showing how far, during the last sixty years, that these great Agencies of Enfranchisement have been in operation, the work of Reform has been completed. The total acreage of the kingdom of Prussia has been estimated to be seventy-three millions of acres, and out of this vast total, nearly forty-five millions of acres of land were in some form or other brought under the influence of this special Legislation. Nearly thirteen Lakhs of persons have commuted Team of Hand Services, by consenting to land allotments or making money payments. This change alone represents a saving of the labours of the Peasant class for thirty millions of days. In respect of Rights of Common, seventeen Lakhs of owners consolidated or settled their Right of Common over forty-one and a half million acres during the whole of this period of sixty years. Only one-twentieth of this work remained to be done in 1867. The tendency towards dismemberment has been thus counter-balanced by the encouragement towards consolidation, and in the end it has been found that the danger of excessive sub-division of Land has been avoided. In 1860 fifteen per cent. of the total area of sixty-five and a half millions of culturable land belonged to the Crown, the State Forests, or to the Church, or to municipalities; forty-four per cent., or twenty-eight Millions to non-peasant Proprietors, *i.e.*, the holders of large estates; thirty-five per cent., or twenty-four millions, were Team Farms of Peasant Proprietors, and five per cent. or three and a half millions, were smaller Holdings. The aggregate average of Peasant Properties is thus nearly the same as that of large Properties. The transfer of land effected by the Disfranchisement Legislation may thus be said to have roughly divided the land equally between the rich Landlords and the poor Free men. There are, now about fifteen thousand owners of larger estates, and more than four Lakhs of Middle-class Proprietors, who own from twenty to two hundred acres. There are, further, fourteen Lakhs of Peasant Proprietors with only sixty thousand Tenants of superior Holders, and about twenty Lakhs of Agricultural

Labourers. The proportion of Rural to Urban population in Prussia is seventy per cent. of the former to thirty per cent. of the latter. Heavy indebtedness. the attendant evil of small Proprietors, has been found to prevail in Prussia as in other countries, though the redeeming feature about Prussian Economy, is, that this indebtedness has been due chiefly to the efforts of the people to liberate and improve their Holdings, and it has a tendency to diminish, as the charges created by the Land Legislation and by loans borrowed for improvement are being gradually redeemed. Taking the value of landed estates at seven hundred millions, the amount of mortgage debt was three hundred and seventy-five millions, of which about twenty-five millions were represented by the Loans made by Rent Charge and Debenture Banks, and the remaining three hundred and fifty millions were due to Private Creditors. The proportion of Mortgage Debt to the value of land was formerly two-thirds in place of the present proportion of one half. The figures given above, include the debts due from the Privileged Holdings as also from Peasant Properties. Peasant Properties are, in fact, in many parts of the country less heavily charged than Privileged Estates.

In the words of a Parliamentary Blue-book, from which much of this information has been gathered, it may be stated, in concluding this review of Prussian Legislation, that the Prussian Nation, in the early part of the century, found itself burdened by a cumbersome Feudal System, and writhing in the agonies of Serfdom. Prussian Statesmen, accordingly, set themselves to a manifold task, which in sixty years was fully accomplished, the task of converting the Feudal Serf into a Free Proprietor, of removing the restrictions which the Privileged Owners of land felt so heavily, and making them unencumbered Lords of their properties, of abolishing all the confusion of Tenures, Charges, and Services, of relaxing Entails, of commuting Rights of Common, and of encouraging improvements with State help and State compulsion, and facilitating the free exchange of land. And all these great Reforms, have been carried out without imposing any serious burden on the State's resources, without any violent disruption of the economical relations of different Classes of Society, and without the shock of Revolution or internecine class struggles.

Here in India, we sadly need the help of similar statesmanship. With a growing Population, and limited resources, the struggle for existence is already being felt, as a strain on the Social System. Meanwhile, the experiments that have been undertaken to remedy these disorders are not suggested by any broad view of the future, or any just consideration for vested rights. We refer, especially, in these remarks to the proposed Legislation in the Lower Provinces of Bengal and Behar, which present the largest analogies to the condition of Prussia in the early part of the Century. There, as here, the old customary rights of property have suffered a depression from long disuse, and the rise of a moneyed and privileged class of Landlords, who have invested in land on the faith of solemn pledges, and are naturally anxious to turn their bargain to their best advantage. This class often press heavily, as in Behar, upon the Peasant majority of the population. There can be no doubt that remedial Legislation is urgently required to check these evils, and, quite independently of the saving Clause contained in the Law of 1793, which extended the Permanent Settlement to these Provinces, there can be no doubt that the Government, in its capacity as Sovereign, has every right to undertake Legislation intended to remove admitted and general grievances. We cannot, however, approve of the direction and spirit of the Legislation embodied in the proposals which will soon come on for discussion before the Supereme Legislative Council, in respect of this Bengal Tenancy Bill. The proposed Legislation is based on lines which are diametrically opposed to the principles we have described above, as having influenced the great Prussian Chancellors. While the one sought to disencumber Land, and encourage the growth of absolute property both in the Landlord class and in the Peasantry, the proposals embodied in the Tenancy Bill are intended to increase these mutual encumbrances and the existing complexity of rights and interests. While the Prussian Legislation was guided by the principle of allowing compensation for the abolition of all Rights, Services, and Charges which were not of the nature of personal slavery, the Bengal Proposals reject all idea of compensation. While the Prussian Statesmen have tried their best to minimize executive interference in the settlement of class relations, the theory, underlying the Bengal Bill, is that the State Executive and Judicial machinery must prescribe and regulate every little incident of the relations between the Owners and Tenants of land. The only result, and, to some extent, the intended result, will be that the existing confusion will be still more confounded, class will be set against class, the sacredness of former pledges will be violated, the Landlords ruined without compensation, and reduced to the class of Rent-receiving Pensioners, and the Rayats taught to look more and more to the State as their sole Landlord, without acquiring the training necessary to raise them to a sense of their position. We shall try to make our meaning more plain in the sequel of this paper. We shall only premise here, with a view to prevent all possible misunderstanding, that we do not side with the optimist advocates of the existing condition of things. We freely allow that an urgent Reform, and a radical Reform, is called for, but our contention is that the lines on which the Legislature proposes to proceed are radically mistaken, and will never lead to any real settlement of the present disputes.

The first portion of the Tenancy Bill is devoted to the consideration of Khamar and Rayati lands. What it seeks to do in this connection is not only to register existing Rights and Tenures, but to stimulate the growth of Rayatwari Holdings, and to contract the area of Khamar land, that is, the land in the actual possession of the proprietor, and not let by him to a Ryot for cultivation. The Law is to presume that all land not shown to be Khamar is Rayati land. The Landlord's powers over Khamar lands are absolute, while in regard to Rayati lands, his powers will be greatly controlled by the proposed Legislation. Even when Rayati land is forefeited for default in the payment of Revenue, and bought in by the Landlord, it cannot be divested of its Rayati character, unless the Landlord keeps it in his own hands. The moment he lets it to a Tenant, its Rayati character revives by force of law. So far as the record of existing rights is concerned, we see no reason to object to the proposals of the Government. But, this exaggerated value set upon the reduction of Khamar land, and the creation of new Rayati lands, appears to us to be thoroughly wrong in principle. It is true, some customary incident of ancient times is pleaded as an excuse for the revival of this Policy. But circumstances have so altered since then, that its revival cannot fail to be mischievous. Our own view of the matter is that, while respecting all existing ancient rights, there should be no artificial discouragement to the growth of absolute property in land. If the Rayati land is insufficient to meet the existing wants of an increasing population, by all means encourage the Ryots to buy Khamar lands for consideration, by paying compensation regulated on a system of Real Charges, and extended over a long term, to the Landlord class, who have invested in land on the faith of a strict observance of their purchased Rights. Rayati land pre-supposes a limitation and complexity of Rights, while the tendency of all remedial Legislation should be to make as many Holdings, Khamar or Jerait, as possible. Land gains in every way, and loses nothing by being made the absolute property of the owner. The Prussian Legislation was based on this principle, and we cannot but strongly deprecate the suggestion that a contrary Policy should be inaugurated in Bengal at this day. The proportion of Khamar land is actually so small, being less than ten per cent., that it appears to us to be extremely unfortunate that this apple of discord should be wantonly thrown as a temptation in the way of the agricultural population of Bengal and Behar.

The next two chapters of the Bill relate to the rights of subordinate Tenure-holders and are open to the same objection, that the Bill seeks to make much more complex the relations of parties in place of simmplifying them, and allows relief to one class at the expense of another without providing compensation. It is well-known that the Permanent Zamindari Settlement of 1793 was made on the basis of exacting nine-tenths of the average Revenue of the estate as Land Tax, and allowing one-tenth to the Zamindar for the expenses of collection, and the risk and responsibility he incurred on that account. The Zamindars created subordinate Tenure on the same principle of recovering a fixed and a much larger proportion of the Revenue. This reservation, it is now proposed to limit by fixing thirty per cent. as the limit of the profits of a subordinate Tenure-holder, which should not be encroached upon by any enhancement of the payment claimable by the Zamindar from him. In the case of Jangalbari, or waste lands generally reclaimed at the expense of the Zamindar, this limit is fixed at twenty per cent. Over and above these provisions, it is proposed to rule that no enhancement shall at once double the former rate, and that no enhancement shall take place except at the interval of ten years. At every stage of the process, the Civil Court's intervention is made compulsory, and in the matter of registering these tenure rights and their transfers, the Collector's authority is interposed at every step. It has been estimated by competent authorities that there are in all about eleven and one-third Lakhs of Tenure-holders against two and a half Lakhs of Zamindars and Revenue-freeholders, and that they represent an income of eight Crores of Rupees as against thirteen Crores, which is the income of Zamindars and owners of Revenue-free Lands. These Tenure-holders are thus a very important class, and are well able to take care of their own interests. By their education and intelligence, they are far removed from the state of helpless dependence, which to a large extent is pleaded as a justification for the active interference of the Government on behalf of the Ryots, or other cultivators of the soil. The change, if necessary, in their condition should have been in the direction of enabling these classes to become full Proprietors by private arrangement with the Zamindars, or by permitting compulsory purchase on the basis of a fair and equitable compensation. A balance of mutual liabilities and advantages ought to be struck, and according as that balance turns in favour of the Zamindar or the Tenure-holder, a money payment should be made in a lump sum, or a Rent Charge spread over years, or an Allotment made of an equivalent portion of land, followed thereafter by an extinction of all the inconveniences of subordination and division of interests and rights. Any one of these arrangements would certainly have a more satisfactory result in the general advancement of the country, than the plan of tinkering with existing rights in the assumed interests of one class, to the prejudice of the Zamindars, as at present proposed. The perpetual interposition of Civil Courts and Revenue Authorities can only result in paralyzing private efforts, and increasing the sense of dependence on the State as the only regulator of private rights, than which nothing can in the end prove more prejudicial to all classes concerned.

By far the most important portion of the Bill relates to the position of the Ryots. The evident and avowed intention of the proposed Legislation is stated to be the creation of a large class of what are called Occupancy Ryots. The old Khoodkhast Ryot, no doubt, did possess customary rights and interests in Land long before the Permanent Settlement was made, and he was not in principle subject to arbitrary enhancement and eviction. His position was seriously damaged by the Settlement, which, in order to secure the prompt payment of the Revenue under the Sunset Law, armed Zamindars with extraordinary powers, and these powers made serious encroachments on the Ryot's independence. The Khoodkhast Ryots were like the Mirasdars of the Deccan. Just as in consequence of the Bombay Survey Settlement, Mirasdars have disppeared, and the old *Upari* Tenants have been turned into Occupancy-holders, the old Khoodkhast Ryots were by force of circumstances transformed to a large extent into Tenants-at-will. After a long period of depression,

Act X. of 1859 first conferred Occupancy Rights on all Ryots who occupied any particular Holding for twelve years at a fixed rental, and it is now proposed to confer this Occupancy Right on all Ryots who are residents in the village for a term of twelve years. The status of the holder determines the status of the Holding, and confers on the land a privileged character, thus reversing all past traditions and invariable practice, by which the Tenure of the land regulated the status of the cultivator. The Bill further proposes to confer special privileges upon this class. Their lands will be heriditable as well as freely transferable and they may also sublet the land without restriticons. Their rents can be raised, but the limitations are so many and so complicated, that private contract will cease to regulate these enhancements in the majority of cases, and the interposition of Settlement Officers and Civil Courts will become a *sine qua non* at every step. The occupancy Ryot's rent cannot be increased except after a resort to Courts ; he cannot be ejected even for default in payment, except by a similar interposition. The right of pre-emption, left to the Landlord as a counterpoise to these large powers, is similarly clogged with conditons, so that it can only be exercised with safety after a resort to the Courts. The very price is to be fixed by the Courts if parties do not agree, as they will not in the majority of cases. Even when the Landlord buys in the land, the moment he lets it to a third party, that party acquires the status of a Ryot as freely as though he had succeeded by transfer from the former occupant. In regard to enhancements of rent, it is provided that no rent can exceed one fifth of the gross produce; that no enhancement can double the rent; that no enhancement can take place except by a contract approved of by the Revenue Collector, or by a decree of Court; and the Revenue Collector is to determine the rates of land up to which enhancements may be made, and these rates are to be accepted by the Civil Courts as conclusive in all cases. An increase of rent claimed by reason of a general rise of prices is to be shared half and half, provided the half is not more than the proportion of the rise of prices to old prices. No rate can be doubled at any single enhancement, and an enhancement once made must hold good for ten years.

These are some of the provisions intended to protect the interests of the Ryot classes. Our objection to the change is not based on any indifference to the interests of the Ryots. These Ryots number more than ten millions in all and pay a rental of twenty-one millions to the Zemindars and Tenure-holders, and, as we have said, they hold ninety per cent. of the lands owned by the Zemindars. Such stupendous interests claim all the protection which farsighted statesmanship can confer on them. Our principal contention is that the Landlord's rights, sanctioned by usage and by law, will be adversely affected by these changes without providing any compensation to these classes, and that the permanent peace and advancement of the Country will not be promoted by provisions which at every step set class against class, and compel resort to the Courts, or to the Collector's agency. The interest and ownership in land will still continue to be as divided as before between quarrelsome partners, and no real improvement will take place. Our own proposal is that, as far as possible, the entanglement of private relations should be simplified, and the occasions of conflict and sub-divided ownership should be minimized. We would confer full Proprietory rights on the Ryots of whatever degree who hold Rayati lands, *i.e.*. non-Khamar, but these full rights should extend only over a limited portion of the estate so held, and will have to be purchased for a proper equivalent in the shape of resigning in the Landlords favour all rights over the other portion not so reserved. The liabilities and rights of the Ryots and the Landlords must be duly weighed one against the other, and on the principle of a sliding scale, we would apportion the land between the two classes, assigning one and the larger part absolutely to the Ryot, another to the Landlord, and if a balance is still left due, we would provide compensation in money Rent Charges, by which means all conflict wlll cease, and both the Ryot and Landlord will be made to feel increased interest

20

in their absolute properties. The more practical question relates to the way in which this liberation of the land from its present entanglements can be brought about. Our own proposals are based on the recorded experience of similar undertakings which have been successfully carried out in other countries. In the first instance, we would encourage the redemption of rent and other charges paid by the Ryots to the Zamindars, and Revenue-free and Tenure-holders. The present value of the payments made by them to these classes comes to about twenty-one Crores. These twenty-one Crores paid to the Zamindars and Tenure-holders are, on an average one-fifth of the gross value of the annual agricultural wealth of Bengal, which has been roughly estimated by Major Baring—now Lord Cromer—at one hundred Crores. As there are about ten millons of Ryots, this represents an average gross production of one hundred Rupees for each cultivating Ryot's family, out of which he has to pay at present twenty Rupees or one-fifth share. Estimated in acres, and taking the yield per acre to be ten Rupees, it follows that each Ryot cultivates about ten acres, and pays two Rupees an acre out of a produce worth ten Rupees per acre. In the case of the Occupancy Ryot, we would divide his Holding into three parts, make two of these parts over to him in absolute right, and hand over the third as absolute Khamar land to the Landlord. In the case of other Ryots we would divide the Holdings half and half. As this arrangement will not settle the account of their mutual rights and liabilities, the balance will have to be made up by money Rent Charges. The Ryot, left in possession of his one half or one-third Holding, should be required to pay his old rent on the reduced Holding for a period of thirty or forty years, so as to repay balance of the purchase money with interest. If the parties cannot be made to agree to this slow method, the Government could easily render them this help by advancing the money wherewith the Ryots might be enabled to purchase out their Landlords' claims. The capitalized value of half of twenty-one Crores will be about two hundred Crores, and that of one-third of twenty-one Crores will be one hundred and forty Crores. The Government could safely float any loan at four per cent., and pay off the Zamindars for the loss of their rights over the reserved portions of the Ryots' Holdings, and recoup themselves by levying six per cent. interest from the Ryots for a term of thirty-five years. Purchase on these terms will be compulsory, and the Landlords will more easily be reconciled to it than consent to see themselves deprived of a valuable property without any compensation, as the present Bill proposes to do. Thrifty Ryots might be allowed the option of redemption at an earlier period by the inducement of a considerable reduction in the total capitalized value. This latter plan has been successfully adopted in Russia, in respect of the Serfs who received one-third of their master's lands in Free-hold right. The other plan would set of the mutual liabilities and rights of the two classes, and according as the balance inclined in the Zamindars' favour, an equivalent allotment of land made once for all, or a Rent Charge created for a term of years with a provision for a Sinking Fund, would have to be arranged. This was the principal feature of the Prussian plan of Enfranchisement, and it has this advantage that no liability is thereby thrown on the Government. Even under the Russian plan, the liability of the Government is only nominal, as it only intervenes in place of private money-lenders because its credit is exceptionally good, and its powers of levy are proportionately more effective. In this way we could achieve the liberation of the Ryots in Bengal in a generation or two without any violence to vested rights, and our plan would above all train and educate the people by a slow discipline of thrift to retain their newly acquired status. The present proposals of the Bill simply confiscate the interests of one class to benefit another, and can only be justified on Socialistic or Communistic principles.

The elements of national prosperity are wanting in a country whose principal resource is Agriculture, and that agriculture is in the hands of a thriftless and poverty-stricken Peasantry, who are weighted down with heavy charges, and whose life and labours are not cheered by the charm and strength inspired by a sense of property. If this country sadly wants a proud and independent Yeomanry as the backbone of its strength and prosperity, it no less equally needs the leading and the light of Propertied men. A complete divorce from land of those who cultivate it is a national evil, and no less an evil is it to find one dead level of small Farmers all over the land. High and petty farming, with an upper ten thousand of the holders of large landed estates, and a vast mass of peasant farmers, this mixed constitution of rural Society is necessary to secure the stability and progress of the Country. The Bill under consideration robs Peter to benefit Paul, and at the same time, it creates an hostility of interest, where entire union should prevail, and it clogs the land with a variety of interests and ownership, and entangles mutual relations in such a manner as to drive both parties constantly into Civil Courts. We know our suggestion is so far out of the lines within which the discussion has been hitherto conducted, that it is not likely to attract favourable attention on the part of the extreme advocates either of the Ryots or the Zamindars. Our perception, however, of the perilous nature of an obstinate persistence in a *laissez faire* policy is so keen and our disapprobation of the revolutionary proposals now made is so radical, that we have deemed it necessary to scatter this seed on the field of discussion, and wait to see if it falls on good soil. A settlement based on the plan advocated by us will successfully accomplish all the ends that the Government has in view, and the Zamindars will not be in a worse position than they are now. They will get full compensation for the loss of their rights over one portion of their estates, and their dominion over the other half will be of a character which could never hereafter be questioned. On the other hand, if the present Bill passes into law, the restraints on the Landlord's power in the matter of enhancements and evictions, in the levy of rent, in the claim for improvements, and disturbance, will soon succeed in gradually lowering the status of the Zamindars to the level of pension receivers. Such a state of things will keep up and intensify all the elements of strife, and just as the riots and disturbances in Eastern Bengal have paved the way for the present legislation, further disorders will suggest more drastic and retrograde remedies in the future. It is, above all, important to put an end to this irritation, and this can only be done by the adoption of one or other of the alternative plans of settlement which we have ventured to propose. Let each man's land be as much his absolute property as his house or clothes, and things will settle down themselves agreeably to the interests of all parties concerned. The British Government in India, powerful as it undoubtedly is, cannot command the power to retrace its steps in such matters, and throw the Country backwards a hundred years. This attempt to revolutionize in a retrograde direction is bound to fail, and will fail only to suggest a further repetition of the same unsuited remedies.

To sum up the points in which our proposal possesses undoubted advantages over the present Bill,—

(1) Both would effect a Redistribution of Land, but while the Bill would make this allotment without compensation, our proposals are based on the grant of adequate compensation to the parties who might be deprived of their existing rights ; (2) while the present Bill would perpetuate the existing conflict, and create fresh confusion and complication of interests in Land, our proposal would simplify this entanglement, as far as may be possible ; (3) while the Bill would create an artificially defined class of subordinate Tenants tempted on all occasions to throw off their subjection, and a Landlord class hemmed in on all sides by inconvenient obligations, we would create an entirely independent Peasantry trained by thrift to prize its independence, and at the same time confer an absolute property in their lands on the Zamindars and Tenure-holders ; (4) while the Bill would drive both classes into Civil Courts and the Kacheries of Revenue and Settlement Officers at every

step, we would simply lock up the doors of these coercive Agencies by taking away the usual inducements for strife and dissension, and make Custom and Contract the measure of the obligations binding one class to another, instead of a harassing and penal Law ; (5) while the Bill would create fresh Occupancies, and destroy Khamar land, we would increase the latter, and raise the former once for all, to their full status ; (6) while the Bill would in the end cover the land with one dead level of pauper Tenants, we would ensure their more hopeful existence, aspiring always to attain a higher standard of comfort, along side of a rich Middle and Upper Class of great Territorial Lords.

One word more before we conclude. The present Bill makes no provision for the rights of the Government Tenants in Khas Mahals. There is no indication that the Government is prepared to bind itself by the restrictions it so generously imposes upon Zamindars to receive less than one-fifth of the gross produce as rent, or to refrain from ousting Tenants without resort to the Courts, or from doubling the rent at once, or to pay for improvements, or give ten years' rent as compensation for disturbance. The condition of the Ryots in these Khas Mahals does not compare favourably with the Zamindars' Ryots in Eastern Bengal. The Ryots' advocates in Bengal should certainly not content themselves with partial Legislation, which makes it possible for Government to refrain from dealing towards itself the same strict measure of equity which it proposes to deal to others. And as we are on this part of the subject, we may well ask whether, under the periodical Assessments, the State Landlord is prepared to concede as against itself the same measures of restriction and moderation which it is so anxious to provide for the Tenantry of the Zamindars. Here in this Presidency, Government doubles and trebles, in many cases quadruples, the Assessment at a leap, the Assessment has to be paid punctually on pain of forfeiture of all interest in land, there is no limit that the Assessment in all cases shall not exceed one-fifth of the gross produce, and no payment is made for improvements or disturbance when a Ryot is ousted from his ancestral lands. In all these respects, the Revenue Administration in other parts of India must be put on a more equitable footing before Government can with clean hands ask the Zamindars in Bengal to surrender the Proprietory Rights guaranteed to them by one hundred years' continuous possession, and on the faith of which most of the settled estates have changed hands to such an extent, that the idea of depriving the present race of landlords of their advantages, without compensation for the loss thus thrust on them, savours very much of a Communistic and Latter-day Saints' Revolution, than which, in a country circumstanced as India is, nothing can be more disastrous and perilous alike to the people and to their Rulers.

XII.

THE LAW OF LAND SALE IN BRITISH INDIA.*

THE question of the Law of Land Sale in British India has been the subject of a standing controversy for the last twenty-five years and more, and the new Act for the Relief of the Deccan Agriculturists has raised the subject from one of speculation into a matter-of-fact reality in its relation to this Presidency. Prior to this period, the tendency of British Indian Legislation and Administration had been generally to assimilate the Laws and Institutions of India with the latest innovations in Europe. Usury Laws were abolished in 1855, because Mr. Bentham and others had denounced them in England, and the English Legislature had removed those restrictions on the universal freedom of Contracts. Local Cesses and Octroi Duties were abolished not only in British India, but also throughout the Native States, becauss they interfered with the freedom of Trade. Inam Commissions were set up, and so-called Settlement operations were carried on with a view to equalise taxation on all classes without distinction. It

* Published in 1880.

was a part of this same system that led Government to abolish the old Mirasi Tenure, to abolish the Joint Liability of the village, and substitute in its place the Survey Occupant's Tenure, and when the first Settlements were introduced, much credit was taken for conferring on the Ryots the most unrestricted power of transferring their interests in land. This tendency to innovation and the levelling up of Oriental Institutions to the requirements of the most radical theorists in Europe was in its full swing before the Mutinies, and the Annexation Policy and the Denial of Adoptions were only the Political phases of this same spirit. The fearful blaze of that period of troubles opened the eyes of the ruling Authorities to the great mistake that had been committed, when the Conservative traditions of the first conquests, the policy associated with the memories of Elphinstone, Munro, Malcolm, and Metcalfe, was given up for new-fangled ways of thought and revolutionary action, recommended by men like Bird and Thomason in the North-Western Provinces, and in our Presidency by Goldsmid, Hart, Cowper, and Willoughby.

With the reversal of the Political Maxims which had till then obtained sway in regard to Native States, a similar reaction was for the first time, seen to influence what may be called the Home Administration of the Empire. In consequence of the law which made land, both ancestral and acquired, freely alienable for the debts of its owner, a great change was slowly but steadily taking place in the status and position of the Proprietory Classes. All over India, lands were sold for arrears of Revenue by the Revenue Officers, and for decreed Debts, both secured and unsecured, by the Civil Courts, through the coercive process of Sales, and this change was visibly tending to the impoverishment of the old Proprietors and transferring the lands into the hands of strangers and non-residents, who generally belonged to the mercantile and trading classes, and bought up the land for no other attraction than its character as a paying investment. This change of possession had excited some attention even before the Mutinies began, especially in the North-Western Provinces, but at that time the Government of that Province expressed its inability to do anything more than to watch the natural and unrestricted course of the free transfer of property. During the height of the Mutinies, it was, however, noticed that in many cases the ousted proprietors had re-entered into possession, and that the old Tenantry had sympathized with them, and sided with them against the new purchasers. In August, 1858, this matter attracted the notice of the Court of Directors. They observed that the rapid transfer of lands from the hands of the old proprietors to those of persons with no local influence was a source of weakness to the Government, and without suggesting immediate measures of relief, they recommended the subject to the attention of the Government of India. The Government of India, in forwarding the Home Despatch to the Government of the North-Western Provinces, suggested the advisability of restricting coercive Sales of Land to mortgage decrees, and the Sadar Court of the North-Western Provinces was also in favour of a similar restriction. No further steps, however, appear to have been taken at the time with reference to this suggestion. Early in the next year, Lord Stanley (afterwards Lord Derby), sent out a Despatch which may be said to be the starting point of this controversy regarding the policy of permitting land to be freely sold for all secured and unsecured debts of the owner by coercive process of the Civil Courts, or of his own will and choice. After noticing that the freedom of transfer had been a source of weakness to the Government, inasmuch as the new purchasers had no hold on the Tenantry who sided with the ousted proprietors, the Despatch suggested that in respect of past transactions efforts should, if possible, be made to bring about compromises, and in regard to the future, it was recommended that the powers of the Judges of the lowest Courts should be restricted to suits for money and movable property, that no execution against land should be permitted for decrees below a certain amount, and that lands should not be sold without the sanction of the District Judge, as had in fact been the practice in the case in those Provinces before 1834.

This Despatch was forwarded by the Government of India to the Local Authorities, who in due course elicited the views of their Chief Revenue Officers, and, through the Sadar Court, of the District Judges, with reference to the questions raised in it. As might be expected, the Revenue Officers gave their opinions in favour, more or less, of Restrictive Legislation, while the Judicial Officers for the most part maintained the wisdom of masterly inactivity in this matter. The minutes recorded by Mr. Reade, Mr. Muir, and Mr. Strachey (since Sir W. Muir and Sir J. Strachey), on one side of the question, and by Sir G. Edmondstone, the then Lieutenant-Governor, and Mr. Pearson (since the Hon'ble Justice Pearson), on the other, may be said to exhaust all that can be said for and against the measure of allowing land to be freely sold in execution of decrees. The most noticeable feature of this correspondence is, that while the chief Judicial authority of the Province, the Local Sadar Court, sided with the views of the Revenue Officers to a great extent, the Chief Executive Officer, the Lieutenant-Governor of the Province, minuted strongly against all the proposals made by the Revenue Board, and suggested only slight improvements in procedure as a sufficient palliative for the disease.

We can only present a short summary of the views held by the several officers who took part in this discussion.

Mr. Muir suggested that there should be no restriction on voluntary mortgage or sale, or on the action of the Courts in enforcing such contracts. In the case of simple debts, he was of opinion that the person and movable property of a debtor, and his houses and town gardens, might be attached and sold, but not his lands. In the execution of decrees on mortgage bonds, it was suggested that the Collector should try to secure satisfaction by transferring the property for a term of years, on the payment by the transferee of a sum equal to the decree, or by making over the land to the mortgagee creditor for a term of years to pay himself out of its usufruct, and have his claims discharged. If neither of these alternatives were possible, the land should be sold, or the debtor and his estate should pass through the Insolvency Court, which should be allowed to count the usufruct of the land for fifteen years among the assets of the estate. Mr. Reade, who was then Senior Member of the Revenue Board, suggested that Sales might take place in execution of even money decrees after all attempts had failed to secure payment by selling the movable property of the debtor, and by letting his lands on farm for a period of years, but that such sales should not be ordered without the sanction of the District Judge. The creditor should be required to pay ten per cent. upon the value of the decrees to reimburse the Government for the trouble of realizing his debts. Mr. Thornhill, Commissioner of Allahabad, disapproved of the sale process, and suggested that the best way to ensure a check was to tax extravagance in marriage expenditure. Mr. Cocks, Commissioner of Jabalpur, suggested in addition to the prohibition of Sales by Civil Process of the Lower Courts, that no alienation by a Proprietor should be held valid, which had not the consent of his next two generation of heirs. Mr. Pinkney, Commissioner of Jhansi, thought that the transfer of land from the old Proprietors to the mercantile classes was not capable of being remedied. Mr. Williams, Commissioner First Division, approved of the proposed prohibition of transfers of Land by decrees of Courts on the ground that it would check extravagance, and in the meanwhile, suggested that the Civil Courts should be directed to try first the effects of temporary attachment of the profits of Land by way of satisfying the Decree. Mr. Harvey, Commissioner of Agra, suggested that under strict Hindu Law it was only the usufruct that was liable to be sold in payment of the debts of each Hereditary Holder in possession and that no larger interest should be sold. Mr. Batten, Commissioner of Rohilkhand, was of opinion that the political evil of such transfers was much exaggerated, and that any restrictive Legislation would be a confession of error and weakness, and opposed to the teachings of Political Economy. If a change were to be made, he would only restrict the exemption to Decrees below three hundred Rupees, and in suits above that amount the execution against Land should be in the hands of the European Judge, who should refer the adjustment to the Collector. Mr. Gubbins, Commissioner of Benares, proposed to extend the exemption to Sales for arrears of Revenue along with those under Decrees of Court. In the first case, the Sales should hold good for twenty years at the most, after which the property should return to the owner. In the case of Sales under Decrees, including simple and mortgage debts, only the life interest of the debtor should be transferable. If he and his heirs join, the alienation might hold good for two lives, but beyond that period, it should not be binding. Even private alienations should be void beyond the period of two generations. Mr. Currie, Collector of Boolandshar, suggested the necessity of the introduction of a Law of Entail to take up the place of the obsolete provisions of the Hindu Mitakshara Law of Joint Property as the only effective remedy. Mr. Mayne, Collector of Banda, disapproved of the proposal regarding Entail as being opposed to Native feeling, and maintained that the necessity of borrowing was forced upon the Ryots by the pressure of the Revenue assessment. He accordingly suggested that the Assessment should be lightened. He was of opinion that the political conseqnences of free transfer were exaggerated and that there were benefits arising from the infusion of stranger blood. At the same time, he considered that the change, as far as it had gone, had been sufficient, and that, if possible, the further destruction of the old proprietors should be prevented, and while upholding private contracts, he suggested that Decrees for simple debts should be satisfied by a temporary transfer or farm, and not by the sale of land. The Collector of Cawnpore, Mr. Sherer, was of opinion that the evil complained of was due to the direct engagement of the Government with proprietors of small estates, and that no prohibition of Sale could remedy it. Mr. Strachey, Collector of Moradabad, in a very suggestive minute, urged that the evils complained of, were owing to the novel and rigid Revenue System that had been introduced, substituting individual rights and liability, in place of the old joint responsibility and the absence of the power of Alienation. The change was not in all cases from bad to worse, for stagnation would mean impoverished Proprietors, and the curse of Landlords, impotent for good, would be doubly heavy in a country which was almost entirely an agricultural one. The evil, in Mr. Strachey's opinion could not be remedied by merely Legislative changes, or the reform of the

Procedure of Courts. The Government must take upon itself all the functions of a wealthy Landlord. He, accordingly, advocated the plan of Government agricultural Banks on the model of the French *Credit Foncier*. As far as Legislative relief could legitimately be extended, he thought that the Government had done enough by enacting Sections 194, 243 and 244 in the new Code of Civil Procedure.

The North-Western Provinces Government, after eliciting the views of its Revenue Officers, referred the question to the Sadar Court, who consulted the District Judges upon the matter. Mr. Pearson, Judge of the Sagar and Narbada Territories, in an exhaustive minute, discussed both sides of the question, and gave his opinion against the proposed restrictions upon Sale and the proposed substitute, namely—temporary transfer or farm of the profits. Mr. Wynyard, Judge of Shajehanpore, suggested that Sales in execution of decrees could not well be abolished, as long as the Government retained that process to recover its arrears of Revenue, and that all that could be done by way of remedy was to take steps to secure the attendance of both parties when the suit was tried, and to make the District Judge's sanction necessary in cases of sale for decrees exceeding three hundred Rupees. Mr. Lean, Judge of Mirzapore, expressed his doubts about the validity of the Political argument urged for a change of the

Law, and he concurred in all essential points with Mr. Pearson. Mr. Vansittart, Judge of Bareilly, maintained that although the mischief was chiefly owing to the Revenue System with which the Civil Courts had no concern, yet, as political expediency required it, he would vote for the change, and exempt all Revenue paying lands from liability to any Process of the Courts. Mr. Plowden, Judge of Ghazeepore, also suggested that the remedy for the evil complained of was to be sought in a reform of the Revenue System. The Revenue System broke up the Talukdaries, and violated the principle of the joint liability of village Communities, and substituted individual ownership in its place under the *Pattedari* and *Halkabandi* system. Mr. Ross, Judge of Farrakabad, urged that under a settled and strong Government, the evil complained of was unavoidable under the operations of a Law of equal succession. While, therefore, a complete check was impossible, he suggested, as palliative measures, the necessity of registering all bond affecting land, of increasing the powers of pre-emption, and exempting lands from Sale for debts below one hundred Rupees, and lastly, he advised that a preliminary inquiry should precede the Sale with a view to ascertain and define the interest sold.

The Sadar Court of the North-Western Provinces expressed themselves in favour of compelling the creditor first, to exhaust the Personal Property of the debtor, and then of limiting Sales of Land to decrees in which the property to be sold had been distinctly hypothecated, and to cases of fraud on creditors. They were also in favour of declaring the exemption of land from liability to sale in respect of decrees for small amounts, and requiring the Munsiffs to secure the sanction of the District Judge, before proceeding to sell the land. The Lieutenant-Governor of the North Western Provinces, in reporting his views upon the whole correspondence, expressed himself strongly against all the heroic remedies, and thought that the provisions of Sections, 194, 243, and 244 of Act VIII of 1859 were sufficient for the present, with a slight amendment of Section 244, so as to dispense with the necessity of finding sufficient security, and he suggested that it was desirable to watch their effects for some years, and to be content till then with a direction to require that, in all executions of decrees for money, process shall in the first instance issue against the movable property, and that the interests to be sold should be carefully ascertained by the Collector, so as to secure to the purchaser a carefully defined title.

This summary of the views of the Revenue and Judicial Officers in the North-Western Provinces will show the wide diversity of opinion that prevails on the subject among persons in every way competent to judge about the issues involved in the dispute. All varieties and shades of opinion are represented in it, from the extreme conservatism which would abolish entirely the powers of even voluntary transfer, and make the Ryot a Serf of Government lands, or revive the system of Entail, to the extremely radical principles of a *laissez faire* policy of doing nothing by way of interference between man and man. A strong consensus of views appears, however, to be in favour of a middle course, which, while restricting the enforced Sale of Land to decrees, which by their express terms affected it, would uphold the power of private transfer by way of sale or mortgage, but would, even in cases where sales might be necessary and proper, first try the effects of a temporary attachment and farm of the profits. This view, it will be seen, was first suggested by Sir W. Muir, and coincides in all essential details with that which has received the sanction of the Legislature in the Deccan Agriculturists' Relief Act.

To proceed, however, with the history of the Land Sale controversy, the Government of India appears to have taken no further action in the matter, on the conflicting views of the North-Western Provinces Officers, and to have contented itself with watching the effects of the new Code of Civil Procedure for some years as recommended by the Lieutenant-Governor. It must be remembered, however, that the revulsion of feeling caused by the Mutinies suggested the introduction of Sections 194, 243, and 244 in the

Code, and these Sections may well be reckoned as the first acknowledgment of a change of policy on the part of Government in this connection, and a recognition of its obligation to respect the national sentiment regarding Ancestral Land, and its duty to preserve the old Hereditary Proprietors of the same in their possession. It was hoped at the time that by making the decreed amount payable by instalments, and by permitting temporary attachments of the lands either through a Receiver appointed by the Courts or through the Collector of the District, sufficient time and consideration would be secured to help the involved Proprietor to redeem his lands and retain his status.

In its newly acquired Provinces, the Government of India proceeded a step further in the declaration of this new Policy. In the Punjab, a Circular Order, having the effect of law, was issued as early as October 1858, directing that no hereditary or jointly acquired property in land should be sold in liquidation of a sum decreed in the Civil Courts without the sanction of the Judicial Commissioner. In 1866, when the Code of Civil Procedure was extended to the Punjab Provinces, a proviso was ordered to Section 208 (which declares all rights in lands as liable to attachment and Sale)—to the effect "that no immovable property should be attached or sold without the sanction of the Commissioner of the Division, and no

Hereditary of Jointly-acquired Property in land should be attached or Sold without the sanction of the Chief Court." Similar provisions were introduced by the Government of India in its Proclamations, extending the Code of Civil Procedure to the other Non-Regulation Districts. In the Central Provinces and in Oudh it was added that no ancestral property in land should be sold in satisfaction of a decree without the sanction of the Judicial Commissioner, and no self-acquired property in land should be sold without the previous permission of the Divisional Commissioner. In the Chota Nagpur District of the Bengal Provinces, under orders of the Government of India issued as far back as 1833. Immovable Property was not sold in liquidation of debts, but under the order of the Political Agent of the Province the estate of the debtor was sequestrated, and the assets were appropriated to the payment of the creditor after allowing a small maintenance to the indebted Proprietor. When the Code of Civil Procedure was extended to this Province, these powers of the Commissioner or Political Agent were expressly reserved, and without his sanction no sale could take place. In the Berar Districts, the sanction of the Divisional Commissioner and of the Resident respectively, was required before ancestral or self-acquired land could be sold. It was only in the so-called Regulation Provinces of Bengal, Bombay, Madras and the North-West, that no legal restriction was placed upon the freedom of Sale. In all the other Provinces, the power of allowing Sale was left to the discretion of the Chief Revenue and Judicial Authorities. The necessity of such sanction acts as a deterrent upon Money Lenders, who seldom, if ever, succeed in making out a case sufficiently strong to satisfy the higher Authorities. As the introduction of Sections 194, 243, and 244 was the first step in the way of securing the restriction of complete freedom of transfer in land, this requisition of superior sanction might well be regarded as the second decisive step taken by the Government with a view to protect the old Proprietory Classes from being deprived of their lands by the superior enterprise and intelligence of the Money Lenders.

In course of time, it was, however, discovered that the checks sought to be imposed in both the ways above mentioned proved comparatively ineffective in operation, and this led to what may well be called the next phase of this Land Sale controversy. The subject was first broached by the Judges of the Chief Court in the Punjab, who complained that the discretion vested in them by law required some definite rules to guide it in a spirit of uniformity throughout the Territories, and they asked for a legislative measure which would define more particularly the circumstances in which the sanction should be given or refused, independently of the question, whether the other assets of the land-owning classes were sufficient or not, which was the only point inquired into in practice. This reference reopened the larger question of the desirability of such restrictions upon the freedom of Sale. Mr. Justice Boulouis expressed himself strongly in favour of absolutely refusing permission to the Sale of Land in a Zamindari or Bhayachari Village, in respect of money debts, unless the land was mortgaged to the decree holder. Mr. Justice Simpson went further, and desired that there should be no exception even in cases of mortgage bonds. The Divisional Officers who were consulted on the point, reported their views with the same diversity which has been already noticed in respect of the North-West Provinces. The Commissioner of Delhi was of opinion that the Sale of Land should be prohibited in all cases except under decrees for arrears of Revenue, in which cases, as the Government claimed the right to oust owners for such arrears, there could be no hardship in selling the land at the instance of the private suitor. The Commissioner was not inclined to make any exception in favour of mortgage. The Deputy Commissioner of the same Division expressed himself in favour of reserving the mortgagee's right, and would only extend the prohibition to sales for money decrees. The Deputy Commissioner of Goorgaon was inclined to object to the restriction proposed, but would allow one year of grace to the involved debtor to stave off the Sale.

The Deputy Commissioner of Karnal would dispense with all restrictions, as also with the necessity of sanction, and was of opinion that the provisions of Sections 243 and 244 were quite sufficient restrictions in all cases. The Commissioner of Hissar was also inclined to take an equally favourable view of the Zamindar's position, and was content to watch the effect of the provisions of Sections 243 and 244. He was, however, opposed to the policy of allowing Forced Sales in cases of decrees for arrears of Revenue, and for money borrowed for improvements. The Commissioner of Jallandar, on the other hand, would prohibit all Sales of Hereditary and jointly acquired land under all circumstances. The Commissioner of Amritsar thought that Mr. Boulouis's proposal to forbid Sales in respect of money decrees, and to allow them in case of mortgage debts, would simply prove futile, and lead only to an increase of mortgage transactions. The Commissioner of Lahore was in favour of the total prohibition of Sale under all circumstances. Mr. Griffin, Deputy Commissioner of Lahore, would restrict the prohibition to Ancestral Property only, leaving jointly acquired property to take care of itself. The Commissioner of Rawal-Pindi was in favour of Mr. Boulouis's proposal. The Commissioner of Derajat was opposed to prohibitory Legislation, and thought that the restrictions under Sections 243 and 244 were sufficient. Mr. Brandereth,

Commissioner of Multan, thought that our Revenue arrangements were chiefly responsible for the indebtedness of the Zamindar classes, and that as long as these arrangements continued, ancestral lands should not be liable to coercive Sale on account of simple debts and mortgage transactions. Mr. Barnes, officiating Commissioner of Multan, thought that there was no need of amending the Law, and that the present restrictions were sufficient.

The Financial Commissioner of the Punjab, Mr. P. S. Melvil, reporting his own views upon the reference, urged that the Punjab had passed through its stage of pupilage, and had entered upon vigorous manhood, and that the people were growing in intelligence and wealth; he was of opinion, therefore, that it was not necessary to have recourse to retrograde Legislation, and that the security of land should continue to exist for all debts for which no special security was provided, but that it should not be sold in execution till all other arrangements to pay the decree within a reasonable period of about fifteen years had failed. He, accordingly, suggested that the existing Law should remain unchanged except that the requisition about adequate security in Section 244 should be done away with. The Lieutenant-Governor of the Punjab, however, in reporting upon the whole correspondence his own views, expressed himself strongly in favour of an absolute prohibition of the Sale of all hereditary and jointly acquired lands in execution of decrees, and suggested that the term for temporary Alienation under Section 244 should never exceed twenty years. The Judges of the Chief Court were requested accordingly to submit a draft of the proposed amending Law. These Judges, however, differed among themselves. While Mr. Justice Boulouis and Mr. Justice Simpson were in favour of further express prohibitory Legislation, Mr. Justice Lindsay was strongly disinclined to move in the matter, and took his stand upon the Financial Commissioner's dissent, and the Report made by the High Court of the North-West Provinces, in regard to the satisfactory working of Sections 243 and 244 in those Provinces, as palliative measures. In consequence of this conflict, no further action was taken in this connection. This closed what may be called the Second stage of this Land Controversy.

The Third stage of this Controversy began in 1870, with a reference from the Government of India to all the Subordinate Governments requesting an expression of their views, in regard to the success which had attended the working of Sections 243 and 244, since the new Code became Law. These Sections, it will be easily seen, were in the first instance suggested by the land systems of the Northern and Eastern portions of India, where individual Zamindars, as in Bengal, Behar, and Benares, or Zamindaris held by Village Communities, as in the North-West Provinces and the

Punjab, were sufficiently large in extent to allow a Prospect of their being profitably managed by means of Receivers and Collector's agents under Attachment. This state of things did not exist in the Ryotwari Districts of Bombay and Madras, where the system obtains of small holdings and individual responsibility, and in their case it was to be expected that the Sections would prove inoperative and obsolete. The Reports of the two Governments and of the Judicial Officers subordinate to them confirmed this anticipation. The Madras Authorities reported that Sections 244 had never been extended to their Provinces, and that Section 243 also, was not much resorted to. The Bombay Authorities also made a similar report. In the Non-Regulation Districts of the Punjab, Oudh, the Central Provinces, and the Berars, the Sections were inoperative on another account. These provisions presupposed a division of authority between the Judicial and Revenue Services. In these Provinces, however, both these functions were combined in one and the same Official, and while the check of superior sanction was in operation, Section 244 was found to be unworkable in its practical application. In the North-West Provinces and Bengal also, Section 244 was proved to have been either not worked at all, or to have been abused. As regards Section 243, however, the Authorities in both the Provinces reported that it had secured on the whole beneficial results, by way of mitigating in a considerable percentage of cases the extreme severity of the Law implied in the final resort to the Sale Process ; yet, even in these Districts it was observed that the Sections worked less satisfactorily in the case of small than in large estates.

It was in the course of this inquiry into the working of Sections 243 and 244 that the Authorities of the Central Provinces ventured on their own account to re-open the Land Sale Controversy, and the views of Colonel Keatinge, Chief Commissioner, Mr. P. S. Melvill, Judicial Commissioner, Mr. (now Sir Charles) Bernard, Commissioner of Nagpur, and Mr. Brooks and Mr. Nicholls, Deputy Commissioners, were elicited upon the general merits of the Policy of restricting the Freedom of Sales in execution of decrees. In view of the fact, that the Settlement had been recently introduced in these Provinces, and that property in land had been a new creation of the Settlement, Mr. Melvill saw reason to change the views he had expressed as Financial Commissioner of the Punjab, and urged the necessity of a Restrictive Measure by which lands would be exempted from Sale for debts contracted prior to the Settlement. He, further, proposed that after due notification during which all debts contracted since the settlement might be cleared off, all Sales of Land in execution of decrees should be prohibited without any distinction of ancestral or self-acquired lands. Colonel Keatinge, the Chief Commissioner, was not prepared to go so far as Mr. Melvill. He would confine the exemption to estates yielding more than three hundred Rupees as annual rental. All smaller estates should be left to be dealt with under the existing Law which requires sanction before Sale. The two Systems of Freedom and Restriction of Sale would, he thought, be thus working side by side, and serve to educate the people out of their tutelage. The Chief Commissioner also differed from the Judicial Commissioner on another point. He proposed to make a distinction between Ancestral and Self-Acquired Lands, and to regard all lands, howsoever acquired, as ancestral after fifty years' possession or two successions of heirs, and to exempt only the Ancestral Lands so defined from Sale. In the case of large ancestral properties preserved from sale, the Chief Commissioner proposed that the debts of the owners should be paid off by an attachment of their profits, or by handing them over to the creditors for a term of twenty-five years at the most, to be in the end restored back to the owner free of all claims. In these sever always the inevitable change would, he thought, be sufficiently retarded to avoid all political inconvenience and any sudden Social Revolution. Of the minor authorities consulted, the Deputy Commissioners of Jabalpur, Chindwara, Nimar, and Narbada Division, were of opinion that no change in the existing Law was called for. Mr. Bernard, Commissioner of Nagpur, however, proposed to exempt all lands, whether ancestral or acquired, from compulsory Sale by process of Civil Courts. Mr. Brooks, the Commissioner, and Mr. Nicholls, Assisstant Commissioner, Seoni, were inclined to make distinction between ancestral and Self-Acquired property, and while exempting the one from Sale, when there were heirs living and subjecting it, instead, to temporary alienations, they did not think any protection should be extended, to the other, whether it was joint or divided, and they would extend the same law to Mahomedans as well as Hindus.

Here, this Fourth stage of the Controvesry ended for the present without leading to any practical result, so far as the Central Provinces were concerned. In 1872, Sir William Muir became Lieutenant-Governor of the North-West Provinces, and in connection with the new Rent and Revenue Bills, re-opened the whole discussion. The Honourable Mr. J. D. Inglis, Mr. C. A. Elliott, and Mr. Reade wrote strongly in favour of Restrictive Legislation. Mr. Inglis suggested that, after a certain time, Personal Property alone should be held liable for unsecured debts, as also for arrears of Revenue, that Ancestral Property should be exempted from Sale, on account of unregistered mortgage debts; and that decrees founded on registered mortgage bonds should be satisfied as far as possible, by a temporary transfer of the property, which should be only sold when such an arrangement was impossible. Mr. Reade was of opinion that mortgage transactions should be respected, and that in regard to the past, simple debts also had a claim to be satisfied out of land. He, therefore, proposed that a term of two years should be fixed for the realization of all previous unsecured debts, and that, after that term, simple debts should be only realized from the person and out of the movable property of the debtor. In regard to motgage debts, he proposeed that there should be no interference when the property mortgaged was Self-Acquired. Where it was Ancestral, the claim should be paid off by a farm or attachment of profits for a term not exceeding thirty years. Mr. Elliott urged that the Zamindar should be regarded as a person holding land burdened with a public duty, and that while all claims in respect of old debts should be respected, it should be declared for the future that the Civil Courts would not lend their help to realize new debts by the Sale of the Land or by any process severer than a thirty years' farm, the Zamindar holding during the farm as a privileged tenant.

In the meanwhile, Sir William Muir had learned to moderate his old extreme views, and he contented himself with the proposal that lands should be exempted from sale for unsecured debts, that there should be in every District a Court for the relief of encumbered estates, like the Court of Wards, and that '*Seer*' Lands should be inalienable beyond the life-time of the holder. These views were referred to the Judges of the High Court, Allahabad, two of whom, Mr. Justice Turner and Mr. Justice Pearson strongly condemned retrograde measures, while the third Judge, Mr. Justice Spankie, gave a very doubtful support. Sir William Muir afterwards toned down his proposals still further, and contented himself with recommending that the execution work in the case of Land Sales should be transferred to the Collectors, who, if they found the Lands hopelessly involved, should proceed with the Sale. If there was a hope of rescuing the estate by good management within twenty-five years, the Collector should assume such management. Eventually, Sir William Muir with-drew all his chief proposals, so far as the North-West Provinces were concerned, on the ground that it was now too late to think of prohibiting the Sales of Land for unsecured debts, and expressed himself satisfied that a better execution of the powers conferred under Sections 243, and 244, or an enlarge-ment of these powers, was all that was required under the circumstances. The effect of this unconditional surrender on the part of the Lieutenant-Governor was that in the North-West Provinces Rent and Revenue Acts of 1873, the only new provision that was inserted was in Section 7, relating to ex-Propreitory Tenants, by which Proprietors who lost or parted with theirs Lands were recognised to have the status of Privileged Tenants in Seer Land, holding at a rent of four annas in the Rupee less than that paid by Tenants-at-Will, and this rent could not be enhanced except for specific reasons laid down in the Law. This was the only outcome at the time, so far as the North-West Provinces were concerned, of all this lengthy controversy. Subsequently, as suggested by Sir William Muir, in amending the Code of Civil Procedure, the Legislature took care to enlarge the Collector's powers, and to lay down Specific Rules of Procedure for his guidance, in the matter of the execution of Decrees against Land, the absence of which rules was so much complained of by the various Subordinate Governments who were consulted about the working of the Sections 243 and 244 of Act VIII of 1859. In Oudh, however, a Relief Act in favour of the Talukdars was passed in 1870, by which special provision was made as to the way in which Revenue Officers were to assume the management of encumbered estates, and to arrange for the liquidation of the estates. The Broach Talukdar's Act, passed in the next year, was modelled on the same principles, and later on, we have had several Acts in the same spirit for the benefit of particular classes, notably the Zamindars of Sind and Chota-Nagpur. Before the Deccan Agriculturists' Relief

Act was passed, the Acts named above were the only outcome of this long discussion.

The Land Sale Controversy, however, did not end with the enactment of these measures. It was re-opened in the Central Provinces in 1874 under the Chief Commissioner, Mr. (since Sir John) Morris when the subject was started in connection with a new Revenue and Tenancy Bill for those Provinces. The Minutes recorded by Mr. Morris, Mr. Grant and Mr. Carpenter, Commissioners of Jabalpur Mr. Jones, Commissioner of Nagpur, and Mr. Low, Commissioner of the Narbada Division, go over the whole ground of this most controversial subject, and might be said in some degree to complete the literature of the Restrictive School of Thinkers and Statesmen. As the Government of India was not prepared to prohibit all involuntary transfer of landed properties, the discussion at this time was confined chiefly to the devising of means by which the evils of a too rapid transfer might be obviated. Mr. Grant, for instance, proposed that the best way to protect the Ryots' interests, and deter Bania purchasers from investing their spare cash in land, was to hold that no absolute proprietory title to land could be recognized in India, and to enforce upon the purchasers the full responsibilities of the holders of land by placing a check upon the choice of managers, and in the last resort by cancelling the Settlement, if necessary, and pensioning off the dispossessed holder by a part payment of the Jamma. These drastic remedies alone could, in his opinion, check the evil; all the other measures only touched the surface symptoms of the disease in the body Politic. The necessity of sanction, for instance, enforced in the No-Regulation Provinces, had become, in the course of time, impotent of effect. Mr. Jones also proceeded on the same track, when he laid down as one of his postulates that the mere exemption of lands from Sale for money debts would be an insufficient remedy. He, however, thought that Mr. Grant's Scheme would effect too sweeping a change and it would be impossible to work it. The land might be protected, but the produce of it from year to year would be sequestrated. He, accordingly, proposed his own Scheme which would allow private transactions of Sale, but put a stop to involuntary transfer by Civil Process, except in the case of debts expressly secured on the land, and with a view to secure a check upon extravagant loans, he would require that all loans, for which ancestral property was to be mortgaged, should be contracted only under the Collector's supervision and should be held to be void and of no obligatory force without such consent. Further he would leave parties to exercise their rights freely, in respect of self-acquired land, except that he would encourage Family Entails and Settlements. In respect of past transactions, he would constitute each Deputy Commissioner's Court into an Encumbured Estates

Court, and help the speedy release of estates by loans from Government. Mr. Grant thought that Mr. Jones's Scheme about investing Collectors with the power of certifying good and legitimate loans would be found impossible to work, though he thought better of the Encumbered Estates Scheme. Mr. Low thought that the old Proprietors, were ruined not by the Banias so much as by the excessive temptations to borrowing placed in their way by the Settlement. He agreed with Mr. Grant in thinking that the best way to reduce these temptations was to enforce the responsibilities of proprietory possession. After this was done, the next step was to limit the power of alienating Ancestral Land to one quarter of the estate at the owner's pleasure, and to declare the remaining three-quarters inalienable. The only form of alienation that Mr. Low would permit under his Scheme was a lease for ten years only. Involuntary alienation of ancestral estate by Civil Process would only be allowed in cases when the original bond had been certified by the Collector as having been passed for sufficient consideration, and the property charged did not exceed one-fourth of the owner's possessions. Mr. Carpenter, Commissioner of the Jabalpur Division, contented himself with a more modest and certainly less involved Scheme of Reform. He thought that the evil would be best checked by insisting upon the creditor the necessity of filing a written statement of his account with his debtors in the Registrar's Office, and he would also have a register of all properties, showing how far they were encumbered or free. He disapproved of all strong remedies, but, if further Legislation was desired, he expressed a strong opinion in favour of exempting Lands from Sale, but leaving them liable to the attachment of their profits for eight or ten years. Finally, Mr. Morris, the Chief Commissioner, discussed all the views of his subordinates, and found more or less fault with them all, as being either unworkable, or undesirable, but at the same time he refused to take upon himself the responsibility of suggesting any particular measures for adoption. He, however, made alternative suggestions to the effect that all property in land should be declared exempt from sale in execution of civil decrees, and that the only alienation which should be allowed to the owner was a lease for a term of less than ten years, which lease might be transferred to the creditor in satisfaction of his claim. If the latter measure seemed to be too radical, he suggested the establishment of Encumbered Estates Courts, and was of opinion that the Civil Courts should refuse to recognize all alienations save those certified by the said Courts. This concludes the Sixth phase of these Land Sale Controversies.

None of these discussions of 1859, and 1873, in the North-West Provinces, of 1869, in the Punjab, of 1871 and 1874 in the Central Provinces, seem to have produced much effect upon the Legislature, except in measures of partial operation for the relief of particular classes, which were never recognized to be anything but temporary expedients. The general law for the Presidencies of Bengal, Bombay and Madras continued to be one of unfettered freedom. Sir A. Hobhouse very justly characterized the extreme proposals of the Officers of the North-West and the Central Provinces as violating the spirit of all sound Legislation, and advised more cautious proceedings. The subject was, however, not to be laid at rest by the dictum of the Law Member, and the Government of India was soon after forced to take action in the last stage of this controversy which had its rise this time in the Bombay Presidency. The immediate occasion which attracted public attention to the subject in this Presidency was the outbreak of the riots in the Deccan Districts in 1875. The inquiries undertaken by the Commission included this among other topics, and they raked up the whole of the past literature on the subject as far as this Presidency was concerned. It appeared from this research into past records that as early as 1844, Captain Anderson of the Revenue Survey had complained of the mechanical action of the Courts, and urged the necessity of getting a valuation of landed property made by independent assessors, prior to the issue of the order of Sale and compelling judgment creditors to accept it at that price. Mr. Frere and

Mr. Rose recommended the establishment of Usury Laws, and the opening of licensed Government Pawn-broker's Shops. Mr. Rose further urged the justice of exempting Houses and Mirasi Rights from being sold in execution of money decrees. Usury Laws had obtained in the Madras and Bengal Presidencies and in the North-West Provinces, but they had found no place in the Bombay Code of 1827. Accordingly the Enactment of a Usury Law limiting interest to a maximum rate of twelve per cent., also the introduction of some provision requiring all bonds to be registered, and transferring houses and lands into the creditor's possession, to pay himself out of the usufruct thereof, in a term of years,—these measures were suggested as palliative remedies in 1844, in the interests of the Ryots. The Government of Bombay, however, negatived all these proposals. In 1852, Captain Wingate took up the subject of the Compulsory Sale of the Ryots' lands in execution of decrees, and urged a change of the law on the ground that such Sales were unknown in the times of the old Rulers, were further opposed to Native feeling, and were but rarely resorted to till the land Settlements were made. He advocated the policy of declaring that lands should not be sold on account of unsecured debts, though they might be freely mortgaged and sold voluntarily, and in such cases, decrees might be specifically enforced in regard to them. Captain Wingate also recommended a Usury

Law and proposed to invest the Courts with a discretion, any power to allow proper interest. He suggested the advisability of reviving the Institution of Panchayats to try Summary Suits valued at less than thirty Rupees and the extension of a general Insolvency Law. These recommendations remained unnoticed for nearly thirty years, but it is strange that almost every one of the proposals then made by Captain Wingate has of late received the sanction of the Legislature. The Usury Law, the Exemption of Lands from Civil Process for Unsecured Debts, the Panchayat Courts, a liberal Insolvency Law,—these are the leading features of the new Deccan Agriculturists' Relief Act. To proceed, however, with the history of the subject, in 1859, Mr. Tytler recommended the establishment of a Registry of the Ryots' debts in the Mamlatdar's Office, with a view to check fraud, and show all Payments made by the Ryots. In 1860 Mr. Jacomb submitted a plan of Government savings and Town Banks to help needy Ryots with easy interest. The Government of Bombay did not support either of these proposals. For the next twelve years, Bombay Officers seemed not to have thought much of this subject as the prosperity brought on the Country by high prices secured a sensible advance in the comfort of the people. In 1872-73, however hard times returned, and Mr. (now Sir Raymond) West published his pamphlet "The Land and the Law of India," which gave birth to a long discussion, both in and out of the Presidency. Mr. West proposed that the power of alienating land should be limited. He urged upon the Government that it should declare all assessed land to be expressly inalienable except with its assent, or reassessable to a rack rent on such alienation for the benefit of the public. If this might be deemed to be too strong a measure, he proposed to confine the power of alienation with the Collector's consent to the surplus land, *i. e.* land exceeding a certain fixed necessary minimum for comfortable subsistence, and it was this excess land alone which was to be liable to Attachment and Sale. The Dwellings, and the Crops, and the cattle of the Agriculturists should also be exempt. His next proposal was that mortgages and leases for more than one year be subjected to the same rules as Sales. Mr. West further proposed to limit the right of enforcing a Specific Partition of Property. The necessary minimum requisite for the support of a family should not be partitioned, but the separating sharers should be paid off in money. A system of Family Settlements for large estates, and a liberal Law of Insolvency, crowned the edifice of these proposed sweeping reforms. Mr. Pedder also contributed his mite to the literature on this subject. He argued for a reformed procedure, a Law of Bankruptcy, and finally the exemption of Land from Sale in execution of decrees.

This exemption, however, was not to apply to the crops or profits of land. We next have the inquiries conducted by the Deccan Riots Commission, of which the immediate outcome has been the Deccan Agriculturists' Relief Act of 1879. As far as the subject of Land Sale is concerned, it is to be noted that the Commission reported in favour of abolishing Sales of Land in execution of money decrees. They further suggested the necessity of a liberal Insolvency Law, of the abolition of Civil Imprisonment, and the establishment of Public Notaries and registration of all payments in Pass Books. The Bombay Government, under Sir Phillip Wodehouse, however, negatived the recommendation in regard to the exemption of Land from Sale, as also the proposal to abolish imprisonment for debt. When Sir Richard Temple, however, became Governor, he took up the subject again, with his usual energy, and urged the necessity of giving effect to the recommendations of the Commission in the matter of a law exempting Lands from Sale in execution of money decrees except when they had been specifically pledged. He also pressed for a more liberal Insolvency Law, and a Law for Limiting the Rate of Interest. These suggestions were approved by the Government of India, and the Deccan Agriculturists' Relief Act was passed into Law.

We have thus reviewed the whole history of this lengthy discussion for the past twenty-five years in the

North-West Provinces, in the Punjab, in the Central Provinces, and finally in the Bombay Presidency. There can be no question that the relief so tardily given is in accordance with the conservative instincts and traditions of the people. A thorough review of the whole discussion like the one we have now summarized can alone bring out all the bearings of this most important question. The Government of India has shown great practical wisdom in refusing to lend its support to the more extreme proposals of its Revenue Officers. Mr. Justice West, Mr. Elliott, Mr. Grant, Mr. Jones and the other authorities appear to us to have ignored the main conditions of the problem. The Country is in a transition stage, passing from semi-Feudal and Patriarchal conditions of existence into a more settled and commercial order of things, from a period of disturbance and wars into one of peace and tranquility, from payments in kind to cash payments, from the laws of custom to the rule of competition, from a simple to a more complicated Social Organization. No Economical Legislation can succeed under such circumstances, which seeks to run against the current, or stem the torrent. In all countries property, whether in land or other goods, must gravitate towards that class which has more intelligence, and greater foresight, and practises abstinence, and must slip from the hands of those who are ignorant, improvident, and hopeless to stand on their own resources.

This is a law or Providence, and can never be wisely or safely ignored by practical Statesmen for any fancied political on sentimental considerations. As long as the difference in the habits and education of the saving few represented by the Bania and Brahmin classes, and the spending many who count by millions among the Military and the cultivating classes remains good a property will gravitate from the one class to the other, notwithstanding all prohibitory Legislation. The utmost that Government can safely venture to do is to regulate this inevitable transfer, to temper the change so as to avoid all immediate hardships. An Insolvency Law cannot benefit anybody, where none but the castaways and waifs of Society wish to degrade themselves to seek its advantage. A Law of Forced Entails cannot be expected to work when the notion of equal inheritance by birth-right is so thoroughly engrained in the national mind. A minimum sufficient for subsistence cannot be fixed when the natural conditions of soil and climate permit of the lowering of the standard of necessary comfort to any conceivable limit. The force of resistance must well forth from within, and cannot possibly be super-imposed. The forcible prohibition of all transfer of real property, voluntary and involuntary, can never mend matters—it can only stereotype existing poverty and aggravate existing helplessness. The Government of such a lage Empire cannot afford means to be the Banker of its millions of

Insolvent Tenants, and cannot equalize the changing conditions of bad harvests and scanty or irregular rainfall. As we have said above, it can only adopt temporary expedients, and watch anxiously the effects of its experiments. It must accept as inevitable the tendency to concentration of the landed capital of the Country, and only limit its agency to the minor work of smoothing the gradual change. The only settlement of the Problem that is possible is not to its taste. It should withdraw from its position as Landlord, and look upon the land tax as a tax like any other monopoly taxes. A permanent Ryotwari Settlement fixed in grain which the land produces, and commuted into money values every twenty or thirty years, can alone furnish a solution of this Agricultural Problem. If differences subsequently spring up between class and class, as they have on occasions sprung up in Bengal, the Government can interfere as a mediator, and right matters by protecting the weak against the strong. It will not, however, for fancied Political considerations accept this position or allow Middlemen to come between itself and its Pauper Tenants, and its attempts to undo the legitimate influence of the saving classes can only end in a great disaster. The Deccan Agriculturists' Relief Act can hardly bring any permanent real relief, while the standing cause of all the embarrassments of the Ryots continues at work with untempered rigidity. It is hoped that the new Régime, from which all hope so much, will turn its attention to this aspect of the question and devise a remedy which will establish an accord between the Economical, Social and Intellectual conditions of the population, and secure the real advancement of the Country on a permanent foundation.

KING GEORGE'S SPEECHES IN INDIA

A COMPLETE COLLECTION OF ALL THE SPEECHES DELIVERED IN INDIA DURING HIS TOUR AS PRINCE OF WALES AND IN CONNECTION WITH THE RECENT CORONATION DURBAR

This is a complete and up-to-date collection of all the speeches delivered by His Majesty the King-Emperor during his first tour in India as Prince of Wales and his second tour in connection with the Coronation Durbar. No speech of any importance relating to India has been omitted; and to make this handy collection of His Majesty's Indian Speeches doubly valuable, a useful Appendix has been added, containing among others, the text of the announcement relating to the Coronation Durbar Boons; the Proclamations of H. M. King George, Queen Victoria and King Edward the Seventh on their accession to the throne and the messages of Queen Victoria and King Edward to the Durbars of 1877 and of 1903. The book contains a fine portrait of Their Majesties as frontispiece and seven other illustrations. We hope that this handy volume will be welcomed by the millions of His Majesty's subjects not only in India but all over the Empire.

With eight Illustrations.

Re. One. To Subscribers of the "Indian Review," As. 12.

G. A. Natesan & Co., Sunkurama Chetty Street, Madras.

Central Hindu College Magazine. These energetic publishers have thus added one more to the list of books that every household should possess. Many people will be glad to read His Majesty's own words.

The Punjabee. These speeches are valuable as they contain many expressions of appreciation of India, its people and their loyalty. It is also valuable as they contain many encouraging hopes and words of sympathy expressed by the Royal mouth.

The Rast Goftar. The publication would be welcomed throughout India, and should come handy to publicists and journalists, especially.

Speeches by Eminent Indians

Dadabhai Naoroji's Speeches.—An up-to-date, exhaustive and comprehensive collection. With a portrait. Rs. 2. To Subscribers of the "Indian Review," Re 1-8.

Gokhale's Speeches.—An exhaustive and comprehensive collection of his speeches, with a biographical sketch and a portrait. Over 1,000 pages. Crown 8vo. Rs. 3. To Subscribers of the "Indian Review." Rs. 2-8.

Dr. Rash Behari Ghose's Speeches.—An Exhaustive and Comprehensive Collection. (*With a portrait*). Price As. 12. To Subscribers of the "Indian Review," As. 8.

Swami Vivekananda.—An exhaustive and comprehensive collection of his speeches and writings. With Portraits. Cloth Bound. Third Edition Rs. 2. To subscribers of the "Indian Review," Re. 1-8.

The Indian National Congress.—An account of its origin and growth. Full text of all the Presidential Addresses. Reprint of all the Congress Resolutions. Extracts from all the Welcome Addresses. Notable Utterances on the Movement. Portraits of all the Congress Presidents. Cloth Bound. Over 1,000 pages Crown 8vo. Rs. 3. To Subscribers of the "Review," Rs. 2-8.

G. A. Natesan & Co., Sunkurama Chetty Street, Madras.

The Indian Nation: —Cultured, energetic and enterprising publishers of Madras.

The Provincial Times:—Messrs. G. A. Natesan, Publishers, Esplanade, Madras, have issued a series of books not alone of interest to a general reader, but of value as references and historical records.

The Sanjvartman. There are very few firms in India that take the trouble of being up-to-date, or by the variety of their publication to form and direct the public taste or to diffuse, useful and interesting knowledge among their constituents. Among these few Messrs. Natesan and Company of Madras undoubtedly occupy the place of honour.

LIFT-IRRIGATION

BY ALFRED CHATTERTON,

Professor of Engineering, on Special Duty, Madras.

CONTENTS. Introduction, Water Lifts. Underground Water-Supply, Well Irrigation with Oil Engines, Irrigation from Artesian Wells, The Value of Wind-Mill in India, Experiments with Wind-Mills, Wind-Mills Irrigation in America, The Cost of Power, Cost of Lifting Water, Flow of Water in Sand, Well-Boring, Steam Pumps in the Kistna Delta, Development of Lift-Irrigation, Lift-Irrigation, Irrigation by Pumping, Progress in Irrigation by Pumping in Madras, Irrigation by Pumping in the United States.

PREFACE TO THE SECOND EDITION

Some years ago, Messrs. G. A. Natesan & Co. reprinted a number of papers and articles which I had written at various times on the improvement of the methods of lifting water for irrigation. The little volume apparently served a useful purpose as it met with a ready sale and has been out of print for some time. The demand for information, as to the methods to be pursued and as to the results which have been achieved, still continues and in the absence of any formal treatise on the subject, a fresh compilation of papers has been made which it is hoped will to some extent supply what is needed.

Price Rs. Two.

To Subscribers of the "Indian Review," Re. 1-8.

G. A. Natesan & Co., Sunkurama Chetty Street, Madras.

The Hindu. The Papers contain a good deal of valuable information useful to the agriculturists of the Presidency and elsewhere in India also.

Capital. Contains in lucid and succinct form an account of all the various methods for raising water for irrigation purposes now used in India and in the United States. There are millions of bullocks employed every day in India in lifting water. But it has been proved beyond doubt that the cost of pumping even on a small scale with oil engines is less than one-half that of the bullock-power, and on a larger scale the cost is not even one-tenth. Water-lifting by windmills is also fully described and the results of the various experiments described.

THE

VAISHNAVITE REFORMERS OF INDIA

CRITICAL SKETCHES OF

THEIR LIVES AND WRITINGS

BY

T. RAJAGOPALA CHARIAR, M.A., B.L.

CONTENTS.—Nathamuni; Pundarikaksha; Yamunacharya; Sri Ramanujacharya; Sri Vedanta Desika; Manavala Maha Muni; and Chaitanya:

These are a Series of Seven Essays on the Lives and Writings of the principal religious reformers of the Vaishnavite or Visishtadwaita School of India. The treatment is critical and historical; but special prominence has also been given to the literary side of this School's activity. A clear account of the growth of Vaishnavaism is intended to be conveyed by these Lives of Eminent Reformers, and reference has throughout been made to the development of doctrines. A special chapter is devoted to the exposition of the Visishtadwaita philosophy according to Ramanuja. The growth of Vaishnavaism in Northern India is briefly dealt with in the last Essay, that on Sri Chaitanya, wherein that great Saint's career is also fully described.

Re. 1. To Subscribers of the "Indian Review," As. 12:

G. A. Natesan & Co., Sunkurama Chetty Street, Madras.

Bombay Guardian. This little book can be recommended to all persons who care about the subject, for its interesting biographical notes, its abundance of Hindu lore, and its perfect lucidity.

The Rangoon Spectator. The above work by Mr. T. Rajagopala Chariar, M. A., B. L., outlines in seven Essays of exceptional ability, the development and influence of a great school of Indian philosophy.

Aspects of the Vedanta.

CONTENTS.

***Price As. 12.** To Subscribers of the "Review," As. 8.*

G. A. Natesan & Co.. Sunkurama Chetty Street, Madras.

International Journal of Ethics. **Valuable little book............The whole book is worthy of careful study by everyone interested in theology or philosophy.**

The Theosophical Review. **This useful little volume**

The Prabuddha Bharata. **A worthy compilation.. .... It will repay perusal.**

The Englishman. **Will interest readers who make a study of Oriental thought. There are six essays and they are all appreciative and meant to stimulate one to believe in the eternal principles of the Vedanta.**

The Indian National Congress

An Account of Its Origin and Its Growth
Full Text of all the Presidential Addresses
Reprint of all the Congress Resolutions
Extracts from all the Welcome Addresses
Notable Utterances on the Movement
Portraits of all the Congress Presidents

This is an exhaustive and complete Collection of all the Congress Presidential Addresses and the Resolutions passed at the sittings of all the Congresses. The book also contains extracts from the Welcome Addresses delivered at all the Congresses and several Notable Utterances on the Congress Movement by men like the late Charles Bradlaugh, Robert Knight, Sir William Hunter, Mr. Justin McCarthy, Sir Richard Garth, Lord Cromer, Sir Charles Dilke and others. An attractive feature of the book is a collection of the portraits of all the Congress Presidents. Cloth Bound. Over 1,100pp. Crown 8vo.

Price Rs. 3.** To Subscribers of the "Review," **Rs. 2-8.

Lord Ampthill.—The book seems to me a very complete and well-chosen summary and it is one which will be useful to many people besides myself for the purpose of reference.

Sir Herbert Roberts, M. P.—The record of the work of the National Congress is not only of extreme interest but will be most useful in future as a source of information as to the progress of enlightened opinion in India upon many questions deeply affecting the welfare of the people.

G. A. Natesan & Co., Sunkurama Chetty Street, Madras.

The Hindustan Review.—**The Indian statesman, politician, or publicist could scarcely have at this time of the year a better book on his shelf than that designated "The Indian National Congress." It is obvious that no public man or publicist's book-shelf of works of reference can be complete without a copy of Mr. Natesan's excellent compilation of the Congress literature. Considering its bulk and matter, it is cheaply priced at Rs. 3.**

Glympses of the Orient To-Day

BY SAINT NIHAL SINGH.

Preface.—The following pages are the record of a recent ramble through Asia, the author having personally visited all the lands about which he writes, with one or two exceptions.

It is a collection of impressions formed as the writer slowly journeyed from one land to another, living amongst the people, as one of them.

The book falling into the hands of the Indian youth—for whom it is especially designed—will be the means of inspiring him to work for the uplift of his land.

Contents :—Asia's Spell Broken; How Disillusionment Came; Asia a Menace to the West; Japan's Imperial Dream; Oriental Trade Supremacy; Autocracy to Limited Monarchy; The Modern Oriental Woman in the Making; Where Woman Has The Upper Hand; The Modernization of Japan; Flaws in Japanese Modernization; Education in Japan; Japan's Material Prosperity; Japan: China's Gadfly; The Celestial Student Abroad; Exit the Old, Enter the New in China; Evolution, Not Revolution in India; The Spirit of Maya Leaving Hindustan; To-Day in Afghanistan; Persia Evolving Cosmos Out of Chaos; Rural Life in Iran; Egypt's Agitation for Autonomy; Egypt's Preparation for Self-Government.

First Edition. Price : Re. One.

To Subscribers of the "Indian Review," As. 12.

G. A. Natesan & Co., Sunkurama Chetty Street, Madras.

The Guzerati.—Mr. Saint Nihal Singh tells us how the impact of the West upon the East has shaken the Oriental out of his metaphysical musings and taught him to think of the world of to-day, how the new awakening is to be traced in all Eastern countries. He is an optimist and in favour of an all-sided progress. The spirit that runs through the whole book is commendable and deserves to be imbibed by the Indian youths for whom the book is intended.

My Indian Reminiscences

By Dr. Paul Deussen

EXTRACT FROM THE INTRODUCTION

In recording my impressions of my trip to India in the winter of 1892-93, and thus presenting them to the public I have yielded to the wishes of my friends, partly because, notwithstanding the shortness of my stay in India, I was enabled, being favoured by circumstances, to get a deeper insight into the life of the natives than a European usually gets.

My knowledge of Sanscrit, the study of it had been to speak, my daily bread for the twenty years previous to my trip, was of immense service.

What was to be of still greater use to me in India than the knowledge of the ancient and sacred language of the land, was the fact that I had happened to have spent the best energies of a number of years in entering into the spirit of the Upanishads and the Vedanta based upon them.

CONTENTS

Introductory; From Marseilles to Bombay; Bombay; From Bombay to Peshawar; From Peshawar to Calcutta; Calcutta and the Himalayas; From Calcutta to Bombay *via* Allahabad; From Bombay to Madras and Ceylon; Homeward Bound. APPENDIX:—Philosophy of the Vedânta. *Farewell to India*: A POEM.

Crown 8vo. 270 pages, with a frontispiece.

Price Re. 1-4. To Subscribers, Re. 1.

G. A. Natesan & Co., Sunkurama Chetty Street, Madras.

The Merit of the Book.—Dr. Deussen's account of his tour throughout India, his description of its principal cities, its shrines, pilgrimages and its many holy spots, its leading men of various communities and classes afford much interesting reading. The language in which he describes the customs, ceremonies, manners, traits and traditions of the Indian people—notwithstanding the shortness of his stay in India—shows his profound admiration and love for the land which, to use his own words, "had for years become a kind of spiritual mother-country" to him.

2

Notable Books on India

My Indian Reminiscences.—By Dr. Paul Deussen, Professor of the University of Kiel, translated by A. King. Dr. Deussen's account of his tour throughout India, his description of its principal cities, its shrines, etc., afford much interesting reading. The language in which he describes the customs, ceremonies, manners, traits and traditions of the Indian people—shows profound admiration and love for the land which, to use his own words, "had for years become a kind of spiritual mother-country" to him. Price Re. 1-4. To Subscribers of the "Indian Review," Re. 1.

Glimpses of the Orient to-day.—By Saint Nihal Singh. In this book, Mr. Singh describes the transition that has taken place in Asia, during the last few decades, traces the causes of the awakening and offers a prophecy as to its ultimate effect. Price. Re. 1. To Subscribers of the "Indian Review," As. 12.

All about Delhi.—An Exhaustive hand book compiled from authentic sources. With 36 Illustrations Re. 1-8. To Subscribers, Re. 1-4.

Essays in National Idealism.— By Ananda K. Coomaraswamy, D. Sc. Popular Edition with 6 illustrations Re. 1. To subscribers of the *Indian Review*, As. 12.

The Swadeshi Movement.—A Symposium by Representative Indians and Anglo-Indians. An excellent and authoritative collection of official and non-official views. Re. 1. To Subscribers of the "Indian Review," As. 12.

G. A. Natesan & Co., Sunkurama Chetty Street, Madras.

Moulmein Advertiser. Every one of the volumes, big and small, Messrs. Natesan have of recent years published, contains views of India and Indian current history and forms a most reliable reference of the great social and mental movements now pulsating throughout India.

Sanjvartman, Bombay. Not a month elapses but this enterprising firm brings out elaborate volumes on every kind of subject that affects the interests of India and they are generally the work of men who know what they are writing about.

Indian Political Literature

Essays in National Idealism.—By Dr. Ananda K. Coomaraswami with illustrations. Re. One. To Subscribers of the "Indian Review," As. 12.

Morley's Indian Speeches.—With an Appreciation of Lord Morley, and A Portrait, Crown 8vo., 240 Pages. Re. One. To Subscribers of the *Indian Review*, As. 12.

Gokhale's Speeches.—With a biographical sketch and a portrait. Over 1,000 pages, Crown 8vo. Rs. 3. To Subscribers of the "Indian Review," Rs. 2-8.

The Indians of South Africa.—By H. S. L. Polak. Re. One. To Subscribers of the "Indian Review," As. 12.

Dadabhai Naoroji's Speeches and Writings.—With a portrait. Rs. Two. To Subscribers of the "Indian Review," Re. 1-8.

Glimpses of the Orient to-day.—By Saint Nihal Singh. Price Re. 1. To Subscribers of the "Indian Review," As. 12.

The Indian National Congress.—An account of its origin and growth. Full text of all the Presidential Addresses. Reprint of all the Congress Resolutions. Extracts from all the Welcome Addresses. Portraits of the Congress Presidents. Over 1,200 pages Crown 8vo. Rs. 3. To Subscribers of "The Indian Review," Rs. 2-8.

Indian Military Expenditure.—By Mr. Dinshaw Edulji Wacha. As. 4.

Recent Indian Finance.—By Mr. Dinsha Edulji Wacha. Price As. 4.

Indian Railway Finance.—By Mr. D. E. Wacha. As .4.

G. A. Natesan & Co., Sunkurama Chetty Street, Madras.

The Indian People.—By collecting the speeches and writings of Dr. Rash Behari Ghose, Swami Vivekananda, the Honorable Mr. Gopal Krishna Gokhale, Lord Morley, he has done a distinct service to both the younger and elder generations of Indians; for, these are books which the younger people like to have constantly by their side to study and the elders to refer to occasionally.

The Harvest Field. Anything that will make India more beautiful appeals powerfully to us.................... The Essays are interesting.

The Christian Patriot.—All are thoughtful and inspiring articles and stimulate the reader to think of new paths for the rising generation and avoid beaten and overcrowded tracks in which many young men are still content to walk.

AGRICULTURAL INDUSTRIES IN INDIA

BY MR. SEEDICK R. SAYANI

WITH AN INTRODUCTION BY

SIR VITALDHAS DAMODAR THACKERSEY

Contents:—Agriculture; Rice; Wheat; Cotton; Sugar-Cane; Jute; Oilseeds; Acacia; Wattle Barks; Sunn Hemp; Camphor; Lemon-Grass Oil; Ramie; Rubber; Minor Products: Potatoes; Fruit Trade; Lac Industry; Tea and Coffee; Tobacco; Manures; Subsidiary Industries; Sericulture; Apiculture; Floriculture; Cattle-Farming; Dairy Industry; Poultry-Raising; An Appeal.

Sir Vitaldhas Thackersey writes:—

Mr. S. R. Sayani, I think, has given valuable information regarding the present state and future possibilities of the principal cultivated crops of India.

Re. 1. To Subscribers of the "Indian Review," As. 12.

Mr. W. H. SHARP, DIRECTOR OF PUBLIC INSTRUCTION, BOMBAY. "Agricultural Industries in India" by Seedick R. Sayani, price Rupee One, and published by G. A. Natesan & Co., Esplanade, Madras, is recommended as a book suitable for the Libraries of Secondary Schools in this Presidency.

H. E. THE GOVERNOR OF BOMBAY hopes that it may have a wide circulation and stimulate the introduction of the improvements which are so necessary if India is to reach its full economic development as a producing country.

G. A. Natesan & Co.. Sunkurama Chetty Street, Madras.

The Provincial Times:—Messrs. G. A. Natesan Publishers, Esplanade, Madras, have issued a series of books not alone of interest to a general reader, but of value as references and historical records.

The Indian Witness:—G. A. Natesan & Co., Madras are making quite a name for themselves by their varied publications.

The Empire:—That ferociously enterprising firm of publishers, Messrs. G. A. Natesan & Co., Madras.

Indian Arts, Industries and Agriculture

Agricultural Industries in India.—By Seedick Rr Sayani. With an introduction by Sir Vitaldas Damoda. Thackersey. Re. 1. To Subscribers of the *Indian Review* As. 12.

Essays on Indian Art, Industry and Education.—By E. B. Havell, Re. 1-4. To Subscribers of the "Indian Review," Re. 1.

The Swadeshi Movement.—A Symposium by Representative Indians and Anglo-Indians. Re. 1. To Subscribers of the "Indian Review," As. 12.

Essays on Indian Economics.—By the late Mahadev Govinda Ranade Rs. 2. To Subscribers of the "Indian Review," Re. 1-8.

Industrial India.—By Glyn Barlow, M. A. *Second Edition*. Re. 1. To Subscribers of the "Indian Review," As. 12.

Lift-Irrigation.—By A. Chatterton. Second Edition Revised and enlarged. Price Rs. 2.

Indian Industrial and Economic Problems.—By Prof. V. G. Kale, Fergusson College, Poona. Price Re. One to Subscribers of The "Indian Review" As 12.

The Improvement of Indian Agriculture.—Some Lessons from America. By Cathelyne Singh. Price Re. 1. To Subscribers of the "Indian Review," As. 12.

G. A. Natesan & Co., Sunkurama Chetty Street, Madras.

The *Christian Patriot*:—Part of the present interest in industrial matters in Southern India at least is due in considerable measure to the assiduity of this well-known firm in this direction for years past ever since the industrial problem began to attract notice.

***Kaiser-i-Hind.* We do not think we are guilty of any exaggeration when we say that there is no Indian firm of publishers which can surpass Messrs. G. A. Natesan and Co., of Madras in point of utilitarian enterprise of a most patriotic character. The firm's great aim is how best and most expeditiously to serve the public.**